Billie Holiday

JOHN SZWED

Billie Holiday

THE MUSICIAN
AND
THE MYTH

VIKING

VIKING

Published by the Penguin Publishing Group

Penguin Random House LLC

375 Hudson Street

New York, New York 10014

USA | Canada | UK | Ireland | Australia | New Zealand | India | South Africa | China

penguin.com

A Penguin Random House Company

First published by Viking Penguin, an imprint of Penguin Publishing Group,
a division of Penguin Random House LLC, 2015

Grateful acknowledgment is made to the Estate of William Dufty for permission
to reprint excerpts from *Lady Sings the Blues* by Billie Holiday with William
Dufty (Doubleday, 1956) and selections from published and unpublished
writings by William Dufty.

LIBRARY OF CONGRESS CATALOGING-IN-PUBLICATION DATA

Szwed, John F., 1936–

Billie Holiday : the musician and the myth / John Szwed.

pages cm

Includes bibliographical references and index.

ISBN 978-0-670-01472-9

1. Holiday, Billie, 1915–1959. 2. Singers—United States—Biography.
3. African American women singers—United States—Biography. I. Title.

ML420.H58S99 2015

782.42165092—dc23

[B]   2015001092

Printed in the United States of America

10 9 8 7 6 5 4 3 2 1

Set in Arno Pro

Designed by Francesca Belanger

To Heather, Matt, and Miles

Contents

$\mathcal{M}$any books have been written about Billie Holiday—over forty in English, French, and Italian. All those who have attempted to write about her have discovered that there are many Billie Holidays: one lively and joyful, another bitter and doomed to heartache; there is a Billie with a little girl's cry, and one with an older woman's growl; an early Billie, a middle, and a late one; a race woman and an internationally known chanteuse; a Billie who was one of the jazz boys, another one elegantly backed by violins. Put fifty or sixty photos of her on a table and you will see a heavyset woman and a sylph in silk, an African American and an Asian, a saucy miss and a broken drunk, a perp in a mug shot and a smiling matron posing with a pet. In some pictures she's completely unrecognizable.

During her brief forty-four years she managed to gather a dizzying number of names and personae. Look for her and you'll find Eleanora Fagan Gough, Eleanora Harris, Eleanora Fagan, Eleanora Monroe, Billy Holliday, Billie Halliday, Billie Holiday, and Lady Day. And just as there are different Holidays, there are different audiences for her singing: jazz fans, feminists, classical musicians, black militants, beats, gays, night-club sophisticates, political leftists, showbiz insiders, punks, pop stars, each with its own particular image of her.

Unlike other singers of her day, she never had a big hit record and appeared in film and on television only a few times. Nonetheless, dozens of singers were influenced by her in her own time, most notably Peggy Lee,

Anita O'Day, June Christy, Rosemary Clooney, Dinah Washington, Doris Day, and Frank Sinatra, who said she was the most important influence on singing in twenty years. Today she and Sinatra are the only singers still fully alive to us from over sixty years ago, still attracting biographical interest. Meanwhile, new reincarnations of her continue to arrive—Sade, Macy Gray, Erykah Badu, Tori Amos, Madeleine Peyroux, Amy Winehouse, Dee Dee Bridgewater, Audra McDonald, Annie Lennox—along with newer singers who drop her name to gain credibility.

All of her recordings are still available, many of them on YouTube. Her voice survived the shift in public taste during the rock era, and it still comes at us in coffeehouses and restaurants, on movie soundtracks, in musicals about her life and songs, countless tribute albums, rock allusions (such as U2's "Angel of Harlem"), even in TV cartoons (the Simpsons once sang "God Bless the Child") and video games (*Grand Theft Auto*). As a character in films and novels, she represents an era, a style, a state of being. Her recordings trigger and guide emotions in affairs of the heart and affairs of state. Barack Obama heard in her music a willingness to endure and the strength not to be hurt. Monica Lewinsky said that Holiday's "I'll Be Seeing You" was a song that she and Bill Clinton bonded over.

Much of what we think we know about Holiday, however, is questionable, and over time accounts of her life have been bent to serve some other purpose than telling her story. The sources for our image of her are biographies, her recordings, her choice of songs, filmed clips of her performances, interviews with those who knew or worked with her, journalists' and critics' commentaries, a handful of brief interviews with her, and a few articles written under her own name. But most of our picture of Holiday comes from two key sources. The first, her autobiography, *Lady Sings the Blues*, is a book that still puzzles close readers. Given the usual option of writing a tragedy or a romance—a story of triumph over great obstacles and odds, or a description of defeat—she chose to do both in one book, and did so with attitude. In the 1950s, when her autobiography first appeared, this was an unprecedented choice. Compare her autobiography with Bing Crosby's cheery *Call Me Lucky* or the spate of press release–like biographies such as Barry Ulanov's *The Incredible Crosby*. As a columnist in the *Los Angeles Mirror* suggested in 1950, "There has been the strangest conspiracy among even the gossip columnists to protect Bing . . . from any unfavorable stories." The other crucial source for Holiday is the tireless research of her would-be biographer, Linda Kuehl, which produced well over a hundred interviews, extensive notes, documents, and many pages of writing completed before her tragic death ended the project. Much of her work subsequently appeared in print, though scattered through several biographies.

There is a powerful urge to treat performance as a form of autobiography, and since most love songs, in particular, are part of a long chain of melancholy, they are often interpreted as expressions of pain by the singer in question. Even when the same song is sung by dozens of different performers, one of them is usually singled out as the most authentic, often the one who is believed to have lived the song most fully. Holiday understood this inclination better than others, and as she grew older, she seemed consciously to choose songs that underlined what she had become for many: Our Lady of Sorrows.

Racism, drug and alcohol abuse, and the brutality of some of the men in her life were sufficient to justify her mournful repertoire and a style that reinforced it. But suffering and pain are neither necessary nor sufficient to produce a great artist. Holiday was the singer she was because she knew how to rise above the easy pathos of so many of the songs that came her way and to bring a dignity, depth, and grandeur to her performances that went far beyond simply displaying the bruises she suffered. As Stanley Crouch put it, the double consciousness of African American singing assures that melancholy can coexist with rhythmic exuberance, sorrow with swing, and Holiday treated this not as contradiction but as a means of transcendence.

Holiday is justly considered to be the greatest jazz singer of all time, though she never abandoned words to scat sing and improvise as freely as a horn player, a standard stylistic device of many jazz vocalists. She was also frequently referred to as a blues singer, though she sang very few blues. She did cite Bessie Smith and Louis Armstrong as influences, but many of her songs were also borrowed from theater and cabaret singers like Ethel Waters, Libby Holman, Fanny Brice, and Helen Morgan. Yet she personalized the styles of every singer she drew upon, black or white. Three songs that are often identified closely with Holiday are hardly the usual jazz fare: one, "My Man," an account of the lover who beats and scorns her; the other two (both sometimes banned from radio when they were first recorded) recount a suicide ("Gloomy Sunday") and a lynching ("Strange Fruit"). The simple truth is, stylistically, she ultimately owed very little to any singer who came before her, black or white, yet she is perhaps the only one among them who jazz fans of all generations can agree is a jazz singer.

Most of the writing about Billie Holiday thus far has wrestled with the apparent contradictions of and the enigma posed by her many selves. Some have sought to assess the actual degree of her victimization by claiming that there were fabrications in her autobiography and attributing them to her cowriter, to her editor, or to her. Others have become mired in the quest to understand her childhood in Baltimore and the facts of her parentage. The timeline that biographers typically develop for a subject is a problem in Holiday's case, as she left something of a jagged trail rather than an unbroken line. Even her FBI file is thin, confused, taken from newspaper clips, and inconclusive. Such is the mystery of Billie Holiday, and the problem she presents to any writer who tries to portray her.

Given her acknowledged stature as a musician, it is odd that many of the books on Holiday have only secondary interest in her music. But then again, maybe not so odd: music writing today is increasingly focused on lifestyles, as if the events of artists' lives are enough to explain their music, and the songs they record are treated primarily as documents in support of a given biographer's argument. In Holiday's case, the focus on the emotional power of her interpretations has tended to reduce her artistry, creativity, and enormous influence on the history of jazz to merely her ability to express feelings through music.

Most biographers look for those moments in an individual's life that unlock its secrets or at least sum it up, then weave a narrative that focuses on these moments and ignores or downplays those that don't support their analysis. Many also tend to concentrate on the individuality of their subject, without attempting to understand her in the context of her time, her own society. But it could be worse: Some of the writing on Holiday that has appeared recently is heavily fictionalized.

From my perspective, these tactics for approaching Billie Holiday are now exhausted. I don't mean to say that the existing biographies are not valuable. Many of them have presented important facts and interpretations, and deserve to be read. Nor do I think that there will never again appear a biography that offers more interesting interpretations of her life. But that will be a difficult task because most of the witnesses to her life are gone; the existing interviews with those witnesses often conflict wildly, and some of them were not as close to her as they claimed, or they led lives that left them with something they wished to hide.

What I have tried to do is write a different kind of book, one that attempts to widen our sense of who Billie Holiday was, one that sets her life in the particular framework of the world in which she lived and in that specific musical time. But it also seeks to stay close to her music, to her performance style, to the self she created and put on record and onstage. It is not, therefore, a biography in the strictest sense, but rather a meditation on her art and its relation to her life. New material about her life has surfaced in the last decade, and while I have included it here, I hope that it will primarily be of interest in telling the story of her art. I have also drawn on a number of important writings by academics, most of which have not appeared in books or in easily available form; articles by Holiday herself and others close to her that have apparently not been previously consulted; books on Holiday in French and Italian; unpublished interviews and autobiographies by musicians; my own interviews; and the writings and notes of Linda Kuehl deposited in the Institute of Jazz Studies at Rutgers University–Newark by her editor, Frances McCullough.

Holiday's autobiography, *Lady Sings the Blues*, has been pored over for years by biographers in search of the truth, with special attention paid to areas in which her coauthor, William Dufty, went wrong. But contrary to the usual viewpoints, most of the key sources for her book were actually newspaper and magazine interviews with Holiday, which confirms that it was she who was the source of at least some of the book's fabrications or misrememberings. There are other questions about *Lady Sings the Blues* that might be more productive, such as, if she did falsify some information about herself, why did she do so? Why is her book so similar to other jazz autobiographies or jazz-inflected novels that ambivalently describe the world of pimps and prostitutes—books such as *Miles: The Autobiography*, or Charles Mingus's *Beneath the Underdog*? What are these writers/musicians trying to communicate about themselves and others when they magnify or even glorify The Life, and then back away from it? Was it part of an effort to be authentic? (When Holiday was pressed about the authenticity of her book, she, like Miles Davis, ducked the question by saying she had never read it.)

What interests me most about *Lady Sings the Blues* is its musical detail, Holiday's ideas about the meaning of music, the ideology of jazz, her understanding of race in jazz and America, and her accounts of what shaped her musical development. But more important, I'm drawn, in an effort to see her authority restored, to attempting to understand what she hoped to accomplish with the publication of the book and how she went about it.

David Margolick's book *Strange Fruit* opened up the subject of Holiday's politics and the considerable impact of that particular song, but there is more to be said about her understanding of race. Holiday's life changed markedly when she began performing in downtown New York and on Fifty-second Street, where she came into contact with writers, Broadway actors, artists in the Village, society folk, and film people. It seems as if at one time or another almost everyone who knew her in New York City wished to write about her, paint her, perform with her, or marry her. Composer Ned Rorem worked her into his art songs and discussed her in his prose works. Jack Kerouac wanted to write about the woman he called "The Heroine of the Hip Generation," and contended with John Clellon Holmes to be the first to build a novel around her. (Holmes won, with his book *The Horn*.) Meanwhile, unbeknownst to both of them, Frank Harriott, a black writer uptown, had already begun such a novel, but never lived to publish it. Today, Holiday herself is seen by some as a literary figure, along with Zora Neale Hurston, one of the first to fashion complex narratives about the lives of black women, and therefore a predecessor to the likes of Toni Morrison and Ntozake Shange.

It is these and other issues that continue to make Billie Holiday a mystery, and that have led me to write yet another book about her.

The
Myth

CHAPTER ONE

The Book I: *Lady Sings the Blues*

*W*hen Billie Holiday's *Lady Sings the Blues* was published in 1956, it received a surprising amount of attention for a jazz singer's autobiography. It was written in a direct and often streetwise style, and its apparent openness and honesty was shocking to many. The book was widely reviewed, but often condemned for just those qualities.

By 1956 jazz had moved from being *the* popular music of 1940s America to a more rarefied place in the public's view. It was on its way to becoming a minority music in every sense of the word. Its stars could still occasionally be found in the news, but it was now being guarded by a new breed of critics who were promoting jazz as America's only true art form. Most of the writers were closet high modernists who wanted no mention of drugs, whorehouses, or lynching brought into discussions of the music. To them the content and even the style of Holiday's book seemed misguided, and they saw the financial motivation for it as a personal affront. It was more than they wanted to know about Billie Holiday. Ralph Gleason in the *San Francisco Chronicle* questioned the "pseudo-frankness laced with profanity that made it sensationalized reading, and the blind resentment that made it compelling." The *Saturday Review*'s Whitney Balliett questioned the "high decibels in which the reader is given only a superficial picture of the author and virtually nothing about her art." Harvey Breit in the *New York Times* regretted that the tragic sense she so powerfully demonstrated in her songs was lacking in her book. Her integrity and sincerity were not enough to move a sensitive reader: "The hard surface of her manner prevents Miss Holiday from pausing in her narrative to discuss, say, a song, a delivery, an esthetic response, a disinterested observation." Orrin Keepnews in *Record Changer* criticized the book as a betrayal of the whole cause of jazz and of those who fought the "constant negative battle to keep jazz from being so completely publicly misunderstood." When Holiday wrote, "I guess that I'm not the only one who heard their first good jazz in a whorehouse," she was speaking the truth, but it was a cliché that a generation of jazz writers had attempted to forget. Linda Kuehl's unpublished judgment of the book was the harshest. "She was writing for money to support a drug habit, and for publicity to make it appear that she was off the habit and to get her back her cabaret card." (The cabaret card was a license required of all performers who worked in showplaces that served alcohol, and one for which they were fingerprinted and photographed when they applied for it. Holiday had lost hers in 1947 after conviction on drug charges and had not appeared in a New York City nightclub for the previous eight years.) Nat Hentoff was one of the few willing to accept the book as a cautionary tale and observed in *Down Beat* magazine that it would "help those who want to understand how her voice became what it was—the most hurt and hurting singer in jazz."

Later, attentive readers began to discover that some of the events and dates in the book were wrong, or, worse, possibly fabricated, and *Lady Sings the Blues* has been clouded by doubt ever since. The trouble began in the first paragraph: "Mom and Pop were just a couple of kids when they got married. He was eighteen, she was seventeen, and I was three." Readers shook their heads in dismay at the vision of little Billie as a flower girl at her parents' wedding, but her account was not correct. When Billie was born, her mother was nineteen, her father seventeen. They never married and had never lived together in a little house with a picket fence on Durham Street in Baltimore. She was born not in Baltimore but in Philadelphia. Some questioned her claim of having been raped at age ten. Music world insiders took issue with some of her rough comments about fellow singers and managers. A number of songwriters were angry over her claims of partial authorship of their work.

As time went by, newly discovered evidence supported some of her claims. But the fundamental questions remained: Why should an autobiography cause so much discomfort and suspicion? What could be reasonably expected from an autobiography? Shouldn't an author have the right to create a self different from what readers think they already know about her? If an autobiography is an account of a woman's experiences, those experiences may be felt in one way as they happen, but in a completely different way later in life.

What was perceived by some as lies or exaggerations in Holiday's book were largely matters of interpretation, childhood memories, and slips of fact, not the sort of self-serving rewritings of personal history common in many autobiographies of the famous. French chanteuse Édith Piaf, for example, lived a life that paralleled Holiday's own in its poverty, alcoholism, and abuse by men. Piaf also developed a persona of tragedy and sorrow that radiated from her songs, wrote two autobiographies that apparently fabricated stories of childhood blindness and life-long destitution, and answered charges that she was a collaborationist by claiming heroics in helping prisoners escape from the Nazis.

One response to the question of truth in Holiday's book was to regard hers as different from other autobiographies. Robert O'Meally, in *Lady Day: The Many Faces of Billie Holiday*, viewed what she had written as "a dream book, a collection of Holiday's wishes and lies," a book that had to be interpreted in that light, as one of many faces she presented to the public. As a vocal artist, O'Meally suggests, she had approached songs as a series of "confrontations," in which she creatively reshaped the musical material and the traditions that lay behind it. The power she discovered in doing so became her way of capturing an audience's attention and belief. More recently, Farah Griffin, in *If You Can't Be Free, Be a*

Mystery, asked how those who believe the book was written entirely by her coauthor can also accuse her of lying.

Another way of putting it is to see *Lady Sings the Blues* as a form of autobiographical fiction. Much of what we read about her elsewhere tells us that this was really Billie Holiday speaking in the book. But a certain amount of withholding of certain aspects of her life or changing of facts was a form of editing on her part. Although the Doubleday editors struck out some passages in fear of potential lawsuits, Holiday's own changes or omissions were perhaps a means of preventing readers from knowing too much, of distancing herself to keep from being too closely identified with how others saw her, and especially from what the press had written about her. She chose *not* to see herself as others did, and what might appear to be a private communication between the writer and the reader is ultimately as illusory as believing a singer is communicating directly to a listener in her audience.

From the beginning, Billie posed for photographers together with William Dufty, her collaborator on *Lady Sings the Blues,* as coauthors. Dufty gave interviews on his own before and after the book came out, addressing many issues concerning it in interviews and newspaper articles, including questions about particular facts and his own role in the writing. At the time, Harry S. Truman was publishing the first of his memoirs with Doubleday, and Dufty responded to the matter of errors or lies in Holiday's autobiography by asking what cowriter was going to tell President Harry Truman that *he* should check his facts. Are the subject's memories of experiences not sufficient to create an autobiography? Who was responsible for making the decision about truthfulness when a subject's memories failed to square with those of others? If the uniqueness of an autobiography is that it is built on the personal memories and observations of the subject, should the cowriter or ghostwriter question the subject or urge her to change her thoughts on her own past?

Dufty said he was not going to be a fact-checker for Billie; the words were hers. But that was part of the problem, for when errors were discovered in the book or material was found objectionable, many chose to believe they were not, in fact, her words. Some have insisted that she couldn't write, and she sometimes did apologize for not being able to write better. Yet she did compose some lyrics, and sent letters to music business people, her editor, and friends, though many to the latter were unpunctuated. Others even questioned her ability to read, and quoted her one remark about never having read her own book—which has in fact been a standard dodge of many celebrities when they don't wish to discuss or justify a topic in a coauthored book. She had certainly read *Lady Sings the Blues,* since she commented on many portions of it, both in galleys, at the insistence of Doubleday, and in published form, in her letters and in comments to the Duftys and to journalists. She also read reviews of the book and complained about some of them in detail.

There was also the issue of Dufty's being a *white* coauthor, an issue that has plagued African American autobiographical writing at least since Solomon Northup wrote *Twelve Years a Slave* in 1853, when otherwise sympathetic readers suspected that the truth of his narrative was clouded by the conventions of antislavery writing and the expectations of abolitionists. A hundred years later, some of the same doubts arose about the autobiographies of jazz musicians such as Sidney Bechet and Louis Armstrong, who also had white cowriters.

Some of those suspicious of Holiday's book point out that William Dufty was a tabloid journalist, and thus a "hack." Dufty did indeed write for a tabloid-size newspaper, but it was the *New York Post,* when that publication was still staffed by some of the best journalists in the city. He came to the paper with a background as a labor organizer for the United Automobile Workers, an editor of the union newsletter *The CIO News,* and a publicity director for Senator Hubert Humphrey. He had won awards for his *Post* articles on J. Edgar Hoover's troubled leadership of the FBI, the plight of new Puerto Rican immigrants in New York City, and the failures of drug laws and medical treatment—a twelve-part series called "Drug Addicts, USA." When he ended his career at the *Post,* he was assistant to the editor. He coauthored over forty books, including biographies of the Lehman brothers, Gloria Swanson, and the son of Edward G. Robinson, as well as those of an ex-model and an ex–Catholic priest. He contributed to *You Are All Sanpaku*, the bible of macrobiotics, and wrote *Sugar Blues*, two books that fed the fears of those in the sixties who saw conventional food as an enemy, books that also landed him in the company of food cultists John Lennon, Yoko Ono, and Gloria Swanson, whom he later married.

Dufty met Billie Holiday through his first wife, Maely Daniele, a Jewish war camp refugee who found her way into several different lives in America—a writer, a TV talk show hostess, and a civil rights activist who booked jazz musicians and worked to get their drug charges dropped. Later she was involved with various social action groups in Harlem and the Navajo Nation. When she met Dufty, she had just divorced the former child film actor Freddie Bartholomew of *Little Lord Fauntleroy* fame, for whom she'd been a press agent. In 1955 Maely invited Billie to use the Duftys' fifth-floor apartment on West Eighty-sixth Street (just as she had used some other apartments in New York City) for a place of refuge from the police, her husband Louis McKay, reporters, and the various unsavory figures who haunted her life. "I knew enough to keep my trap shut about anything she was doing in my place or anywhere," Dufty recalled. "She was always involved in some love triangle."

Both Billie and Bill were raised as Catholics, and Dufty felt that they shared enough Irish in their DNA, religious experiences, and senses of humor that despite their very different backgrounds they could work well together. Billie was staying with the Duftys when their son Bevan was born, and she became the child's godmother.

In the mid-1950s Holiday was in financial trouble: She owed money to her record companies and the IRS, she was still unable to work in New York City nightclubs, and her reputation as an unreliable performer reduced the offers she received from venues in other cities and countries. Books by stars who revealed their afflictions and miseries were then selling well and breaking the hold that publicists had long had on what the public could know about them. Lillian Roth's *I'll Cry Tomorrow* and Diana Barrymore's *Too Much, Too Soon* had been successful enough to be turned into movies. Several people had already approached Billie about writing her own book, the latest one a writer from Miami she'd met while appearing at the Vanity Fair Club, but Billie found him impossible to work with, as she had the others. She was especially put off by the writers at *Ebony* who had ghosted first-person articles under her name and, according to Dufty, had her "sounding like a freshman at Sarah Lawrence."

When Billie returned from some performances in Florida in June 1955, Bill began handling correspondence for her, writing to bookers and club owners on her behalf and sometimes finding musicians for her gigs. While she was staying in his apartment, she read a bit of a manuscript he was working on, and they began to talk about it and her own story, and the trouble she had had with previous writers. He suggested that he could write it for her, to which she agreed, and when he asked her how she wanted to approach the project, she replied, "You're the writer, I'm the singer. You write it." A contract was drawn up in which she got 65 percent and he 35 percent, with his expenses "securing court records and other data for the work" to be taken from the first royalties. Billie retained 90 percent and Dufty 10 percent of all other rights. She agreed to work jointly with him and give him her life story. Any differences between the two of them on content and style were to be resolved by the publisher. It was agreed that "no agent or broker brought about the Doubleday agreement."

With this understanding, they began to get together at regular hours after he came home from work at the *Post*. Billie made it clear that she did not want to have her conversations recorded on tape. "She would always reprimand you for not paying attention. You had to go along with her way of doing things. That's just the way she was. . . . She had an air of total dignity, her wit was situational . . . she was absolutely, defensively, herself. . . . At times it was very frustrating. She wouldn't be in the mood and would get angry at something I said, and leave my apartment . . . but as she stepped into the elevator the remarks she made in anger to me would illumine a whole passage."

When Dufty asked her if she had ever read anything written about her that was accurate, she recalled "The Hard Life of Billie Holiday"— an article based on an interview she had done with journalist Frank Harriott for *PM* newspaper in 1945. Dufty discovered that the material in it was rich enough to be the basis for the first three chapters of the book, often using what had been written verbatim or changing it slightly to standardize the narrative. When she read what she had said ten years before, it set Billie to recalling things long forgotten. Dufty went on to find other interviews she had done for *PM*, *Metronome*, *Down Beat*, and elsewhere that he could draw on.

The opening line of the book, "Mom and Pop were just a couple of kids when they got married," was reshaped from the 1945 *PM* article. In it Billie was asked to talk about her life, and she began by saying that she was born in Baltimore in 1915 of parents who were "just a couple of kids." When asked what she meant by that, she replied:

> "Mom was 13 . . . and Pop was 15." She paused. "Mom's and Pop's parents just about had a fit when it happened. They'd never heard of things like that going on in our part of Baltimore. But they were poor kids, Mom and Pop, and when you're poor you grow up fast."
>
> Billie turned her eyes to us, smiled, and her frown disappeared. She lighted a Chesterfield, and began speaking rapidly, between short, reflective pauses.
>
> "Mom and Pop didn't get married till I was three years old," she said . . .

The British magazine the *New Statesman* later reprinted those sentences and offered prizes for the best "similarly explosive first or last sentences from a real or imagined biography." Over a hundred readers gave it a try, but the *New Statesman* awarded only consolation prizes and declared that the contest was more difficult than they had imagined:

> Miss Holiday's explosiveness ... is no simple formula. In 23 su-
> perbly chosen words, she has established her background, re-
> corded at least five relevant facts, illustrated (by her method of
> doing so) one facet of her own character and made firm friends
> with the reader by a breathtaking and slightly naughty dénoue-
> ment. Too many of her imitators felt that vulgarity or sheer im-
> probability were satisfactory substitutes for the artfully conjured
> impudence and shock which characterized the original.

Once the first chapter and a short outline of Holiday's book were completed, they were sent to Lee Barker, an editor at Doubleday, who bought the book immediately on the basis of Dufty's skill at capturing Billie's voice. An advance of $3,000 was given to Billie, and $1,050 to Bill. Though Barker didn't know much about Holiday at the time, he had been an editor of Ethel Waters's autobiography, *His Eye Is on the Sparrow*, and saw the potential for black celebrity books.

As Dufty began writing in June, he wrote Norman Granz, the owner of Clef Records, her record producer in California, to involve him in the project and give him an idea of the plans for the book:

> We have been working for a week now pulling stuff together. She
> has been dictating huge patches of terrific stuff. I have dredged
> the [newspaper] morgues and clip files; we have played old [rec-
> ord] sides for clues. And the project has gone well—something I
> never believed quite possible, almost an accident of timing. . . .
> She is concerned that the book be done right and that it be the
> truth, at long last. There had to be a gimmick, of course. But in

the context of all the phony spurious ghosted biogs current; the spate of paste-up slapdash jazz histories; and all the nonsense and myth that has gained currency about Lady over the years, I'm not sure the truth itself at long last isn't itself the gimmick. And I can say, on the basis of stuff in hand, that publication day will be novelty night at the Book of the Month Club. We are dredging ancient court records, so it can be whole. And it is my journalistic guess that a few of the Judges, public dignitaries involved in the sociological sense in this story—those who are not dead may wish, some that they were.

In late August Billie left New York for California, and when she returned, the book was ready to send off for final editing in November 1955.

Billie and Dufty had shaped the autobiography in a confessional mode, with drug addiction as what Dufty called the "gimmick" to sell it. It was the year in which Otto Preminger's film *The Man with the Golden Arm* broke through the Hollywood codes to portray the life of a heroin-addicted jazz drummer, and articles by Billie such as "How I Blew a Million Dollars" in *Ebony* and "Can a Dope Addict Come Back?" in *Tan* magazine were driving magazine sales. Using drugs as the means of attracting an audience was nonetheless a tricky business. The revelation was shocking at the time to most who read it, but in the effort to create a naturalistic account of the suffering, pleasure, and crazed romanticism of the quest for drugs, it was easy for such a book to turn into a narrative of addiction, a tedious account of narcotic business practices. (Such would be the weaknesses of the autobiographies of Miles Davis, Art Pepper, and many celebrities to come.) In Holiday's case, however, the drug dealing was done not by her, but by her fans, sycophants, lovers, and the musicians she hired, so there was not much she could tell. Although Holiday falsely assured her readers that she had put drugs behind her, if her book was successful, she might find herself forever expected to write and talk about that experience—a life reduced to drugs.

. . . . .

After the manuscript was turned in to the editor, Billie and her husband began to read the final drafts, and Louis started dropping by the Doubleday offices to check on progress. They then surprised Barker and Dufty by hiring an attorney, Harry A. Lieb, to advise them on the contents of the book. Lieb seemed genuinely shocked by the life that she had led, and appeared to want to protect her from herself. After he met with Barker and Dufty several times, Billie wrote Barker that she had been reading from the book and talking to her lawyer, and there were changes that she wanted to make. She forwarded a letter from Lieb that had been sent to her and Louis McKay:

December 27, 1955

Dear Mr. Barker,

Since my meeting with (William) Dufty and you, I have had no word regarding the suggested deletions and additions to the manuscript. It is extremely important that it be read and re-read carefully before publication to make certain that possible libelous statements be deleted. Incidentally, has Billie read the entire contents of the book herself? Although my function is not of a critic, I should like to give you my opinion of the book as presently written. I must preface my remarks by telling you that I have heard Billie sing on records and radio and her voice is just beautiful. There is so much of human suffering, sensitivity and music in her voice. The book, therefore, comes as a disappointment, as if in her autobiography she had written to put herself in the worst possible light. The first 50 pages are very good, but the rest is a series of gripes, with a few scandal items. It is bitter and even the cuss words get very tiresome when they are repeated over and over again. Now I cannot believe that that is all there is to Billie. Her story must surely be dramatic and touching and it should evoke sympathy, pity and understanding. This book, in my opinion, does not do this. It doesn't give the reader the faintest inkling of what a drug addict feels or suffers, nor does it portray her as the great singer she is. It would seem that some of the wonderful notices she has received could be woven into the telling of the story. I feel that Billie doesn't just want to show her tough outer shell or that is the way she wants the world to regard her. There is a great story in Billie and it would seem to me that Billie and Dufty should be able to produce it. The above is just my opinion. I may be all wrong, but take it for what it is worth. I have only your best interest at heart.

Harry [Lieb]

Once the suggested reediting and deletions were completed, however, Holiday and Louis McKay were still unhappy with the results. McKay claimed that certain passages had been deleted only after threats had been made against Billie. Lawyers for Doubleday had insisted that some passages be sent to various people who might find them objectionable, and Charles Laughton, Tallulah Bankhead, and Billie's former manager and lover John Levy each responded with demands to have any references to them deleted. Even more ominously, McKay insisted that Billie's many difficulties with the law were the result of pressures brought to bear by persons who knew that she possessed information about them that she intended to make public. Billie now blamed what she saw as shortcomings of the book on the publisher's deletions: She told her friend the songwriter Irene Kitchings that "when they got through cutting that book, it wasn't fit for anybody to read."

Others were complaining even before the book was out. Her agent, Joe Glaser, a "shtarker" famous for manipulating his clients and making them money, thought it was bad for business (though after its publication he rushed to buy the film and dramatic rights). After Norman Granz had read some of the manuscript, he wrote Dufty to say that he knew Billie needed money, but he, too, feared the sensationalism of the narcotics material might backfire and make it harder for her to get more work. Dufty reassured him that only a small part of the book—less than one tenth—would concern narcotics, and he had been advised by the publishers that the subject would sell well.

When it was published in 1956, the *New York Herald Tribune* said that it was "a hard, bitter and unsentimental book, written with brutal honesty and having much to say not only about Billie Holiday, the person, but about what it means to be poor and black in America." When she read it, Billie said, "I can't help it. I just told what happened to me. A lot of my life has been bitter. You ought to read what they left out of the book. I told everything, but they had to cut some of it."

She was even more upset when the *New Yorker* called her book "as bitter and uncompromising an autobiography as has been published in a long time . . . a largely authentic, if almost indigestible social document." Dufty said she wondered how life in a black neighborhood in America could be both authentic and palatable. She was particularly stung by a review in the *Baltimore Afro-American* by the eminent African American professor and literary critic J. Saunders Redding, who was offended by the book's realism and her willingness to share so many details of her life. He opened his review by declaring, "I suppose Billie Holiday has a right to sing the blues, and whether she has or not, she has assumed that right for reasons that she considers sufficient. . . . [The] opening paragraph is a sort of sardonic summary of all that tragically disordered background that Billie Holiday came from and of all she went toward." He followed with a summary of the details of that "disordered background," but without mention of her music or what she had accomplished, and concluded, "This reviewer is no squeamish prude, but Billie Holiday and William Dufty use language so raw with so little warrant that there were times when this reviewer got 'real sick.'" Billie wrote Bill and Maely and asked if they had seen the review: "Well I don't know if you have been digging it but my book is just a bitch. Did you see that shit that man from my birthplace Baltimore wrote? He even said that my Mom and Dad were stinkers for having me. I am sick of the whole goddamn thing. You tell people the truth and you stink. I didn't hurt anyone in that book but myself. . . . Please have Bill to look into this for me or I will take other means to take care of him. He needs a lesson . . ."

The opening words of Holiday's book were undoubtedly shocking and certainly memorable; they are still quoted today. But there was precedent for such blunt frankness. Five years earlier Ethel Waters's autobiography, *His Eye Is on the Sparrow*, had an equally stunning opening:

> I never was a child.
>
> I never was coddled, or liked, or understood by my family.
>
> I never felt I belonged.
>
> I was always an outsider.
>
> I was born out of wedlock, but that had nothing to do with all this. To people like mine a thing like that just didn't mean much.
>
> Nobody brought me up.
>
> I just ran wild as a little girl. I was bad, always a leader of the street gang in stealing and general hell-raising. By the time I was seven I knew all about sex and life in the raw. I could outcurse any stevedore and took a sadistic pleasure in shocking people.

Waters's memoir's opening, like Holiday's, seemed to promise the complete story of her life. She, too, had been raised a Catholic, had been raised in Philadelphia, and grew up poor and a witness to poverty, alcoholism, drug addiction, crime, and public sexuality. Like *Lady Sings the Blues*, Waters's book also evaded any mention of her same-sex relationships, the date of her birth was wrong, her cowriter was a white man, and both books had the same editor and publisher. But the reaction to *His Eye Is on the Sparrow* was markedly different. It was a Book of the Month Club selection, and excerpts were published by the *Ladies' Home Journal* and the *Atlantic Monthly*; author's luncheons were sponsored by the *New York Herald Tribune* and the American Booksellers Association; the American Library picked it as one of the year's notable books. The difference in reception was a reflection of attitudes toward the authors and their public personae. Waters cast her autobiography as a confession but also as a conversion experience, a woman who found faith's triumphant rise from the ruins of her childhood, and was a credit to her race.

Dufty once spoke of Ben Franklin's autobiography as being a model for Billie's account of her own self-creation, but her description of her early life is more reminiscent of Dickens, filled as it is with miseries and rejections in a neighborhood in which houses of prostitution were the elite establishments. Her narrative of her artistic successes, tinged with bitterness toward the music business, the police, the courts, the press, and her mother, did not make for motivational reading. Nor did her revelations of her husbands as con men, pimps, and possible drug dealers sit well with her attempts to move beyond them near the end of the book.

Still, *Lady Sings the Blues* sold respectably, some twelve thousand to fourteen thousand copies the first year, along with a nineteen-page condensation of the book in *Coronet* magazine and a serialization by the British newspaper *The People* under the title "Body and Soul." *Lady Sings the Blues* has remained in print ever since, and for many it is something of an American classic.

CHAPTER TWO

The Book II: The Rest of the Story

*I*n the beginning, the editing of her book was light, with very few changes in style or wording. A few family and celebrity names and a date or two were corrected. A paragraph on the origin of her stage name "Billie" was added, some details on the judge who first sentenced her in New York City were expanded, a bit more was added on the clubs of Harlem, and four new paragraphs were written on her first meeting with Louis Armstrong. She had wanted *Bitter Crop* as a title, words taken from the song "Strange Fruit," but the publisher insisted on having the word "blues" in the title for sales purposes. They finally agreed on *Lady Sings the Blues*, even though she continued to protest that she didn't want to be known as a blues singer.

Billie was annoyed when the editor suggested that the word "bitch" was used too often. He was not swayed when told that she thought of it as a neutral term for women, and regularly used it in referring to herself. In the end, she wrote in the margin of the edited draft, "Change 'bitch' to 'whore.'"

The more substantive changes involved deleting certain passages out of fear of litigation, and the addition of a completely new ending. Throughout the editing of the book various "interested parties" came by the Doubleday offices to express their concern about libel. Billie's reputation as an addict had alerted a number of people to guard against being closely associated with her, especially when they themselves were using drugs. The publisher's lawyers by now were fearful that the book might contain libelous material that they had missed or not understood and pressured the editor to use pseudonyms and cut several lengthy passages about various celebrities. In the end there were no lawsuits and all of the concerned people seemed to vanish.

"Getting Some Fun Out of Life," the fifth chapter, was set to open with "I met some wonderful people when I was a little girl singing around Harlem," and follow with a number of portraits of celebrities who frequented there. Though most of them ultimately disappeared from the book, some readers still accused Holiday and Dufty of name-dropping by mentioning stars such as Bob Hope, Ava Gardner, Clark Gable, Clifton Webb, and Lana Turner as a way to inflate Billie's importance. But these were, in fact, among her most avid fans in Hollywood and uptown New York, and often her companions in clubs and at parties. There were many more she could have mentioned: John Roosevelt (FDR's son); composers Leonard Bernstein and Ned Rorem; Harlem high-life figures like club owners Dickie Wells and Clark Monroe, dancer Tondelayo, and singer Thelma Carpenter; far more of the jazz greats she worked with; and any number of people from the art world and society. Once the cuts were made, this chapter was less than five pages long.

The first person to disappear in the editing was Charles Laughton, who visited her at the Alhambra Grill in Harlem. She wrote that she knew he was someone special when he walked through the door but was not surprised to see him there, since a number of other Hollywood actors, such as Paul Muni and Franchot Tone (and his mother), were regulars in her audience whenever they were in town. George Raft had once danced for her in a club when he asked her to sing for him.

Laughton was on his way to London to appear in Alexander Korda's film *The Private Life of Henry VIII*, and John Hammond, Billie's first record producer, had told him to be sure to see her. (Laughton and his wife, Elsa Lanchester, spent weekends with Hammond when they were in town.) But Harlem was not new to Laughton. Billie learned that he kept a black valet to discreetly guide him in his cruising uptown. He stayed after her performance was over, and she said his regal manner and his fearlessness in coming up to Harlem to see her was enough to compel her to take him home for a dinner cooked by Sadie, her mother. When he was leaving at dawn, he rather formally asked Billie if he might have "some of those cigarettes to take to the ladies of London." With the four hundred dollars that he gave her, she went around the corner to the apartment of white jazzman Mezz Mezzrow (himself the subject of a celebrated cowritten autobiography, *Really the Blues*) and bought every reefer he had. She fully expected that Laughton would share some of them with her, but he left without offering her even one stick.

He stayed in the city for a few more days, and Sadie introduced him to some men that she thought he might find interesting, and when he left for London he thanked both of them for their kindness and wrote out a check to Billie for $1,500—a year's wages for most Americans at the time. She was so shocked by it that she was afraid to cash it in case he had made a mistake and canceled the check. Instead, she kept it in a scrapbook her mother had made for her. But two years later, in a fit of desperation over a lack of money, she took the check to the bank:

> I wrote my name on the back, pushed it through the window and waited, all the time keeping one eye on the door. I was half expecting someone to come in and grab me. But it only took a couple of minutes. The man handed me $1500 in bills and said "Thank you." I had played Charles Laughton cheap and I was ashamed of myself. He was only trying to be nice, but he had saved my life.

Her encounter with Orson Welles was to be the next topic in the chapter. In 1942 Welles—writer, director, actor, producer, autodidact, boy genius—was in Los Angeles, having just completed *Citizen Kane*. He was then working on *The Magnificent Ambersons*, *Journey into Fear*, and *Mexican Melodrama*, appearing in his weekly *Almanac* radio show, and had recently returned from New York, where he directed Richard Wright's

Native Son onstage. Like other Hollywood hipsters, at night he headed for the jazz clubs on Central Avenue, the Harlem of LA.

His companion those nights was Billie Holiday, herself new to LA, and working in Billy Berg's Trouville Club, where nightly she sang to crowds that included Bette Davis, Martha Raye, Merle Oberon, Lana Turner, John Garfield, and Orson.

> He was supposed to be getting ready to marry this beautiful Mexican broad Dolores del Rio then, but he spent so much time with me I don't know when he ever got to see her.
>
> When we'd made the rounds, we'd go up to my joint in the Clark Hotel. I'd always have a big bowl of fresh fruit there and Orson loved fresh fruit. And then he'd have a bath. Orson was up to his pockets then making the picture *Citizen Kane*, writing, directing, acting all over the place. By the time we'd get back to my joint, it would be almost morning, and time for him to go on the set. But his damn head would be going all the time. He'd come out of the bathroom in his shorts and start rewriting, redirecting or acting out the picture; moving the furniture around, trying himself on for size in my mirrors. He'd like to run me crazy.

Kane was a great picture, she said, having seen it nine times in her room with Welles in his shorts taking all the parts before it showed in a theater, but since Holiday did not arrive in Los Angeles until October, after the premier of *Citizen Kane*, it was more likely he was acting out *The Magnificent Ambersons*.

Holiday and Welles made a striking pair on the streets of Los Angeles, both of them riding high, all sass and bravura, white and black together, he engaged to del Rio, Billie recently married to Jimmy Monroe (the colorful brother of Harlem club owner Clark Monroe), playing their roles with reckless cool. It was ultimately *too* cool for the folks at RKO, and soon the harassing phone calls began: She was ruining his career, the film, and the studio; she'd never work in films; they'd sic the police on her; he'd be fired from his film and disgraced in the business. The hotel began receiving threats warning of what would happen if they didn't keep Welles out of the building. Señorita del Rio even called to warn Holiday that she was jeopardizing her marriage plans. But Welles laughed it all off: With his film about to open, the studio wouldn't dare risk the bad publicity.

Billie would not see Orson Welles again for years, until he walked into a club where she was appearing:

> I remember the night Orson Welles came into the Onyx. I hadn't seen him in years. He was all grown up and famous, but it hadn't changed him any kind of way. He came in with a girl who looked like a perfect doll. She was such a knockout she just stood there and everybody stared at her while Orson grabbed me in his arms, hugged me and kissed me. Then he introduced this beautiful chick to me as his wife. I'm a real square about newspapers, I hardly ever touch the things so I didn't even know he was married to Rita Hayworth or anybody.
>
> Anyway, Orson and Rita and I sat down at a table for a drink.... When I got up to sing, Orson reached across the table, took my hand and said "You're still my beautiful brown baby." He always called me that. So I said thank you sugar, and wham bam, excuse me, Ma'am, if Rita didn't haul off and slap him smack in the face and walk out.
>
> I felt terrible. I begged Orson to go after her and get her. I sure didn't want to be in the middle of a public hassle over nothing at all.
>
> But Orson didn't bat an eye. He just said, "Hell, let her go."
>
> So this beautiful chick walked out on him and he sat there and let her go.... And Orson and I hung out together for a couple of days.

Once her adventures with Welles were cut from the book, there was nothing left of the planned chapter but a brief mention of her radio acting experience with Shelton Brooks and her friendship with playboy Jimmy Donahue. Too brief, it would seem, since Billie and Dufty expected their audience to know the significance of these people and the occasions they describe.

Shelton Brooks was described by Billie in her book as a songwriter and author of the song "Some of These Days," and, though she didn't mention it, it was a number made famous by Sophie Tucker, for whom it was first written. Brooks wrote many other hit songs and some of the first jazz standards, appeared as a song-and-dance man in Broadway shows, and had his own twice-weekly radio soap opera on CBS Radio. It was on this program that Billie appeared, doubling parts as a wife and a maid.

The party that Billie mentions next in the published version of *Lady Sings the Blues* took place at the East Sixty-first Street home of Broadway musical star Libby Holman, who for years haunted Harlem clubs such as Connie's Inn and Small's Paradise, bringing with her performer friends Tallulah Bankhead, Jeanne Eagels, Beatrice Lillie, and DuPont heiress Louisa d'Andelot Carpenter. Holman virtually owned the torch song in New York, in part because she took it to both sides of the racial line. In 1929 she appeared in the Broadway musical review *The Little Show* and sang "Moanin' Low," set in Harlem and sung as a black prostitute's plea, and danced to it in French apache style with Clifton Webb as her pimp. Although Holman performed the song in tan blackface on Broadway, she was invited by the newly founded NAACP to do so that same year at the organization's fund-raiser, where her blackface was understood by some (such as Walter White, executive secretary of the NAACP) to be an act of solidarity rather than an insulting appropriation. Billie recorded the same song eight years later, in 1937.

Holman was first known to Billie as a fan who frequented small Harlem clubs late at night after Libby's own stage shows ended. Her private life had recently put her in the headlines when her husband, Zachary

Smith Reynolds, the heir to the R.J. Reynolds tobacco company, was shot to death following an argument with Libby when he learned that she was pregnant. She and Albert Bailey Walker, her presumed lover and her husband's best friend, were both charged with murder. But before legal action could go any further, Louisa d'Andelot Carpenter, Libby's sometime lover, turned up with bail money in the small North Carolina town where the trial was set, dressed—as was her custom—like a man, and whisked Libby away to seclusion in Delaware. Holman and Walker were ultimately cleared of murder and her husband's death declared a suicide when the Reynolds family asked that the case be dropped for lack of evidence and to quiet the scandal.

The party at Libby's took place on January 19, 1939. As Billie discreetly put it, "Libby's husband had been dead awhile and she was celebrating her baby's birthday." It was Libby's son Christopher's sixth birthday, and since the boy had a fondness for the swing music that he had heard on the radio, Holman hired Billie's old boyfriend Benny Goodman and his band with all its stars, including Lionel Hampton, Harry James, Gene Krupa, and Teddy Wilson, along with Billie and Helen Ward as singers. The guests were Libby's friends from New York society, Hollywood, and Broadway. The music was hot, the champagne flowing, and Billie, Libby, and Helen Ward together sang "Happy Birthday" to Christopher. But the party was a "dog," as Billie would say, dead on its feet, with a somber tone set by the presence of a weeping Ria Langham, the wealthy New York socialite whom Clark Gable had just divorced in order to marry actress Carole Lombard.

The night was saved by Jimmy Donahue, first cousin and confidant of Barbara Woolworth Hutton, the richest and perhaps saddest woman in America, the million-dollar baby, the poor little rich girl of pop song fame. Jimmy himself was an heir to the same Woolworth fortune, and often accompanied Barbara on her travels where she found husbands, sometimes buying them noble titles to enhance their dicey credentials. Donahue fancied himself an actor and showman, and there were no limits to which he wouldn't go to put on a show, whether flaunting his sexual orientation, buying his way into the middle of a nightclub review, publicly mocking Mussolini in Italy and Hitler in Germany, or living with the Duke and Duchess of Windsor and financially supporting them when they were shunned by the King and Queen of England. He later claimed to have had an affair with the duchess, though friends said Jimmy enjoyed his little jokes. Billie wrote that on the occasion of Libby's birthday gathering he restarted the party by stripping while Goodman's band accompanied him with the old burlesque favorite "A Pretty Girl Is Like a Melody."

"No Good Man," chapter twenty of the published version of Billie's autobiography, was largely devoted to the horrors of living with her manager John Levy. Though he bought her (presumably with her money) the first home she had had since childhood in Baltimore, a fine house in St. Albans, Queens, her suburban dream turned into a prison: He beat her, she said, stole her money, abandoned her and her band on the road, and wrote performance contracts that made her responsible for all contingencies. For ten pages in the original draft of *Lady Sings the Blues* she spelled out a litany of flying bottles, punches, kicks, emergency room visits, abuse, scorn, and public humiliations. The chapter was leavened only by her many references to Tallulah Bankhead, the incendiary celebrity who had just dropped into her life, but these were also edited out.

For seven weeks in the summer of 1948 Holiday was booked into the Strand Theatre on the same bill with Count Basie and the film *Key Largo*. Since she had just been released from jail after having served nine months for drug possession and had been shut out of club appearances by the cancellation of her police cabaret card, it was an important gig, restoring her name to marquees and paying her more than $3,878 a week ($38,000 in today's money). Billie was in the theater seven days a week and eleven hours a day, and onstage five times a day for forty-minute sets. She was off for the two hours between each appearance, not time enough to change and go home, so she was confined to the dressing room and bars and restaurants close to the theater. Around the corner Noël Coward's *Private Lives* was playing onstage, starring Tallulah Bankhead, and when she wasn't there or rehearsing her radio show, she came by to see Billie: "The only kicks I got outside of the forty minutes on stage," Holiday remarked.

Tallulah was the daughter of Will Bankhead, a wealthy Deep South politician who, despite being an important supporter of Franklin Delano Roosevelt's New Deal and prolabor legislation, managed to get reelected to Congress from Alabama many times and rose as high in the government as speaker of the House. She was born on the family plantation but refused to go to college, and with the indulgence of her father moved to New York to find work as an actress, then went on to England, where she quickly became famous for her eccentricities and sexual antics onstage and off. Back in the United States, Bankhead's tricks were less successful in helping her build a name, and she was forced to scramble for work in plays for which she had no affinity: She could turn *A Streetcar Named Desire* into a melodrama, or *Private Lives* into high camp that had gay audience members laughing in places never imagined by the playwright. Offstage she was infamous for her flamboyance and her dandyism, often confusing exhibitionism with glamour, living to shock and never herself be shocked. But she was also deeply wedded to jazz—what other white woman at that time would have written a tribute to Louis Armstrong for *Ebony* titled "The World's Greatest Musician," which scolded black people for not taking Pops more seriously?

Billie had known Tallulah from her Harlem days when the grand lady came striding into cabarets dressed in a homburg hat and a man's suit or a flowing gown, loudly announcing her own presence at the door. Now the two women began sharing their show business miseries over lunch at the Edison Hotel and joining in other liaisons in the dressing room (made public by Bankhead's insistence on leaving the door open).

"Banky was the only person I could talk to; also she was about the only person John Levy couldn't scare away." Something about Tallulah's Southern sass and her growled threats sent Levy running for the door, either in humiliation or fear. Tallulah was also the anonymous guest in Billie's book who made "a nasty crack" at Peggy Lee's party when Peggy gave Billie a song she had written for her. "Well, godammit darling," she said, "you should have written something, considering you stole every goddam thing Billie sings." Billie quietly steered Tallulah out of the club, where Levy had fled in embarrassment. "'Come on darling,' she said to me, ignoring Levy. 'Let's go up to my place in the country. It's too goddam hot in New York anyway.'"

Then Levy made the mistake of interrupting.

"Billie's not going anywhere with you," he said. "She's got a home of her own."

"You call that place a home," she said. "It's just another goddam hotel. Besides Billie is like me, she needs at least four men around her."

Levy couldn't take it. He hollered at Banky. "Another word out of you and I'll kick you square in the ass."

With this, Banky walked up to him and stared him down. "No you won't mister," she said. "Not mine. You might kick Billie's, you bastard, but not mine and you know it."

Billie put her in a cab. "Banky, listen, Billie loves you. Now please go home."

The two women shared several qualities: They were reckless in their social lives, generous to a fault, and often squandered their talents. They were close, but unequally so. Bankhead seemed obsessed by her, and when the Strand run reached its end, she accused Billie of trying to duck her, and sometimes insisted on joining her when she heard she was going to a party or visiting a club to hear some music. She was said to have put up money for Billie's bail when she ran afoul of the law, and at one point she hired Billie's stepmother as her maid. When Holiday was charged with possession of opium in California, Tallulah suggested that she and Billie call J. Edgar Hoover to ask for his help. But as Tallulah talked to Hoover, the request quickly changed to a demand. An account of the three-way phone call was intended for chapter twenty-one of *Lady Sings the Blues*, but was cut.

> After the story [of the drug arrest] hit the papers, the first person I heard from was Tallulah. She knew me and she knew Mr. Levy and she knew better than to believe all she read there. She didn't wait for no lawyers, she didn't think about hurting herself, she went to bat, starting at the top and working down.
>
> She called J. Edgar Hoover, head of the FBI. Then she got both me and him on a three-way telephone hook up, with her in New York, Mr. Hoover in Washington and me in San Francisco.
>
> Mr. Hoover tried to tell Banky it was out of his hands; that the FBI had nothing to do with the Treasury Department which handled narcotics, and besides I was not being prosecuted under Federal laws, but had been turned over to state authorities, and he couldn't interfere. But Banky didn't give up. She begged him to do anything he could for me. She told him what a fine girl I was, how I wasn't to blame. When he kept saying it was out of his hands, she gave him a lecture.
>
> "What do you mean you and your darling G-Men go out and get the people who are smuggling this stuff in the boats and giving it to children? What do you mean it's out of your hands? This girl's life was almost ruined once because they sent her to jail. She makes millions of people happy. And she never hurt a soul except herself."
>
> "Sure," she continued, "she may need a little perking up from time to time, darling, but who doesn't?"
>
> "Cool it, Banky," I tried to say, interrupting her . . . I thought this woman's going to fix it so they put me under the table.

Tallulah followed up the call with a letter to Hoover, shifting into another Bankhead mode entirely, this time the Southern belle:

I tremble when I think of my audacity in approaching you at all with so little to recommend me except the esteem, admiration and high regard my father held for you. I would never have dared to ask him or you a favor for myself but knowing your true humanitarian spirit it seemed quite natural at the time to go to the top man. As my Negro mammy used to say, "When you pray you pray to God, don't you?" . . . I had only met Billie Holiday twice in my life . . . and [I] feel the most profound compassion for her . . . she is essentially a child at heart whose troubles have made her psychologically unable to cope with the world in which she finds herself . . . poor thing, you know I did everything within the law to lighten the burden.

Sometime between 1949 and 1952 Bankhead found the need to distance herself from Holiday, perhaps beginning in 1951, when Tallulah charged one of her maids with stealing her money and took her to court, and her maid countered by threatening to publicly detail her drug use and sexual hijinks. The maid had begun dropping names to the press of those with whom Bankhead had had liaisons, such as saxophonist Sidney Bechet and Harlem playboy and club owner Dickie Wells. Bankhead didn't want to be seen as being close to a person with some of the same wounds and frailties as herself, and her own 1952 autobiography made no mention of Billie. When Holiday's editor sent Bankhead the section of *Lady Sings the Blues* that concerned her, she called him during his Thanksgiving dinner to threaten Doubleday with a lawsuit if her name appeared anywhere in it.

Billie then tried to reach her by phone several times, and when she failed, she wrote Bankhead asking for an apology and demanding that she drop her objection to her mention in the book. If not, Billie threatened, she could call on her own maid and several performers who had witnessed them together at the Strand to publicly embarrass Tallulah.

When Billie died, Tallulah attended the funeral, and was seen leaning over the coffin, whispering to her.

. . . . .

Poet Elizabeth Bishop is not mentioned in *Lady Sings the Blues* or for that matter in any other writings about Holiday, but she lingers in the margins as one of those women in the 1930s and 1940s who had a deep fascination with her. In 1944 Bishop wrote a series of four poems titled "Songs for a Colored Singer" that she hoped someone would set to music so that she could have Billie Holiday sing: "I put in a couple of big words, just because she sang big words well—'conspiring root,' for instance." It was Bishop who introduced Billie to her harpsichord teacher, Yale professor Ralph Kirkpatrick, when she took her to his apartment one afternoon to hear him play Bach. Kirkpatrick recalled her as one of the most intelligent listeners he had ever met.

> While Billie put away the better part of a bottle of rum, I played Bach for her. Her face registered everything, and no manifestation of the music seemed to escape her . . . I could have used her like a precision instrument to monitor my performance of the G Minor English Suite simply by watching the subtle variations of expression on her face show me with an infinitely sensitive instrument to monitor what was coming off and what was not. Her own performances, heard through the haze of cigarette smoke in a nightclub, gave heartrending glimpses of a raw and bleeding sensibility condemned to exploitation on every side, unsustained by the protective bulwarks that education and privilege could have given her, and destined, as I knew from the day I first saw her, to end in the gutter.

Later, the two of them sat together at the keyboard. Since Billie could not read music, he played a piece through first, but only once, so she could sing it. "Holiday had the most extraordinary gift of phrasing that I'd ever heard in a singer," he said. "Once she heard it, she knew exactly how the tune should go."

In retrospect, it is not so surprising that composers of classical music would be drawn to Holiday's phrasing, precise diction, and refined sense of the pulse of a piece of music. Leonard Bernstein wrote the song "Big Stuff" for Holiday to sing at the opening of his dance work *Fancy Free*, Ned Rorem acknowledged writing several songs with Holiday in mind, and Thomas Adès's *Life Story* calls for the singer to use Billie's late recordings as a model.

Louise Crane is not mentioned in Holiday's autobiography by name, but she is there under the name of Brenda, "a rich white girl from Fifth Avenue." Crane was the daughter of a wealthy former governor of Massachusetts and a mother who was a founder of the Museum of Modern Art. Louise used her money to support artists and acted as an agent for a number of jazz musicians. She and Elizabeth Bishop had been classmates at Vassar, and were lovers for many years, visiting jazz clubs almost every night when they were living together in New York. It was Louise who introduced Elizabeth to Billie, and the two of them followed her from club to club wherever she performed. They had a large collection of Billie's records, some of which were privately recorded.

But Crane's fascination with Holiday was far more serious than Bishop's. One night Elizabeth came home to find Billie in bed with Louise, and in a fit of fury threw Billie out of the apartment. Bishop and Crane then moved to Key West in 1937, but Louise traveled back and forth to New York, where Elizabeth was certain she was seeing Billie—and indeed she was, taking her shopping to Bonwit Teller and other midtown stores and giving her presents, including her first fur coat, a silver fox. Louise followed her around, picked her up after each night's work, and even underwrote her mother's restaurant, Mom Holiday's, on Ninety-ninth Street near Columbus Avenue.

She also booked Billie into the "Coffee Concerts" she presented at the Museum of Modern Art, which mixed folk, avant-garde, classical, and jazz music on the same programs. Billie was by now ready to move away from the downtown slummers of Café Society and into real society and the concert hall. Everyone who attended her Coffee Concert was enchanted by her songs, from the *New York Times* reporter who was there to poet Marianne Moore, who came at Louise's invitation, dressed in her black tricorn hat and cape, and was thrilled by Billie's "bacarole" [*sic*] opening number, "Fine and Mellow"—"and of course by her flame-colored skirt and Japanese Mei Lan Fang aestheticism." Moore could famously bounce names and images off the wall, but in drawing a comparison between Holiday's performance and those of a legendary male Peking Opera singer whose female roles featured small but highly expressive hand gestures, she was right on the mark. Moore also asked Crane if she could provide her with "that intimate song of Billie Holiday's about the eyes" (undoubtedly "Them There Eyes").

John Hammond's adventures in jazz were coming home to haunt him. When he learned that it was his cousin Louise who was involved with Billie, he went directly to the Crane family to warn them that their daughter's relationship with the singer might lead to the family being "hurt by unsavory gossip, or even blackmailed by the gangsters and dope pushers Billie knew." Louise's mother subsequently ordered her never to have "any more colored folk in her house, I didn't care *who* it was," and she and Billie ceased to see each other. Hammond said that Holiday never forgave him for it, and Billie angrily describes the affair in her book, offering her theory of what was driving Louise's attentions and how they affected black people such as herself:

> But some girls like Brenda can't love or let themselves go with anybody—man or woman. They can't even be lesbians and work at it. They're incapable of loving anybody—just the opposite of my trouble. And they try to make up for it by buying things for people like me.
>
> It's a cinch to see how it all begins. These poor bitches grow up hating their mothers and having the hots for their fathers. And since being in love with our father is taboo, they grow up unable to

get any kicks out of anything unless it's taboo love. And some Negroes in America walk around with big "Do Not Touch" signs on them, that's where we come in. And I'm telling you it can be a drag.

There were others who could have appeared in the book. Elizabeth Hardwick moved to New York from Louisville in 1943 hoping to become a writer and an intellectual. She shared an apartment with Greer Johnson, a friend from Louisville who had also just come to town, and who later became a producer who created important opportunities for Holiday when work for her was scarce. Hardwick includes a chapter on Billie in her book *Sleepless Nights* that is part essay, part nonfiction, based on Hardwick's and Johnson's idolatry. She wrote of Billie as "the bizarre deity," the phrase that the poet Baudelaire used for his brown-skinned mistress, and as one of those for whom the word "changeling" was invented, an offspring of a legendary being who has been switched at birth for a mere mortal.

Her whole life had taken place in the dark. The spotlight shone down on the black, hushed circle in a café, the moon slowly slid through the clouds. Night-working, smiling, in make-up, in long, silky dresses, singing over and over, again and again. The aim of it all is just to be drifting off to sleep when the first rays of the sun's brightness threaten the theatrical eyelids.

Simone de Beauvoir visited New York City in 1947 and went to Carnegie Hall with Richard Wright to see Louis Armstrong and then to the Downbeat Club, where Billie was appearing with Art Tatum. Attendance at the club had been sparse, and both performers' pay had just been cut for lack of business. Although Billie didn't perform that night, she was there at the club, and De Beauvoir described her in her diary:

She is very beautiful in a long white dress, her black hair straightened by a clever permanent and falling straight and shiny around her clear brown face. Her bangs look like they've been sculpted in dark metal. She smiles, she is beautiful, but she doesn't sing. They say she's on drugs and sings only rarely now.

The last chapter in the original draft version of *Lady Sings the Blues* was moved back to become part of chapter twenty-two, and a new final chapter was added to the published book titled "God Bless the Child." In it Billie describes being once again arrested in Philadelphia for drug possession, along with her husband, Louis McKay, only this time, she says, with no evidence of any wrongdoing. After a night in jail, she went to the Showboat Club, sang her last evening's set, and left by bus for New York. In her concluding paragraphs she says the doctors had told her that she had successfully kicked her addiction—a fact she already knew, she explained, because she now hated television, a true sign of her rehabilitation.

Billie often found herself the subject of attention of the police, who wanted to prove to the public that they were dealing with the drug plague, no matter where it was found, and of the press, which was eager to reveal her true character when she was away from the lights and the glamour. She had become the archetypal black jazz junkie, and there was no way she could deny it. Most of the passages cut from the book concerned her involvement with the white elite, which perhaps would have helped make her case for her rehabilitation and widened her social circle beyond African Americans and junkies of both races. But when they were edited out for fear of litigation, *Lady Sings the Blues* became what we know it to be today: a confession in which she blames no one but herself, and doesn't ask for sympathy.

After Billie's death Bill Dufty wrote several articles in which he cited a number of topics that hadn't been discussed in the book, either because

Billie didn't want them there or because she hadn't remembered them. Some of what she had recalled had been triggered by minor incidents. One day Dufty and Billie were having lunch in a tiny Chinese restaurant—roast duck and 7 Up and gin, favorites of hers—when the waiter brought some mustard to the table.

> Ask him to take away that damn mustard . . .
>
> I hate the smell of mustard. I sat in a tub of mustard for eighteen hours one time, killed my baby so I wouldn't be a bad girl. Having a baby without being married. My mother worried about that. It happened to her. And all she prayed for was it wouldn't happen to me. I didn't want to hurt her so I sat in a damn tub of hot water and mustard. God will punish her, the kids used to say. He damned well did, too. The only thing I ever wanted is that baby.

It was well known that Billie loved children, talked about having them, and openly fantasized about what it would be like to be a mother and have a family that lived in a house with a white picket fence—an image she had carried from her childhood. She enjoyed the company of children so much that she often asked her friends to bring theirs to see her or offered herself as their babysitter. When she lived in Queens, young Miles Davis and his family were her neighbors at a time when both of them were experiencing brief moments of domestic bliss. On Saturday afternoons Miles would borrow a bicycle and pedal over to Billie's house to talk and drink gin. He said she reminded him of his mother, with her light brown skin, long hair, and regal carriage. Billie always asked him to bring his two-year-old son Gregory along with him, occasions on which she happily played with him and never wanted him to leave. She often found excuses to spend time with her friends' children, babysitting for Maya Angelou's son Guy, or Jack Crystal's son Billy, and she was quick to ask to be godmother to the children of the Duftys, as well as to Leonard Feather and Rosemary Clooney. ("It takes a *bad* woman to be a good godmother," she said to Rosemary.) Bevan Dufty recalled Billie doting on him as a child and trying to breastfeed him from her milkless breasts. At one point, she attempted to adopt a child in Boston, and was devastated when she learned that she had been turned down because of her drug conviction.

After the book was published, Dufty read somewhere that Billie had once been a guest at the White House while Franklin Delano Roosevelt was president, but she had never mentioned it to him or anyone he knew. When he asked her about it, she shouted, "Jesus Christ, don't remind me of that damn thing. I don't even want to *think* about it." Her explosive response was puzzling, since Billie had always spoken of FDR as one of the few men she admired. But it was not the president who was the issue. In 1944 Hazel Scott, the pianist and singer who worked with her at Café Society, had talked Billie into going to one of the president's infantile paralysis benefit balls held annually on his birthday, January 30. Billie was concerned about how the staff of the White House, the "dicty Negroes"—what she called the snobbish black elite of D.C.—would respond to her being there. She imagined that every one of them would be watching her, looking for signs of drugs or their traces on her arms. Though she had not yet been arrested for drug use, she knew the rumors of her addiction were widespread in the black community.

Finally she agreed to go, and when she arrived in full finery, she had a long wait ahead of her, with Hollywood stars such as Mary Pickford, Maria Montez, Lucille Ball, Jinx Falkenburg, John Garfield, and Red Skelton roaming in and out of the dressing rooms and bathrooms. After she had finished her song, she couldn't leave until the president had made his appearance. By now she was spending every minute looking for an empty bathroom, and in desperation she stepped into an elevator and hit the button. When it stopped, she walked out and began making her way down a long hall when she heard a voice she recognized from the radio saying, "Well, little lady, you look as though you're lost." There was the president of the United States in a wheelchair pushed by a naval officer. She, like most of America, had never seen the president in a wheelchair, as he was carefully guarded from the public's learning of the degree of his illness. She was shocked to see him looking older, weakened, an invalid. When their eyes met she saw something else:

> These goddamn American doctors don't know nothing about drugs. Here's a man who was President of the United States. He should have the best doctors around. He's got a war to run and all that bullshit and aggravation and you know what they had him on? They had him on morphine. Yeah, morphine. They should have been giving him goddamn heroin.
>
> My God, I couldn't sleep for days thinking about it. I wished I'd never gone near that place. Who the hell could I talk to about it?

To take advantage of *Lady Sings the Blues'* publication, Clef Records produced an album with the same title made up of songs Billie had been working on in the studio over the previous two years, all of them rerecordings of songs she had previously issued, and most of them with titles that were chapter titles in the book. Only one song was new, "Lady Sings the Blues," with music by Herbie Nichols, a little-known pianist who was much admired by musicians for his challenging compositions. They had been brought together by Dufty, and Billie added the words to an instrumental piece by Nichols that he had titled "Serenade."

But the big event to promote the book and provide some work for Billie in New York City was two performances at Carnegie Hall. The concerts were set for November 10 at eight thirty and midnight, and both were sold out, with seats added onstage for the overflow. Don Friedman, the show's producer, asked Gilbert Millstein to narrate parts of the book between her songs to create an autobiographical structure for the event, presumably because Millstein had given the book a posi-tive review in the *New York Times* and was well known as a journalist and a critic in the city. Millstein would read selections over piano ac-companiment, and the spotlight would then swing over to Billie for her to segue into a song. When Holiday arrived that afternoon for rehearsal, it was obvious to everyone that she was not well. Her voice was thin, her suit ill-fitting, her legs and ankles swollen, and she had no interest in singing. She picked the songs for the performances and the order in which they would be sung and then left. Millstein feared that she would never make it through the night.

When the lights went down for the first performance and the musi-cians began to play, Millstein later wrote, "Miss Holiday stepped from between the curtains into the white spotlight awaiting her, wearing a white evening gown and white gardenias in her black hair. She was erect and beautiful; poised and smiling. And when the first section of the narration was ended, she sang—with strength undiminished, with all the art that was hers." Despite the incongruity of a middle-aged white man's reading her words while she stood only a few feet away, the audience seemed to accept it in stride, much as readers had when Wil-liam Dufty wrote in Holiday's voice. In fact they seemed moved and even startled, gasping at words they had never heard spoken at a public gathering.

A heavily edited recording was made from the two concerts that evening and released as *The Essential Billie Holiday: Carnegie Hall Concert Recorded Live,* leaving out some of the rougher parts of her book—descriptions of her addiction and her attempts at drug with-drawal, sentencing and parole, her days with the Count Basie band, the racial tension surrounding her performance of "Strange Fruit," and her hope of having her cabaret card restored (which was strongly ap-plauded). Two reels of tape exist that reveal that, in addition to the ex-cised readings, there were fuller versions of some of the songs on the album, seven songs that weren't included, and, at the end, a presentation to her of a leather-bound and gold-engraved edition of *Lady Sings the*

Blues, along with a plug for the *Coronet* condensation of the book then on newsstands.

Overall it was something of a triumph for Holiday, but one that came at a huge cost. Gerald Early summed it up: "Holiday's concerts were the final public acceptance of jazz as an art form and of the black performer as artist. The life and the art had become interchangeable. And the life and the art had become a kind of voyeuristic tragedy for the audience and a self-conscious tragedy for the artist." As Billie said, "They come to see me fall on my ass."

After her death in 1959, Dufty wrote a series of eight articles in the *New York Post* on the final years of Billie's life that served as a de facto finale to the autobiography, and readers responded to them as such. Among the letters to the editor, the novelist Dawn Powell said the story of the end of her life was "perfect—making the end a triumph and not a defeat," and playwright Lorraine Hansberry praised "the bold and unvarnished, yet sweet humanity in the writing." Dufty wanted his pieces added to the book's subsequent editions to complete her life story, but no publisher has yet chosen to do so.

Holiday's problems were accumulating just at the moment when inexpensive forms of photographic and recording technology were becoming available. The first gossip magazines appeared, and increased police and psychiatric surveillance was introduced along with more extensive means of governmental gathering and exchange of information on individuals and their behavior. The story of her life was made public as part of the first war against drugs. She was being followed nightly by the police, and her apartment building sometimes had an officer at the door warning visitors away. Yet she quickly realized that it was possible for her to use some of the same media and methods to defend and redefine herself.

Beginning in 1947 Holiday began giving more interviews to music magazines (such as "I'll Never Sing with a Dance Band Again—Holiday," *Down Beat*, 1939; "Don't Blame Show Biz!—Billie," *Down Beat*, 1947; "Billie Holiday, Now Remarried, Finds Happiness, a New Sense of Security," *Down Beat*, January 11, 1952), and in the last ten years of her life several articles were written under her name for African American magazines ("I'm Cured for Good," *Ebony*, July 1949; "Can a Dope Addict Come Back?" *Tan*, February 1953; "How I Blew a Million Dollars," *Our World*, March 1953; "Billie's Tragic Life," *Ebony*, September 1956). The articles written for African American audiences deal openly with her failures—drug use, poor business dealings, even poorer choices of husbands, time spent in prison, and her problems finding work in New York City without a police permit. The articles in *Ebony* were particularly important to her, not only because it was the premier African American magazine, but because it was where in 1951 Cab Calloway had published "Is Dope Killing Our Musicians?," warning readers that the sweep of drugs through the black community had left a generation of jazz musicians addicts, who were doomed unless they sought help. Though no names were mentioned in the article, the magazine included a rogue's gallery of drug users' pictures that included Billie along with Miles Davis, Gene Krupa, Dexter Gordon, and others. In all of these publications, as in *Lady Sings the Blues*, she argued for changes in drug laws and rehabilitation, spelled out how her civil rights had been violated by the police and the FBI, and pleaded for her cabaret card to be restored so that she could make a living.

She also spoke openly about life as a woman of color in America, something that was very rare, and even dangerous at that time, and declared herself "a race woman"—one who was committed to the rights of her people:

When you're writing, straighten them out about my people . . . I'm a Negro. I've got two strikes against me . . . I'm proud of those two strikes. I'm as good as a lot of people of all kinds—I'm proud I'm a Negro.

A lot of the real dicty people with talent used to come and hear me [in nightclubs]. They were wonderful, but as usual it only took one cracker in the audience to wreck things.

I hate these East Side clubs that hire colored entertainers and re-fuse to cater to colored customers.... When I go there they put me in a corner together with the rest of the colored customers ... they have a marvelous way of getting us all together where we can't be seen by the whites. Then when they learn that I'm Billie Holiday they immediately become apologetic and switch me to the ringside where I have a perfectly horrible time. I find I can't enjoy the show any longer because of what's happened and I pick up and walk out.

It was slow, this attempt to climb clear of the barrel. But as I grew older, I found those trying to keep me in it were not always the corner hoodlum, the streetwalker, the laborer, the numbers run-ner, the rooming-house landladies and landlords ... They, I found, were the ones who wanted me to "go," to get somewhere. It was their applause and help that kept me inspired ... long before the mink-coated lorgnette crowd of Fifth Avenue and Greenwich Vil-lage ever heard of me.

I never felt inferior to anybody and I couldn't learn to act as if I did. That was my trouble. I never got past the fifth grade in school. If I had, I might have been brainwashed like a lot of brown skinned kids. When I was thirteen I just plain decided one day I wasn't going to do anything or say anything unless I meant it. Not "Please, Sir." Not "Thank you, Ma'am." Nothing. Unless I meant it. You have to be poor and black to know how many times you get kicked in the head just for trying to do something as simple as that. But I never gave up trying.

The last article under Billie's name, "I Needed Heroin to Live," co-written with Dufty, was first rejected by *Esquire* but then published in the infamous magazine *Confidential* in October 1959, for which she was paid $1,500. She had been hospitalized for liver problems, not drug abuse, but was then arrested in her hospital room for alleged possession of heroin and put under twenty-four-hour police guard. The article was originally titled "Heroin Saved My Life" and was her final statement on the media, psychiatry, the medical system, the law, her publisher, and Hollywood.

Lying in bed in Metropolitan Hospital in Harlem, she read her own preobituaries in the newspapers and commented on them caustically. "Billie Doomed" was the title of one, and to the policewoman by her bedside she remarked, "We're all doomed, baby. What the hell else is new?" Another was headlined "Billie Holiday Is Dying of Dope Addiction and Alcoholism." Her comment: "Did they blame Arthur Godfrey's lung cancer on cigarettes? He's through pushing them on TV, God bless him," as she lit up a king-size nonfilter brand. "That's for sure." The article continued: "Her voice is shot—cracked and eroded by the careless years of drug addiction, whisky drinking and other malign influences." "I've never had much voice to begin with," she laughed, "but I've got more today than I ever had"; then, arching her back, she broke into the first few notes of "Night and Day." "Whisky and heroin have taken their toll too," said another press report. "The famed jazz singer lies on the verge of death at 46 [*sic*]." "My mother and father never touched dope in their lives—and neither lived to be as old as me. I've been on and off heroin for fifteen years. Who knows? Maybe heroin kept me alive." When she read that a psychiatrist she had never seen had declared her as self-destructive, the victim of a death urge, she chortled, "I'm not the suicide type. Never have been. Homicide, maybe, but not suicide."

Billie's mordant humor persisted until the end. Dufty said that when he visited her room one day, he saw her motionless with her eyes closed and her husband with a bottle of liquor and saying prayers for the dead. Fearing the end, Dufty withdrew quietly. When he came back later, she was still lying there, but then she opened her eyes and asked "Is he gone?" When Dufty assured her, she said, "I've always been a religious bitch, but if that dirty motherfucker believes in God I've got to think it over."

Throughout *Lady Sings the Blues*, Holiday resists being categorized, typed, and limited by the social constraints placed upon her, and goes to great pains to show how these limitations affected her life and her art. Her primary message is her survival as an artist—what she had come through, but also what she needed to accomplish to keep going. However, the doubts raised about the book's authorship, her literacy, the role of a white man in the writing, the truth of her story, and the possible mercenary aims of the project all added up to undermine her stature as a responsible author and an agent of her own destiny. This is not unique among accounts of jazz musicians' lives, and it is even more common in the lives of African American women artists, who have a long history of difficulty in establishing respectability and legitimacy within a history of slavery, poverty, segregation, and discrimination.

A biographer's task is to develop a life story, and then check facts and correct what she sees as mistakes or lies. Some of those who have written about Holiday saw it as their job to challenge her account of her life and remind the reader of what Holiday *really* was (and maybe how hip they are) by using terms of disrespect such as "whore," "whorehouse," and "junkie." But as an autobiographer, part of Holiday's own task was to present a clear portrait of her place in the society in which she found herself. To her this meant showing how the stigmatized women who work as maids, singers, and prostitutes have their own values. She urges her readers to accept that, even among the lowest in society, characteristics such as strength, dignity, and the ability to survive should be seen as forms of virtue. As much as it was a means of making money (which was also necessary to redeem her), *Lady Sings the Blues* was an act of redemption, an attempt to assert her dignity, as she always did, within a society that had already condemned her to a form of ignominy. As it is, she reveals far more of herself than most autobiographers, and if at times she wanders into pathos, she reminds us (as does Dufty in his articles following her death) that she thought of herself as religious. While asking for compassion for the addicted, she blames only herself for making bad choices and being too weak to resist drugs. Hers was not a victim's story.

CHAPTER THREE

The Image: Film, Television, and Photography

*B*illie Holiday tells us that her first film work was in 1933 as an extra in what she called a "mob scene" in *The Emperor Jones* staring Paul Robeson, though no one as yet has been able to identify her in the movie. Maybe she is there, hiding in plain sight in one of her many identities; maybe she was cut out of the film. Still, there were some who saw an affinity: When Terry Southern adapted *The Emperor Jones* for BBC television in the 1950s, he used her music on the soundtrack.

She does appear prominently in the 1935 film short *Symphony in Black: A Rhapsody of Negro Life*, directed by Fred Waller at Paramount, featuring Duke Ellington as a composer at work, creating a nine-minute or so extended composition in four parts, "The Laborers," "A Triangle," "A Hymn of Sorrow," and "Harlem Rhythm."

The film has the feel of a musical revue in one of the larger Harlem cabarets. Holiday appeared in the second and longest section, playing a sad young woman rejected by her lover or pimp (played by the dancer Earl "Snakehips" Tucker) and thrown to the ground like a dancer in a French apache dance. Following the dramatic setup, she's seen singing "The Saddest Tale," an Ellington song of only nine lines that she nonetheless made the most of, standing motionless with her eyes closed, her face half in shadow, and turning away from the camera at the end. The song is performed with a minimalist, almost method approach to acting, unlike that adopted by many singers on film at that time, who either smiled through even the saddest of songs or acted out their pain with crude gestures.

In her autobiography Billie downplayed *Symphony in Black* as "just a short subject" that no one would see, but it was an important step in Ellington's career, as well as her own. Being featured with the Duke Ellington band before she was twenty years old would have been achievement enough, given that she had made her first recordings with Benny Goodman just the year before (even though her performances with Goodman seemed, by her own admission, somewhat childlike). But her singing with Ellington was remarkably poised, with all the features of her mature style in place—the rhythmic manipulations, her distinctive timbre, melodic inflections, and unsentimental delivery. The song's opening lines—"I've got those 'lost my man, can't get him back again' blues"—would set the tone for much of her repertoire for the next twenty years.

Orson Welles, *The Story of Jazz*, and New Orleans

In the summer of 1941 Duke Ellington made jazz history when *Jump for Joy*, his musical based on themes of African American history, opened at the Mayan Theater in Los Angeles. Though it never got beyond Los Angeles, the musical drew large numbers of Hollywood's elite who were excited about the mixing of social and political themes in a Broadway-type setting. When Orson Welles saw the piece, he approached Ellington after the show and asked to meet with him the next morning at RKO. Orson had been planning a film, to be called *The Story of Jazz*, that would be one section of a sprawling four-part anthology movie. He proposed to Ellington that they write it together, with Duke acting as musical director and composer. Louis Armstrong would appear as himself and be the focus of the film; pianist and singer Hazel Scott would play Lil, Louis's wife; and a long list of New Orleans musicians were to appear as themselves, speaking in their own vernacular. When he met Holiday three months later and struck up an affair with her, he asked her to play the role of Bessie Smith, and invited her to come to the studios with him where he was preparing to start production on *The Magnificent Ambersons.*

Welles began his own research on jazz, songs were selected, the musicians were interviewed for ideas, and Armstrong wrote him a short autobiography. The script was written by Elliot Paul, a writer for Welles's radio shows and a pianist who had studied boogie-woogie with one of its masters, Albert Ammons. In the script that emerged, a young Louis Armstrong is discovered by trumpeter Joe "King" Oliver and develops into the spark that brought jazz into full flower in New Orleans. But then Storyville, the city's entertainment district, is closed by the secretaries of the army and navy in 1917 to protect recruits heading for Europe in World War I from vice and corruption. Now out of work, Armstrong leaves town by a Mississippi riverboat and relocates to Chicago, where jazz flourishes and spreads across the country. It soon becomes a world-wide phenomenon, and Armstrong travels to London and Paris, where he is celebrated as an *artiste.*

What might have been material for a conventional musical biopic was instead intended to be radically innovative, mixing together different styles of jazz, using the surrealist drawings of Oskar Fischinger, and becoming the first film to celebrate the life of an African American.

Before the film could begin production, though, the United States was attacked by Japan on December 7, and priorities shifted everywhere. Even the movies changed almost overnight. Two days after the attack, RKO stockholder Nelson Rockefeller and the director of the Office of the Coordinator of Inter-American Affairs, John Hay Whitney, approached Welles with the idea of going to Brazil as a goodwill ambassador, where he would produce films with the cooperation of the Brazilian government to help stave off the rise of fascism in Latin America. Welles's first thought was to make a film of Brazilian Carnival that could be connected to *The Story of Jazz* and would show the social and cultural importance of the Afro-Brazilian event by paralleling it in the film to Mardi Gras in New Orleans. Both could be a part of the anthology film that he was planning to call *It's All True*. RKO agreed to fund it, with the Office of the Coordinator of Inter-American Affairs picking up any losses. But as shooting of the Rio Carnival got under way, and the studio saw that Welles was highlighting the origins of the event in the poorest sections of the city and focusing on the everyday interaction of races in Brazil, the moguls feared the material would come as an unwelcome surprise to white Americans, and became uneasy with the project. Dr. Maurice Bernstein, Welles's guardian after his parents died, wrote Orson on May 14, 1942, that RKO was on the verge of shutting down the film and not renewing his contract:

> Today, I was at your studio and got an earful. First, that RKO is frantic about your expenses, both personal and in making the picture in South America. One million feet of color film when only 12,000 can be used. And in addition, your mixing of the blacks and whites cannot be accepted by Iowa, Missouri, not to mention all the people the other side of the Mason/Dixon line. You probably know the feeling of RKO better than I on all these things. But your doings are certainly stirring them up.

Filming was halted abruptly within a day or two, and though Welles tried to keep the project alive with his own money, he was unable to finish it. Orson never completed his jazz film but kept the idea alive by hiring the same New Orleans musicians (minus Armstrong, whom even he couldn't afford) as house band for his radio show in the early forties, and by producing *Years of Jazz*, a weekly history of jazz for Armed Forces Radio Service in 1944.

New Orleans Without Welles

After World War II ended, Majestic Pictures, an independent film company working under the RKO umbrella, decided to adapt *The Story of Jazz* using parts of Elliot Paul's jazz script and casting for *It's All True* and merge it with another Paul script, "Conspiracy in Jazz," but without Orson Welles and Duke Ellington. The new film was intended as a conventional history of jazz, jazz then understood as having been invented in New Orleans, with Louis Armstrong as its most important figure. It was aimed at predominantly white audiences in all parts of the country with a story with which they could identify, and if there was enough black presence in the film to pick up an African American audience, all the better. It was a tricky formula, and one that had already produced some bad Hollywood films.

When plans for the film, now titled *New Orleans*, were announced, there was immediate excitement among jazz writers and African American journalists, who foresaw a movie that celebrated black contributions to America and, through its casting, would not involve segregation or dilution of the music. Despite the popularity of jazz in the early 1940s, there was still only a vague grasp of its history and meaning. Was it high art or folk art? Music for dancing or close listening? Vulgar trash or spiritually redemptive? Best when played by blacks or whites? All of these issues were raised by the story line of *New Orleans*.

The script that producer Jules Levey chose centered on Miralee, the daughter of a wealthy New Orleans family who returns from studying opera in Europe and finds her mother's maid (played by Billie) secretly playing the piano and singing "Do You Know What It Means to Miss New Orleans" in their palatial home. This apparent infraction of household rules was more significant then than it may now seem: An African American maid in the 1940s should not have been discovered playing the piano and singing while at work, and most certainly should not have been singing a love song. Fascinated by what she hears, the daughter then orders her maid to take her to Storyville, where she witnesses Holiday singing with the Louis Armstrong band in the cellar of a gambling establishment, and is instantly converted to jazz and life in the underworld. Wringing of hands follows among the whites, but there is no stopping the young woman, who, in the throes of discovery, decides that she will become a jazz singer herself, especially after she falls in love with the club owner and finds the conductor of the New Orleans Symphony also secretly attending these nightly jam sessions. Against better judgment, she insists on performing one of Holiday's songs as an encore at her first concert of classical music in the city and watches the audience walk out in disgust.

When Storyville is closed, the black performers of the district march out together, with Billie singing in the lead (with what is said to be the voice of an uncredited Ethel Waters dubbed in for Holiday's). A diaspora of New Orleans's black musicians follows, and Chicago soon becomes the magnet that draws jazz musicians to the city. Then, in a strange ending, all the African Americans who populated the film disappear; the opera singer performs the Billie Holiday song again as an encore to a classical concert, with the white Woody Herman band and a symphony orchestra and a chorus behind her, only this time to great applause. Jazz had somehow become a lady, and a white one at that.

Work on the film began in early September 1946, when a crew was sent to New Orleans to film local sites and a jazz funeral, while prerecording of the music began in Los Angeles. Holiday arrived late, twelve days after production began, and was in no mood for hanging out with her colleagues. Her addiction was taking its toll, and she was angry at her manager, Joe Glaser, for having signed her up for a part she didn't want. Much of what she had accomplished to that point had been aimed at avoiding domestic labor, yet she was haunted by it. Her mother had been in domestic service, at one point for Ethel Waters and later as a maid for the singer Mildred Bailey. Her stepmother had been Tallulah Bankhead's maid. Shortly after she came to New York, Billie had a part as a maid on a Shelton Brook soap opera on radio. The transition from playing mammies to playing maids did not represent much progress for black women in fifty years of filmmaking. Granted, the role of a maid who is commanded to take her white mistress slumming did signify a shift in the female racial paradigm in the postwar era: from mammies

and their feckless young white charges to maids and their headstrong
employers. In daytime these maids were underlings in the world of
upper-class young white ladies, while at night they might serve as guides
to the underworld. An intimacy existed between maid and mistress, but
it was an awkward one, in which the maid was asked to share the secrets
of her own life with her white employer at the same time she was asked
to protect her mistress by lying about their nocturnal adventures. But a
maid for a white woman was still a maid: Billie complained that her
drama coach for the film was making her try out twenty-three different
ways of saying, " 'Yes, Miss Miralee' and 'No, Miss Miralee' in order to
get the right kind of Tom feeling into it." Years later, that role was still on
her mind. When journalist Murray Kempton visited her shortly before
her death, he found her ironing a shirt for her husband. She stopped,
took a look at her work, and then started over again, remarking, "I suppose that's why I never made it as a maid in the movies. I'm just not the
maid type." She apparently never agreed with Ethel Waters's sentiment
that it was better to play a maid than to be one.

As with the Welles film, RKO once again objected to so many people of
color being featured in *New Orleans*. Producer Jules Levey, siding with
the studio, also took issue with the script and edited out the most important scenes, according to director Herbert Biberman and screen-
writer Paul. One of the first drafts of the script for the film contained a
quite different ending: All of the principal actors moved on to Café Society in New York, where the opera singer improvised words to a tune
played by jazz musicians, and Billie Holiday and the Golden Gate Quartet both sang. In the concert hall ending, Louis Armstrong played in
front of the Woody Herman band and a symphony orchestra.

Biberman said that "Levey was scared to death that too many Negroes will come to the theaters to see this picture because there will
be too many Negro artists in it." In order to change the direction of the
film Biberman was replaced by Arthur Lubin after Busby Berkeley was

ruled out. The resulting movie shows signs of ambivalence toward its subject and of drifting off course throughout, with Billie portrayed at some moments as a servant and at others as a stylish singer. One character is interrupted just as he begins giving an explanation of the history of jazz; some musicians (Lucky Thompson, the Woody Herman band) entered the film without seeming to have any relation to one another, and there is even an odd allusion to Kristallnacht during the closing of Storyville.

When *New Orleans* opened at the Winter Garden in New York, it was presented as an exploitation film, with posters advertising Storyville's "18 Blocks of Sin Dives!" and photos of prostitutes smiling out from their "cribs."

It was Holiday who had the last word on the film. When she heard that Herbert Biberman had been called before the House Un-American Activities Committee and sent to jail as one of the Hollywood Ten, she wrote, "He should have shown them *New Orleans*. With all that Uncle Tom stuff in it, and his name on it as one of the authors, he could have beat that mother-huggin' rap."

Holiday on Television

Holiday made very few TV appearances, but in her first, the ABC series *The Comeback Story* on October 14, 1953, she participated in a reenactment of her life. *Comeback* was an early reality show, one that explored the backgrounds of those who had overcome infirmities and afflictions—a woman athlete who had colon cancer, a blind jazz pianist, an alcoholic radio announcer, a child singer who lost his career when his voice changed, and, in Holiday's case, a singer who overcame heroin addiction, poverty, and racism. Although it was conceived as a victim's story—one unintentionally reinforced by her swollen jaw, the result of an infected tooth, which kept her from saying very much—the presence of some famous friends made the program more interesting than it promised to be. Among those who appeared were Artie Shaw, Louis

Armstrong, singer Mae Barnes, Arthur Herzog Jr., Leonard Feather, Count Basie, and Pod Hollingsworth, the Harlem club owner who first hired her to sing. Benny Goodman, Teddy Wilson, and John Hammond, it turned out, refused to appear on the show, the latter because he thought it was in such bad taste.

Still, the story of Holiday's life that was presented was a candid one, which involved subjects that were largely forbidden on national television. The program's moderator was Georgie Jessel, a showbiz stalwart whose fame far exceeded his accomplishments, a man who was often the butt of rude jokes. Jessel was unflinching in his comments, however, and ended the show by telling the audience that Holiday was not able to work in nightclubs in New York City because she couldn't get a license from the police to perform, even though she had paid her debt to society. Billie, smiling and begowned, exchanged a few words with Jessell and then sang "God Bless the Child."

In 1957 CBS producer Robert Herridge asked jazz writers Whitney Balliett and Nat Hentoff to select the best musicians to appear on a TV show, regardless of how well known they were. They picked Count Basie, Lester Young, Thelonious Monk, Billie Holiday, Gerry Mulligan, Coleman Hawkins, Pee Wee Russell, Jimmy Rushing, Jimmy Giuffre, Red Allen, and others to create an all-star big band and to split off into several smaller groups. It was live television, but it was to be as free-wheeling and improvisatory as possible. (There was no script, and the camera operators were told to shoot whatever they liked.)

The only musician who presented a problem for the producer was Billie Holiday. During a sound check Herridge received a note from a sponsor's representative that said, "We must not put into America's homes, especially on Sunday, someone who's been imprisoned for drug use." Herridge told the representative that if Holiday was out of the show, then he, Balliett, and Hentoff would leave. The show aired with Billie included on December 8, 1957, as "The Sound of Jazz," a special production of CBS-TV's *The Seven Lively Arts*, and it resulted in Holiday's finest moment on television.

Lady Sings the Blues: The Film

After her autobiography was published in 1956, plans for a film about her emerged, shaped by Lester Cowan, whose long career as a director included such films as *One Touch of Venus*, *My Little Chickadee*, and *The Story of G.I. Joe*. The script for *The Trial of Billie Holiday*, by songwriter Ann Ronell, Cowan's wife, begins in 1938 with Holiday traveling with the Artie Shaw band in the South and follows her as she returns to her mother's apartment in Harlem, tracks her time in federal prison, and dwells on her 1949 trial for narcotics and her defense by lawyer Jake Ehrlich. It was as close to film noir as a biopic about a musician could be, but there were no takers for the project.

Cowan tried again by optioning the film rights to *Lady Sings the Blues* to serve as the basis of a script by Ronell and William Dufty. To encourage Billie to agree to the project, Dufty wrote her of his good impression of Cowan:

> This was the first guy who had faced the basic reason why there can't be honest movies about people who stay brown all year round. Loot. Because, it is said, a third of the box office gross of any movie comes from the South, everybody has to trim and trim. Cowan starts with that. He says it's not true, except for cowboy pictures. He starts out with the premise that you write the South off. You tell the people down there that they aren't ready for this movie yet. And when they are, it can be shown down there. In the meantime, he works on the basis that the southern gross can be made up by Europe . . . I hope I'm right, and I think I am, that after Cowan has done your life story in this movie, this cat is going to have to do a new ending for this book. And a happy ending, too. If I'm not, I want you to keep this letter and make me eat it next year.

The lead was to be played by Dorothy Dandridge, a black actress and singer who had fought her way into Hollywood and nightclubs but was desperately in need of a starring role. United Artists advanced money for production, the government of Puerto Rico agreed to fund construction of sets for filming on the island, and Anthony Mann (who had directed *The Glenn Miller Story* a few years before) was hinted to be the director.

When Cowan wrote Holiday to introduce himself and his film about her, he stressed that his movie would avoid the sensational. Unlike some of her autobiography's reviewers, he said he found her book inspirational, a great saga of survival, a universally moving account. It carried the same forceful message as that of Ralph Waldo Emerson's essay "Self-Reliance." His film, he promised her, would not be banned for its drug, sexual, and racial content—a real concern, given the rough treatment censors had given *The Man with the Golden Arm* several years before. With the moral message he saw in her life, it might even lead to New York City's dropping its ban on her performing at clubs that served alcohol. More than that, it would lead to millions becoming aware of "the staggering cost we pay in this country for the foolish notion of treating the narcotic addict as a criminal, and driving sick people through punishment to crime."

As Cowan began to think about casting, he changed his mind about Dorothy Dandridge and let it be known that he was considering actress Diahann Carroll for the role of Billie. But in an article in the *New York Times*, he also said that Holiday might be portrayed by a white actress: "My principal concern as a producer," he explained, "is to find for the role an actress who can do justice to it." Asked if he had discussed the casting with the singer, Mr. Cowan said her only comment was, "I'm not prejudiced." In fact, Holiday had wondered why *she* wasn't playing herself, and "even if they get a white actress the character she plays will still be colored. If they change that there's no story." There was recent precedent for casting a white actress as black, since Jeanne Crain played such a role in *Pinky* (1949). Cowan had also considered Lana Turner for the role of Billie, but United Artists felt that Ava Gardner—who in 1951 had played the mulatto Julie in *Show Boat*—was the bigger name at the moment and the studio said it didn't want to make "just another low-budget second feature."

Dancer James "Stumpy" Cross said that Gardner had tried to get Billie to take her part in *Show Boat*, but she wasn't interested. Gardner may have been contemplated to play Billie because of rumors that she *was* actually black. Years later, James Baldwin recalled that Ava had spoken to him about the part:

> My buddy, Ava Gardner, once asked me if I thought she could play Billie Holiday. I had to tell her that, though she was certainly "down" enough for it—courageous and honest and beautiful enough for it—she would almost certainly not be allowed to get away with it, since Billie Holiday had been widely rumored to be black, and she, Ava Gardner, was widely rumored to be white. I was certainly not making a joke, or if I was, the joke was bitter: for I certainly know some black girls who are much, much whiter than Ava.

When Cowan's film failed to go into production he tried yet again with a script titled *Blue New York* by Dufty and Ronell. This time it was announced that the movie would not be so much a filmed autobiography as it was *"our impression* of Billie Holiday and the meaning of her life." Liberties were taken: Some names and races were changed, one character was invented, and William Dufty would now be a figure in the film. Ann Ronell had written several new songs for the real Billie Holiday to sing on the soundtrack: "Blue New York," "Hungry for Love," and "Happy Birthday All Year Long." Casting was still in question. When Dufty saw Joseph Losey's 1962 film *Eva*, in which Jeanne Moreau played an elite call girl who relaxed to Billie Holiday records between customers, he was so taken by those moments in the film that he wrote Ronell that he was now convinced that Moreau was the only person who could play Billie.

After Holiday died, other producers rushed to put similar films in the works, one stumbling over the other in their announcements: In

1959–1960 Philip A. Waxman and Albert Zugsmith both said they had signed Dorothy Dandridge to play the lead in two different bio movies that each of them was planning, and a Broadway musical with her in the lead was also being promised. Meanwhile, Dandridge was playing a Holiday-inspired drug-addicted jazz singer just out of prison in "Blues for the Junkman," an episode of a noirish NBC-TV film series called *Cain's Hundred*. In the same year John Butler and Carmen de Lavallade danced to her songs with a voice-over narrative that stressed the misery of her life in "For Miss Holiday" on CBS's TV program *Camera Three*.

In 1966 Dufty wrote a stage play, *Harlem: A Musical Memoir*, which focused on Holiday's life in Harlem in the 1920s and the 1940s, with two actresses playing the young and the older Billie. The piece would have been mildly avant for the times, with a rotating stage for rapid time and scene changes, dream sequences, and danced street scenes.

In 1971 another flurry of Holiday film ideas appeared, even though there was confusion over who had the film rights to the book. Actor Ossie Davis's Third World Cinema announced the forthcoming film *The Billie Holiday Story*, starring New York stage actress Diana Sands and directed by John Berry, who had been Orson Welles's assistant and was blacklisted in the early 1950s, as was the proposed scriptwriter Millard Lampell, who was better known as one of the Almanac Singers. John Hammond was to develop the soundtrack using the original Columbia recordings and was doing research in Baltimore to find people who had known Billie as a child. The film would not use the Holiday-Dufty book as a source, and would end in 1940, when Billie was twenty-five. Anticipating that Louis McKay would contest the project, Third World was prepared to ask the courts to rule on whether he was Holiday's legal or only her common-law husband.

Motown Goes to Hollywood

It was Jay Weston, a publicist for the Newport Jazz Festival, who was the most dogged in pursuing a Holiday film. He met Billie at the festival, and when she told him about her autobiography, he optioned the film rights to it from Joe Glaser and held on to the option for years, even when TV producer David Susskind tried to buy it to make his own film, again with the aid of John Hammond. In 1968 Weston produced his first picture, *For Love of Ivy*, starring Sidney Poitier and singer Abbey Lincoln, and believing that Lincoln would be the closest likeness to Holiday that could be found, he asked her to play the lead in his film. When Abbey turned him down because of marital difficulties with her husband, Max Roach, Weston tried for Diahann Carroll, but again no film resulted.

When Weston read an interview with Diana Ross in which she announced she was leaving the Supremes and had long dreamed of playing the role of Holiday in a film, Weston began to shop the idea around Hollywood. At first there was little enthusiasm for the project: Ross didn't look or sound like Billie, there was no evidence that she could act, and she seemed too young and too lightweight for serious contention. Only Berry Gordy, the man who had groomed Ross for success at Motown Records, believed in the idea. He was in love with Ross and had been trying to find a way to get them both involved in a film. But even he had his doubts, mostly about the effect the film could have on her career if Ross played "a black junkie singer." In a time when blacks were making their way into movies with blaxploitation films like *Shaft* and *Super Fly*, he was concerned about Diana's appearing in a film that might be slotted into that genre. What he wanted for her was a crossover film, one that would reach white audiences as well as black, much like Motown Records had done with music. Casting a member of the Supremes to represent Holiday in a biographical film, instead of using an actress from the usual Broadway and Hollywood realms, might also make it a draw for the TV and pop record audiences.

Biopics about entertainers were typically romances, cast as stories of performers who overcame great odds to rise to triumph. The problems with a Holiday film were that her life seemed to Gordy to be a questionable triumph, and that the drugs and alcohol that killed her were taken of her own free will; even if he agreed to show her addiction in a film, it was likely to be censored. This was not what he wanted for the first biopic of an African American woman. With backing from Paramount, a little-known Canadian was picked by Weston as scriptwriter, and another Canadian, Sidney Furie, as the director. The first version of the script attempted to follow the Holiday autobiography, even though William Dufty tried to halt the film with claims of his authorship. (Dufty later dismissed the film in a letter to the editor of a magazine as an autobiographical fantasy of Berry Gordy's.)

The raw facts and complexities of Billie's life remained a concern for Gordy. Furie tried to reassure him: "I told him I didn't want to make a serious, deep, important movie. I wanted to make a piece of entertainment that would make big money for all of us." But Berry was not used to standing on the sidelines, and bought his way into becoming a producer, and then purchased the entire film back from Paramount when it went over budget, paying for it with his own money.

He brought in two new writers from the Motown staff, neither of whom had ever written a script. Three of Holiday's husbands were compressed into one; characters were invented; incidents were fabricated (an encounter with the Ku Klux Klan in the South, a Southern white jazz musician who introduced her to heroin); and Ross's performance of "Strange Fruit" had the most painful and pointed of its lyrics cut from the song. The film gave no indication that she was considered the greatest singer in the history of jazz, let alone that she had recorded hundreds of records. Jazz musician and composer Oliver Nelson was quickly replaced by Michel Legrand, who brought a lush, traditional Hollywood approach to the score.

When Diana Ross complained about the inauthenticity of the film to Gordy, he told her, "The hell with being truthful . . . white people don't worry about changing the facts to make good movies. Why should we be saddled with it just because we're black?" That was true enough, but there were inauthenticities in the film that only compounded the problem, and that worried Ross: Her own singing was far from Holiday's technically in its phrasing and rhythmic feel, nor was there any sign of irony, satire, self-pity, pain, or mature sexuality in her bright interpretation of Holiday's songs. What she did bring to these songs was a pop sensibility, one that evoked in an audience a different realm of musical experience and distanced them from the jazz world of Holiday. Ross belonged to a new idiom of music that was sweeping the world and threatening to turn jazz into a minor art.

How could they make a film that would celebrate Holiday but at the same time also reveal all her weaknesses and failures? One answer was to show that she was not responsible for those shortcomings, which were the product of her tormented childhood, the lack of a real father, as well as poverty and racism. Yet how heavy could such a message be made for white audiences? How could all this be part of a love story? Another possibility was that the film could be framed as a moral lesson, a goal the autobiography had in fact sought to achieve. In the original draft of Holiday's book the last chapter was to be didactic, a don't-try-this-at-home warning that would stand in such sharp contrast to the recollections of the "hip kitty" who spoke in the pages that came before. It was ultimately edited out.

The film opened like a late-fifties film noir, black and white, with a brassy big band playing in a minor key over rumbling rhythms that warned the audience of what was to come: Billie in chains, being fingerprinted, having a mug shot taken, then thrown into a padded cell. When she began to scream and writhe on the floor, she was put into a straitjacket, and the film drifted toward the tropes of fifties melodramas of hysterical women. Billy Dee Williams was cast as Louis McKay, who was presented as her only husband, a kindly, sweet man who would forgive her anything—someone closer to a father than a spouse. The real Billie Holiday, of course, had other husbands or husband surrogates, all of them famously brutal, though none as well documented as Louis McKay. In one note that survives from Billie to McKay, she wrote:

Let's face it, you're not my husband, not even my boyfriend . . . Louie, how much can I take. You're in New York two days and I, your wife, see you five minutes so let's be friends and forget it.

Ross was certainly not bad in her performance, and if anything, she was almost too good—too beautiful, too charming, too full of energy and playfulness to be Billie Holiday. She was dedicated enough to the role to re-create Holiday's bedroom and dressing room in her space on the film production lot, keeping some of Billie's own things in them. Even those who hated the film were able to praise her performance apart from it, and the film received five nominations for Academy Awards.

Today, some forty years later, producer Jay Weston is still thinking of refilming Holiday's biography in a "more authentic version," one that nonetheless includes a fictional affair with the black DEA agent who eventually was assigned to follow her. Jennifer Hudson (who played the character modeled on Florence Ballard of the Supremes in the film *Dreamgirls*) would be cast as Billie.

The Photos

Holiday was one of the most photographed black women of her time, one of the first to have her picture appear in a national magazine, and perhaps the most popular jazz performer among professional photographers. Many of those images are still in wide circulation today, even though there were those who felt she never looked as good in pictures as she did in life.

Carl Van Vechten was apparently in the midst of a project to photograph every leading figure of the Harlem Renaissance—Nora Holt, James Weldon Johnson, Countee Cullen, Nella Larsen, Claude McKay, Zora Neale Hurston, Langston Hughes, and Bessie Smith—and was eager to get Holiday into his studio. Even though she is not normally considered part of the Renaissance, Holiday was widely known by many Harlem artists to be one of their own.

She was not particularly eager to do another shoot, but the Harlem journalist Gerry Major intervened on behalf of Van Vechten and arranged a session in March 1949. Major asked her to wear an evening gown, but she arrived dour and distracted in an everyday gray suit. She was still under indictment in California for drug possession and had just

been denied a New York State Supreme Court order to restore her cabaret card. Van Vechten began shooting, but she was not cooperative. The
conditions of his sessions could be excruciating: He worked slowly under hot lights, moving floral arrangements, pets, and art objects in and
out of the frame, asking for changes of clothing between shots, or no
clothing at all.

He pulled out the photos he had taken of Bessie Smith to convince
her of the quality of his work. She began to cry, and he began to click
away as she explained how important Smith was to her. After a break at
midnight, she returned from her apartment with a sharp change in attitude and her dog Mister, a boxer. Van Vechten filmed Billie in color
(which he usually avoided) peeking out from behind a vase of large pink
roses, wearing an evening gown, and even topless, with her arms folded
across her breasts; she lay down with her head next to her dog's with the
camera on the floor in front of them, and in a dark robe against an angular black-and-silver-striped hanging. He photographed her singing while
seated, or holding an African carved head next to hers. Many of his images suggest that he might be looking back to the exoticism of Josephine
Baker, perhaps even further back to Gauguin's Polynesian paintings.

Van Vechten later wrote that he had "spent only one night photo-
graphing Billie Holiday, but it was the whole of one night and it seemed
like a whole career . . . I took photographs of her crying, which nobody
else had done, later I took pictures of her laughing." Once they had finished, she stayed until dawn while "she related in great detail the sad,
bittersweet story of her tempestuous life."

In the 1940s *Life* magazine was the source for the best photography in
the United States, with a stable of ace news and portrait photographers
like Margaret Bourke-White, Robert Capa, Henri Cartier-Bresson, Alfred
Eisenstaedt, Philippe Halsman, and Edward Steichen, and several who
were especially drawn to jazz, Gjon Mili, Gordon Parks, and W. Eugene
Smith. Mili, something of an avant-garde photographer, staged jam sessions in his loft studio for films such as *Jammin' the Blues* and the still photography he did for *Life*. In 1943 he filmed a jam session to accompany an

article on V-Discs, the government-supported recordings that were sent to military bases across the world. Mary Lou Williams, James P. Johnson, Teddy Wilson, and Duke Ellington were among the musicians, and the singers included Lee Wiley, Josh White, and Billie Holiday. The black-and-white shots are stunningly lit, with black-on-black backgrounds and shimmering whites. Mili's photos of Holiday caught in performance are among the best. An earlier session was devoted to one of the *"Life* Goes to a Party" features that the magazine sponsored from time to time, this one including some of Duke Ellington's and Eddie Condon's musicians, and Holiday as the only singer. If Americans did not yet know who she was, this striking photo of her singing among the musicians instead of in front of them would have made her a memorable figure.

The
Musician

CHAPTER FOUR

The Prehistory of a Singer

*W*hen Billie and her mother moved from Baltimore to New York City in 1929, Wall Street was crashing, Prohibition was radically changing the entertainment business, and the glories of the Harlem Renaissance were fading. As Langston Hughes would write, "We were no longer in vogue, anyway, we Negroes. Sophisticated New Yorkers turned to Noel Coward." But Hughes was only partly correct. Harlem's writers, painters, and playwrights may have lost their uptown allure, and its elaborate revues may have been shrinking or moving to midtown theaters, but its music, which had never been the strongest element in the Renaissance's ideology, was finding new homes in small cabarets and cellars in Harlem, where the ban on alcohol was not consistently enforced. An alternate jazz age to that of the whites downtown was taking shape there, and suddenly it seemed that a great variety of women singers was everywhere. Some were established artists, like the blues singers, coon shouters, and red-hot mamas, all of whom owed much to African American musical traditions. Newer styles were appearing as well, such as the flappers and torch singers, and they, too, had roots in the black community.

The concept of a jazz vocalist did not exist when Billie stumbled her way into a career as a singer. A singer's having a career of her or his own—independent of a band, a musical theater, or a vaudeville company—was only just beginning to be possible. Still, there was then no clear idea of what a jazz singer might be. The women artists that most can now agree on as the leading figures in jazz singing—Bessie Smith, Billie Holiday, Ella Fitzgerald, Sarah Vaughan, Betty Carter—were all quite different stylistically from one another, and all created such individual approaches that they were not easily adapted by other singers without making them seem unimaginative imitators. And yet there was a set of common resources from the past from which all these women drew to craft their own approaches.

By the mid-nineteenth century the full impact of black singing on America was yet to be felt. For most white Americans outside of the American South, the only black vocalizing they might have heard was from a distant church service. Yet the few individuals who did witness more of this music believed they were hearing the future: the dominant feature of a distinctive American singing style that was yet to take shape. As early as 1845 a journalist named J. K. Kinnard declared that the world had not yet heard the best of America's poets, the Negro poets and songsters, nor had they been properly acknowledged even at home. Abolitionists thought the spirituals were the most distinctive and powerful music they had ever heard. In the 1850s Walt Whitman singled out the language of Negroes as having "hints of the future theory of the modification of all the words of the English language, for musical purposes, for a native grand opera in America, leaving the words just as they are for writing and speaking, but the same words so modified as to answer perfectly for musical purposes . . ."

After railroads and the radio connected most of the country and recorded music came into existence, only the most isolated person would not have known that a new kind of singing was emerging, even while segregation made it easy to ignore its origins. But by the 1960s there were those such as music critic Henry Pleasants who declared that the source of the American singing style was primarily black. He went even further with the radical suggestion that when the European tradition of classical music was becoming decadent in America, African American singers surfaced as the vital voices of the future by reinventing the "objectives, criteria and devices of the early Italian masters of opera" by treating song "as a lyrical extension of speech": "They emphasize clear enunciation and conversational phrasing—and to achieve this effect, they employ the same musical devices as their distinguished predecessors, including the appoggiatura, the turn, the slur and the rubato."

Pleasants pointed out two other factors that contributed to the ascendancy of African American popular singers. First, they had the freedom to interpret that had been denied their classical counterparts, who increasingly came under the domination of the composer and the orchestra. And second, they were able to use the microphone to restore much of the charm, intimacy, and virtuosity that had been lost in classical singing when the emphasis changed from the rhetorical to the lyrical.

"Reinventing" was the word that Pleasants used to describe this shift of musical aesthetics, though "creolization" might have been an even more accurate term because it would call attention to the ways in which historically unrelated cultures can sometimes fuse to create a totally new form without concern for origins or a respectable patrimony.

African Americans were leading the way in breaking with European musical tradition, and, strange as it might seem, this break had been anticipated, and maybe even urged, by the minstrel show, the first form of musical theater to reach the whole country. Its history is much longer than the eighty or so years that it is said to have lasted in the United States; its legacy is far more complicated than just a matter of white people copying black people, and even today questions about the sources of this music and its influence remain unsettled. Some minstrels were black, and some of those we now consider white performers were then categorized as nonwhite in one way or another. A few of the white performers who wore blackface, such as Al Jolson or Libby Holman, were very popular among people of color. Minstrelsy reached a much wider audience than just the United States, and it took on different meanings in other countries. In South Africa minstrel performances in blackface have been popular for over a century among nonwhite Africans in Cape Town during Coon Carnival in January of each year. Adolf Hitler's mistress Eva Braun posed in blackface for professional entertainers' photos in imitation of her favorite performer, Al Jolson, who was Jewish. Billie Holiday, like many other black performers of her time, at least once had to darken her skin so as not to look too white when appearing with a band of black musicians before a white audience.

The music and dance of minstrel shows were not copying Negroes so much as they were constructions of imaginary characters in imaginary antebellum settings by white composers and choreographers who put them together from various cultural ingredients. If they believed what they were presenting were simulations of real people, they had failed. More likely, they knew they were pastiches, or parodies, especially because many of the tunes of the minstrels and some of the humor had scarcely concealed origins among the tent and stage shows from the past that had minstrelized the Irish. A New York theater writer in the late 1800s remarked after a minstrel show he had just witnessed that he pitied Negro performers because they had to compete with the real thing!

The subject of theatrical black masking continues to fascinate and remains something of a favorite activity for academic theorists, who develop new explanations for it every few years. But whatever its history and complexity, and however distasteful it is, minstrelsy tells us that something was missing and desperately needed in American singing: the voices of excluded black people. The offshoots of minstrelsy shaped styles and agendas that are in some ways still with us today. In 1961 the great R&B singer Jackie Wilson recorded a tribute album to Al Jolson, *You Ain't Heard Nothin' Yet*. Aretha Franklin's father, the estimable Reverend R. L. Franklin, said his favorite singers were Muddy Waters and Al Jolson, and Aretha herself recorded some of Jolson's and Stephen Foster's songs. Since the heyday of minstrelsy, popular music has continued to be a form of cultural masking, a weird type of passing, a den of exoticism, an arena for vernacular everything but especially speech, and a playground for those who enjoy crossing lines, changing shape, and taking risks.

.   .   .   .   .

By the late 1800s the big minstrel show spectaculars had begun to fade and were replaced by vaudeville or variety shows that presented a series of different performers—singers, jugglers, dancers, comics—who appeared individually, leaving behind the traditional minstrel staging that had every member of the cast onstage at the same time. But minstrel-like performances persisted in new musical forms called "coon songs." A 1920 Victor Records catalog explained the music listed under "Coon Songs and Specialties":

> By "coon songs" are meant up-to-date songs in negro dialect. The humor of many of these songs cannot be called refined, and for that reason we have distinguished them from old-fashioned darky humor, these songs being listed under "Fisk Jubilee Quartet," "Negro Songs," and "Tuskegee."

Coon songs were designed to characterize black Americans in ways that would amuse whites. It was amusement of an especially insidious sort, the humor often approaching a sort of fearmongering never imagined in minstrel shows. White anxiety over the freeing of the slaves and the threat of Reconstruction was boldly put on display. Minstrel fantasies of life on the old plantation were replaced by those of a free people in competition with whites for jobs and social status. Songs with titles like "If the Man in the Moon Was a Coon" and "New Coon in Town" were typical.

Thus it came to be that a jumble of watermelons, flashy clothes, straight razors, gamblers, hustlers, chicken thieves, buffoons, doomed social climbers, bullies, and promiscuous and libidinous characters were ascendant on the stage. From 1880 to 1920 coon songs were a craze, like ragtime and the blues that were yet to come, and hundreds of pop songs were produced to meet the demand. "Pop songs" they were, because they gave rise to Tin Pan Alley, the industrialized song factories that emerged to keep a steady flow of music available for sale to the public. Coon songs were silly and offensive, and crudely made, sometimes with only the word "coon" substituted for another word in an older song to rush out some sheet music for sale. Yet some of the most successful songwriters learned their trade on these songs, and a few continued to write in the same spirit years later: Irving Berlin's 1930 "Puttin' On the Ritz" mocked black social pretensions on Lenox Avenue in Harlem. The song was recorded by Fred Astaire in 1930 and later was "whitened" with new words for Astaire to sing about Fifth Avenue in the 1946 film *Blue Skies*. The original version survives on YouTube in a fuzzy print of the 1930 film *Puttin' on the Ritz*, with Harry Richmond singing in front of white dancers, who leave the stage when a group of noisy and exuberant blackface "real" Negro dancers appear. This kind of revision and sly appropriation of coon songs persisted well into the twentieth century in pop songs like "Hard-Hearted Hannah," "I Ain't Got Nobody," "Big Bad Bill (Is Sweet William Now)," and "Bad, Bad Leroy Brown."

Some coon songs were similar to those that in minstrel shows would have been sung by men playing the roles of both men and women, but now they were being performed by white women, who might appear in blackface, and so took on different emotional weight. The singers who were most successful in the earliest period of coon songs, such as May Irwin, were generally large, respectably dressed, buxom white women who assumed the role of black mammies berating their husbands, or performing the role of men who were aiming to defeat the toughest dude in town. The *New York Times* in 1895 reported that:

> When [Irwin] sang her new darkey songs . . . one forgot her blonde hair, her peaches-and-cream complexion, and her blue eyes; every tone of her voice, every expression of her countenance, every gesture and motion combined to create an illusion now of a lovelorn Virginia darkey, now a dangerous Tennessee "coon."

In a review of Irwin in *Courted into Court* in New York City in 1896, the *Times* said:

The Southern negro she impersonates in "Crappy Dan" and "The New Bully" is not the old plantation darkey, happy in his bondage, primitive in his simplicity, but a product of the new civilization, the bad town darkey of the present age of transition. That he is susceptible to humorous treatment Miss Irwin proves, and the manner in which she puts him before us in all his badness and audacity, without the aid of make-up or scenic effect is, in its small way, a triumph of art. But the same crappy Dan, with his dice loaded for "sebens" and his "quaintance wid a gun," represents a grave social problem.

Other women coon shouters (that is, untrained robust singers) often deliberately assumed ethnically ambiguous personae in their offstage lives. Anna Held, one of the most famous, reached New York from Europe at the beginning of the 1900s under a press agent's manipulated cloud of mixed identity (was she Catholic or Jewish? Polish or French?) to work with Flo Ziegfeld in his *Follies*, doing coon songs with a French accent (that was often undecipherable). But Held never used blackface, instead doing her ethnic signification by means of an extravagant cakewalk and facial imagery. Close behind Held at the *Follies* was Nora Bayes, singing her feature song, George M. Cohan's "Beautiful Coon." She, too, avoided blackface, but sang coon songs in an Irish accent, and spiked Irish songs with Yiddishisms. Later, away from the *Follies* and on her own, she added the plantation cakewalk dance to her act, dressing in a mammy costume and performing in a plantation setting.

There were black singers in blackface makeup who sang coon songs for white audiences as well as black, and white singers in blackface who performed for both white and black audiences. As early as 1903 some white performers began to reveal their white skin under their gloves to the apparent shock of their audiences. But when a white performer revealed her skin in front of a black audience at the Lafayette Theater in Harlem in 1915, she was hissed in disapproval, not because they had been taken in by the makeup, but because they preferred the masquerade.

But none of these new coon shouters could top Eva Tanguay, a French Canadian who made her way to stardom from 1905 to 1929 in whiteface or black with bawdy songs like "It's All Been Done Before but Not the Way I Do It," "Go as Far as You Like," and the brassy, free-spirited "I Don't Care":

You see I'm sort of independent,
Of a clever race descendent,
My star is on the ascendant,
That's why I don't care.

She dressed in elaborate costumes, sometimes literally made of money, other times showing more flesh than had ever been seen on the respectable stage. Her dancing and singing were not the best, but both were done in an explosive style as she romped across the stage tossing out sexual innuendoes. Offstage, her behavior was unpredictable, and she always made sure that her fans knew everything she was doing, whether stabbing a rival with a hat pin, walking out on her own hit show, or being arrested for lewdness. Her private life became so thoroughly public that she was suspected of staging her personal relationships: She was briefly engaged to a popular female impersonator who appeared dressed as her bride, while she was attired as the groom; she had an affair with George Walker, the black stage partner of Bert Williams, the great early blackface singer and comedian; she wrote about her recklessness and trysts in the Hearst newspapers. In her first big New York musical she sang a coon song, "My Sambo," that received such enormous response that when she starred in her next show, *The Blonde in Black*, the title was quickly changed to *The Sambo Girl*. It would be hard to overestimate Eva Tanguay's influence. Mae West started out as a Tanguay imitator, and both Sophie Tucker and Ethel Waters borrowed freely from her.

What Tanguay established was that licentiousness and racial and sexual indiscretions could be forgiven in a performer's private life if she somehow combined energetic and comedic sexuality while in blackface roles. In the process she also demonstrated a fundamental principle of minstrelization, a form of racial and cultural passing in which high-status minstrelizers felt free to *temporarily* mask as subordinates after learning only a minimal number of real (or imagined) cultural characteristics, never fearing being unmasked because they were performing exclusively for their own group. The subordinate, however, was required to have a physical self at least marginally similar to that of the dominant group, and in addition had to fully master the high-status group's cultural characteristics to perform for *them*, though she or he was never free from the risk of being discredited. This was a principle that was so much a part of a society founded on racial inequality that Tanguay, like other white performers onstage, came to realize that it would be possible to minstrelize without blacking up.

"The real thing" was represented by Ma Rainey, who was billed as "the Mother of the Blues." Rainey had worked her way up from early black variety shows like the Rabbit Foot Minstrels to forming her own traveling tent shows, which drew both blacks and whites. She was sometimes also billed as a coon shouter and a "Black Face Song and Dance Comedienne," though she sang no coon songs and wore no black makeup. She dressed instead in costumes and jewelry that radiated wealth, dignity, and pride, and traveled with her own stage sets, a full troupe of dancers, and a choreographer. Her show was filled with comedy skits and eccentric dance acts, but she was unquestionably the main attraction, singing in a powerful voice that reached outside the tent even without a microphone. She flirted with men in the audience, but sang about the pleasures of women together without men. Her repertoire was primarily the blues, with only the occasional pop song. But there was another side of her performances that set her apart from the flamboyant white singers of the era, which Sterling Brown captured in his 1932 poem "Ma Rainey": her ability to turn entertainment into a sacred event by the force of her songs alone. When she sang "Backwater Blues" (probably her account of the devastation and human tragedy caused by the Nashville, Tennessee, flood of Christmas Day 1926), the laughing and cheering of her audiences gave way to a silent collective prayer:

> An' den de folks, dey naturally bowed dey heads an' cried
> Bowed dey heavy heads, shet dey moufs up tight an' cried.

She continued touring and recording until the late 1920s, when her kind of blues fell out of favor with urban African Americans, and she withdrew to where she had begun, in the backwoods of the South. But by then she had influenced any number of singers, including the young Bessie Smith, who spent time as part of her troupe.

Another characteristic singer of the period was the "red-hot mama": physically formidable, tough, wise, holding no illusions about men. These women modeled themselves on white singers like Tanguay and African American blueswomen like Ma Rainey. Although the mamas themselves were typically not very old—most were only in their twenties—they acted in a mature manner, physically taking charge of the stage and the theater the instant the curtain went up. Their songs were didactic, mocking, threatening, and vengeful. They typically began by addressing the women in the audience, and then turned to the men, spelling out their intentions: They sought sexual freedom on their own terms, and no man would ever take advantage of them. Bessie Smith, like Ma Rainey, had some of these qualities, but black women were never given the title of red-hot mama, even though "hot" was a term most often used by black musicians and singers to describe some types of their music. Bessie was nonetheless clearly one of the key models for this kind of singing.

Sophie Tucker was the quintessential red-hot mama, even though she was born in Ukraine and had entered the United States with her family under an assumed Italian name, Abuza. She began her career in show business in blackface singing coon songs such as "That Lovin' Two-Step Man" and "That Lovin' Soul Kiss." She was called by various names (including Ethel Tucker and Solo Tucker), billed under others ("The Southern Coon Singer," "Best Coon Shouter in Captivity"), and in interviews offered differing accounts of her life, especially about where she got her Italian name, why she performed in blackface, and why she eventually abandoned blackface. At one point she, like others, began to expose her white skin by pulling back her gloves onstage, but then followed her glove striptease by announcing that she was Jewish, and not Southern. Finally, abandoning her makeup altogether, she entered the Jazz Age by billing herself as the "Queen of Jazzaration" or "The Queen of Jazz" and shifting to saucy songs that declared her independence. Though now performing as white, her repertoire openly echoed that of Bessie Smith and Ethel Waters, including such numbers as "I Ain't Takin' Orders from No One" or "Mama Goes Where Papa Goes (Or Papa Don't Go Out Tonight)."

There was yet another, smaller group of singers at the extreme opposite pole of other popular artists in the late 1920s and 1930s world of song. They were not considered part of a specific category, but they might be called flappers because they performed as very young, naive, coquettish girls, singing in childlike voices. Helen Kane was the most famous and successful of this group, especially after her recording of "I Wanna Be Loved by You," with its "boop oop a doop" minimalist rhythmic scat line, became a big hit. It was her tiny voice, along with her hairstyling and stage movements, that appeared to be the source for the Fleischer Brothers' *Betty Boop* movie cartoons. This style of singing might seem far removed from African American song, but when Kane sued Paramount Pictures over the *Betty Boop* films, it was revealed that she had likely taken her singing style from the young Cotton Club performer Esther Jones, also known by the stage name Baby Esther. Other black singers with high voices used similar childlike scat effects, such as Rose Murphy, best known as the "chi-chi" lady for one of her own scat interpolations.

Although in *Lady Sings the Blues* Holiday never mentions three other singers who were major forces in her first decade as a singer—Ethel Waters, Mildred Bailey, and Mabel Mercer—there is reason to believe that all three were important to her. She knew them all. Her mother had served as a maid for both Waters and Bailey, not the best of ways for an aspiring performer to relate to world-famous singers. Waters was not known for her kindness to anyone, and once proclaimed that Billie sang as if her shoes were too tight. On another occasion she interrupted Holiday's singing onstage to tell her that she had no right to sing a song that Waters also sang. John Hammond said that Mildred Bailey constantly complained to Billie about her mother's sloppy housekeeping and cooking, in part because it was true, but he felt it was also because it was Bailey's way of dealing with the fact that Billie was such a fine singer. Mabel Mercer, on the other hand, had a small cult following of the very rich and the very talented that Billie admired, but she recognized that Mabel kept a certain distance as a performer, a gentle hauteur that she could never manage. When she first went to see Mabel sing at the urging of her friend Thelma Carpenter, she remarked, "You know I can't be a classy singer!"

Surely, no singer has ever had a career as far-reaching or as fully realized as Ethel Waters. She was born twenty years before Holiday, but their early lives had remarkable similarities. There was nothing in Waters's miserable childhood that suggested greatness, but by means of talent, hard work, and fearlessness she made her way to the top as a blues, pop, and gospel singer, dancer, writer, and stage and film actress. Her successes form a long list of "first black woman to . . ." honors, and if many of these triumphs have been forgotten, it's at least in part due to the fact that she did so much so well.

Her range as a singer was enormous. She excelled in several styles, and used them to challenge her competitors. Langston Hughes was so fascinated by her salty, near-blues "Go Back Where You Stayed Last Night" of 1925 that he urged his readers to become acquainted with her work, which was simultaneously more sophisticated than that of other songsters and far rougher than that of the refined blues singers who preceded her. When the blues began to fall out of fashion in urban areas, with black uplift newspaper writers arguing that they were vulgar and a drag on the race, Waters widened her song repertoire, but with a shrewd eye for fault lines and fissures. Noting that "My Man" was seen by white people as a blues, she realized that there was room to negotiate between the tastes of the two audiences. She introduced many songs that were immediately successful and are still well known, like "Stormy Weather," "Black and Blue," "Dinah," "Sweet Georgia Brown," and "Am I Blue?" Sophie Tucker once paid Waters to teach her about her singing style and choice of songs, since she, like Bessie Smith, was hoping to begin a new phase of her career with freshly minted pop tunes.

In addition to the clarity and breeziness of her singing, what set her apart from other singers of her times was the magnetism of her physical performance. She worked hard to *act* the blues, while most others merely sang. When she moved beyond blues to pop songs, she said she was surprised that she could act them, too. Her eyes engaged everyone in the audience; her smile was unusually warm but also persistently difficult to read (shy? teasing? coquettish?). Her arms were often held straight out from her body like a dancer's, offering openness, but also making room for her shake dance, which engaged most of the parts of her body.

Though it would not be quite accurate to call Waters a crossover performer, by drawing on the work of the white red-hot mamas and merging it with a black aesthetic, Waters shaped the direction of popular music well into the next century, so much so that it's difficult to find a black woman singer who came after her who didn't show her influence. How could it be otherwise when she never flinched at crossing musical territories, experimented with changing tempos within a three-minute recording, mixed the words of one song with another, slipped comedy into unfunny songs, and made casual talk, scatting, and rapping all parts of her interpretations? At the same time, she could mock her competition with devastating imitations, or lovingly copy Louis Armstrong's singing on "I Can't Give You Anything but Love."

Though Holiday did not credit Waters by name, the fact that she recorded songs that Waters had already made famous, sometimes sounded like her (especially on Holiday's first recording, "Your Mother's Son-in-Law"), and borrowed from her songs when she composed her own blues (Holiday uses lines from Waters's 1922 recording "Ethel Sings 'Em" in her "Fine and Mellow" and Waters's 1924 "Cravin' Blues" and 1925 "Down Home Blues" in her own "Billie's Blues") speaks for itself.

On a first hearing of Mildred Bailey, it might not be apparent to most listeners that she was considered an important singer, much less a jazz singer. Her voice is high and light, and she does not seem to offer any particular point of view. But she did improvise, had a clear and sure ability to communicate a song, and could sing the blues in a manner that white and many black people found more appealing than the heavier, more rural-inflected performers. Her sense of swing was secure and had a floating quality that made her fit in comfortably with swing musicians as a new era of jazz began.

Her mother was Native American, Coeur d'Alene, from eastern Washington, and Mildred had occasion to threaten to sue journalists who wrote that she was a Negro. Bailey rose to national fame by performing with the extremely popular Paul Whiteman Orchestra at the same time as Bing Crosby sang with that band, and he remarked at how much she had taught him about singing. Over the years many other singers, such as Rosemary Clooney and Tony Bennett, said much the same about what they had learned from her as a band singer.

Mabel Mercer was an Afro-British singer who reached the United States from Paris and Britain briefly in the late 1930s, and then returned to stay permanently after 1941. She was a singer who genuinely could be called a chanteuse. She sang lyrics with precise pronunciation, rolling her *r*'s like an old-school British stage singer, and delivered her songs conversationally, often sitting in a chair, seldom moving her hands. At the same time she discreetly broke some of the rules of singing by stressing the less important words in a phrase, bringing surprising emotions to lyrics, and allowing long, held notes to drop away at the end of phrases.

Mercer developed a way of looking at the audience without appearing to see it and yet somehow making it feel that she was personally singing to each person in it. For many she was an acquired taste, but she was worshiped by singers such as Frank Sinatra, Nat Cole, Mel Tormé, Tony Bennett, Peggy Lee, Eileen Farrell, and Ethel Waters. Billie resisted going to hear her at first, but once she did, she almost missed her own next set at the club across the street because she didn't want to leave. It was likely Mabel who introduced her to songs like "You'd Better Go Now" and to George Cory and Douglass Cross, songwriters who had written songs and arrangements for her and accompanied her on record. Billie recorded two of their best songs, "I'll Look Around" and "Deep Song."

> And blues were only torch songs
> Fashioned for impulsive ingénues
>> Leah Worth and Bobby Troup,
>> "The Meaning of the Blues"

When Billie performed on the first night that Café Society opened in late 1939, she began to put together a new repertoire, much of which would become part of her performances for the rest of her life. The message of these new songs and her manner of presenting them connected her with torch singing, a new style derived from a mixture of European and African American cabaret performance. Although many fans blamed the downtown venue for what they viewed as her abandonment of her jazz roots, Barney Josephson, the club's owner, said she herself had asked to do these songs and assured him that was what she now wanted to sing.

Torch singing is scarcely more easily defined than jazz singing or blues singing, but it can at least be described as the ability of a singer (usually a woman) to tell a story through a song with emotional conviction. The pieces themselves were typically laments, songs of longing, romantic misfortune, of weariness with life, or even of the pleasures of pain; the words were sung slowly, softly, with confessional intimacy. Their performers revealed themselves as searching for an unobtainable love, perhaps even one free of sexual desire. Unlike the red-hot mamas, torch singers made no bold public proclamations, but instead interrogated their unbearable situation, their enslavement to an ideal of love.

Torch songs are descendants of French cabaret songs from the late nineteenth to the early twentieth century, which often dealt with the sorrows and sad lives of the lower classes, the people of the streets, and were sometimes called realist songs. They were ballads that told stories, or songs in which the singer introduced herself to the audience, sometimes in self-mockery. (Songs told from the point of view of a prostitute were very common, and could be poignant, whining, or camp.) There were also reflections on personal, social, or political topics, and songs of moods and feelings (such as "Autumn Leaves"). These songs were sung in bars or nightspots, spaces small enough to allow the singer to carry on a kind of part-spoken, part-sung conversation with members of the audience. Most French singers of these songs were older, with experiences that would lead an audience to believe that the singer was communicating directly from her life.

The singers of torch songs have been called many things: tragic victims, fallen angels, damaged divas, tortured sound-angels, suicide queens, wounded prostitutes, and ethereal sonic documentarians of our romantic dark sides. It was said that Holiday could turn anything— even "My Yiddishe Momme" or "Strange Fruit"—into a torch song, and it was songs such as these that her audiences would come to interpret as missing parts of her autobiography.

Yet she was called a blues singer for the rest of her life. Was this a mistake, a misunderstanding of blues songs? The names songs are given and the categories they are placed in are often notoriously arbitrary and have little bearing on how they differ from or are similar to other songs. Although "blues" in a song title did not necessarily make the piece a genuine blues, blues and pop songs do share a number of harmonic, rhythmic, and emotional similarities. They were both shaped and formalized at roughly the same time, the early part of the twentieth century. Both types of song do deal with the displeasures and disappointments of love, but they are the only subject of torch songs, while the blues can be concerned with everything from war and poverty to horse racing and the praise of automobiles.

Blues lyrics and their melodic characteristics were sometimes embedded into otherwise ordinary pop songs in the section marked "tempo di blues." What is equally confusing is that elements of many commercially written coon songs found their way into folk blues, as well as into bluegrass, for that matter. Things may or may not have been simpler when different genres of music were more segregated than they now are. Race records were made by black performers for black audiences, but radio leaked them to larger audiences, and jazz musicians always had blues in their repertoires. On the other hand, recordings by whites were distributed and played everywhere. African American women singers were always called blues singers, and their songs were written for them by black songwriters or were already known to them through black folk tradition. The women who sang torch songs were always white, and got their songs from white Tin Pan Alley writers.

There were some who resisted this regimentation. Libby Holman was a close observer of Bessie Smith's, Ethel Waters's, and Billie Holiday's music, and at one point announced that she was giving up torch songs for blues and folk music because they were not self-pitying. It was an interesting distinction, but one that does not bear close scrutiny. Were all torch songs self-pitying, or did they also project a refusal to submit to the pop ethos of love? Could they not be thought of as weapons to be used against life, as Ned Rorem put it? Were the blues free of self-pity? Think of the number of blues songs that begin with lines such as, "Here I am sitting in this one-room country shack, a thousand miles from nowhere" or "Poor boy I'm a long way from home / I don't have no happy home to go home to."

Whatever it was that Holman heard in blues songs, it was clear that she wanted out of the torch role, and eventually went on the road with Josh White accompanying her on guitar. Billie Holiday, on the other hand, who had been familiar with the blues from childhood, discovered how to apply what she had learned from them to pop songs. Her large repertoire was almost exclusively Tin Pan Alley products, Broadway show tunes, or European cabaret songs, and it was she who broke the hold that whites had on torch songs. Many people in the forties and fifties didn't even consider her a black singer.

"Love for Sale" is an interesting example of racial and musical casting at work. It would seem a perfect song for Holiday, one to which she could bring emotional experience and deep feeling. But she recorded Cole Porter's song only once, late in life, and apparently never sang it in live performance. It was written for *The New Yorkers*, a 1930 Broadway revue, and was sung by a white singer, Kathryn Crawford. It was quickly banned from airplay on some radio stations, and a *New York World* critic called the song "filthy" and "in the worst possible taste." A few weeks later Crawford was replaced by Elizabeth Welch, a singer whose racial identity was complex, but since she'd worked mostly in African American musical theater, audiences assumed she was black. The producers also changed the setting of the song from the popular midtown Manhattan restaurant Reuben's to the Cotton Club in Harlem. After that, no one seemed to care how unsavory the Broadway song performance was, and Libby Holman had a hit recording with it.

In both torch songs and blues the singer is the one who expresses the narrative, a convention that sometimes leads audiences to assume the singer's life is the source of the song. There is also the sheer exoticism of the two musical forms and their singers. To many listeners, these genres were inherently strange. The blues were completely alien to the European musical tradition, and while torch songs came from turn-of-the-century France and Germany, and later from Harlem, they were new to most Americans. Even stranger were the torch singers themselves, most of whom adopted the stage identities of urban sophisticates, former femmes fatales, prostitutes, or women who had wandered onto the stage from the French film serial *Les Vampires*. They had borrowed from well-traveled European cabaret and Parisian apache gang members' street styling, and while their makeup, hand placed on hip, dangling cigarette, and head-cast-back stance were elements to which nightclub habitués might have been accustomed, it took their unexplained appearances on *The Ed Sullivan Show* of the 1950s to make them familiar to most Americans.

These were singers who also sought to assume a more complex and somewhat mysterious identity. Libby Holman's performances in black-face did not prevent her from being celebrated by some in the black community for her sympathy to their cause. She sang at the Apollo, did NAACP benefits, told columnist Walter Winchell the blues were her passion, was described in reviews as "Creolesque" and "dusky," and was oddly compared to Ethel Waters as a coon song singer (a type of music Waters seldom if ever performed). Fanny Brice was Jewish and started in blackface, but she developed several different stage identities and was especially known for introducing the hugely popular French song "My Man" to America, along with a pouting streetlight lean that marked her forever as something more than just a funny girl. Whether it was the song, the setting, or Brice's fluid identity, many whites took the song to be a blues.

Helen Morgan was Irish American, or maybe Canadian (part of her mystery), and had her start singing ballads in French in Toronto, atop a grand piano. She was thought by some to be a mulatto—she was not, but the rumor won her the role of Julie LaVerne in the stage musical and film adaptations of *Show Boat*, as well as a song written for her by Noël Coward called "Half-Caste Woman."

When torch singers' songs were laminated to their caustic, reckless, or shadowed lives, as was the case with Helen Morgan, Libby Holman, and Édith Piaf, their real or imagined identities were reinforced. A later group of jazz singers—the Boswell Sisters, Dinah Shore, Kay Starr, and Lee Wiley—were all nominally white but had mixed-race narratives (Creole, Native American, African American) affixed to them by the whispers of fans, the press, and sometimes by their own hints. It is at this strange crossroads where jazz, pop, blues, torch, and jazz identity transformations took place, and where songs were turned into lives, that Billie Holiday's career as a singer was developed.

CHAPTER FIVE

The Singer I

*B*illie Holiday's voice is odd, indelibly odd, and so easy to recognize, but so difficult to describe. In her early years some called it sad, olive-toned, whisky-hued, lazy, feline, smoky, unsentimental, weird. Her first record producer, John Hammond, said that there were many objections when he signed Bob Dylan, but nothing compared with what the music business had to say about Holiday's singing on her early 1930s recordings that he produced—"scratchy," "unmusical," "where's the melody?"

Her voice is so unique that some of her vocal techniques fall outside the standard techniques of musicology and beg for new terms to express them: falling behind the beat, floating, breathing where it's not expected, scooping up notes and then letting them fall. Even her pronunciation can be so unusual that common words would have to be respelled if they were transcribed phonetically. Composer and jazz historian Gunther Schuller flatly says that the Holiday style ultimately can't be properly transcribed in written music:

> [Holiday's] art transcends the usual categorizations of style, content, and technique. Much of her singing goes beyond itself and becomes a humanistic document; it passed often into a realm that is not only beyond criticism but in the deepest sense inexplicable. We can, of course, describe and analyze the surface mechanics of her art: her style, her technique, her personal vocal attributes; and

I suppose a poet could express the essence of her art or at least give us, by poetic analogy, his particular insight into it. But, as with all truly profound art, that which operates above, below, and all around its outer manifestations is what most touches us, and also remains ultimately mysterious.

There may be a certain investment in keeping one's favorite music somewhat mysterious, but Schuller's point is borne out by the inadequacy of many attempts to transcribe her recordings with musical notation.

Billie Holiday's elusive style was not always well received. In the beginning, some habitués of Harlem cabarets thought that she was too rough, too plain, too musically crude to be a singer. There were musicians who were not impressed by the twists she gave to popular songs. Teddy Wilson, an elegant pianist and the leader on some of her best 1930s recordings, thought she copied Louis Armstrong too closely. He preferred clear-voiced balladeers, singers with careful phrasing like Beverly White, an obscure performer who sometimes alternated with Billie in the same small clubs. Even years after she had been acclaimed as a great vocalist, Wilson remained unimpressed by her singing on the records that had helped to make him famous, and said he now preferred Barbra Streisand to Holiday. When Billie first went to Chicago to sing at the Grand Terrace Café, one of the most important jazz clubs in the country, she was told by the manager that she was "stinking up the place . . . you sing too slow . . . sounds like you're asleep!" There was no question that she sang more slowly than most of the singers at the time, and it was sometimes said that it was because of her insecurity. But slow singing, like slow drumming, requires a higher level of skill in holding the time steady, and also exposes any of the singer's pitch, breathing, or phrasing problems. At times, such as in the 1944 version of "I'll Be Seeing You," her tempos are so measured that it almost seems as if she is treating each word as a separate phrase.

Since her first recordings were intended for African American jukebox play, most people in the country did not hear them until years later.

But the audience that was first exposed to her singing was slow to warm to her, and even at her peak in 1945, polls in the Negro press showed that Jo Stafford, a white singer with a silken voice, was more popular than Holiday. She never reached first place in the *Down Beat* poll, the leading magazine among jazz fans. In 1942 the winner was Helen Forrest, her co-singer with the Artie Shaw band; in 1943, Jo Stafford; and in 1944, Dinah Shore. On several occasions Billie said that Stafford was her own favorite singer.

Holiday and Stafford shared many musical characteristics: Billie's vocal gestures were also understated; both singers improvised in a sub-tle and sophisticated manner; the vibrato that many singers count on to show emotion (or hide their problems with intonation) was used selec-tively by both of them in their cool, straight melody lines. But Holiday could adorn those lines with small but unforgettable turns, up-and-down movements, fades, and drop-offs. (Compare Stafford's "I'll Be Seeing You" with Holiday's version of the song: Stafford's is a perfect vocal performance, calm, reassuring, a prime example of what critic Will Friedwald calls Anglo-Saxon soul, but Holiday's pulls the heart and ears in an unimaginably different direction, singing *down*, slower than expected, turning the song into what one might regard as a classic of chronic nostalgia.)

Holiday typically used vibrato to increase the emotional charge of a word or phrase, and perhaps, more often, to swing a single note, as Louis Armstrong did, setting it into motion by increasing the width of vibrato just before moving on to the next note or phrase. Billie was well aware of the importance of vibrato and once commented on it: "When I got into show business you had to have the shake. If you didn't, you were dead . . . That big vibrato fits a few voices, but those that have it usually have it too much. I just don't like it. You have to use it sparingly. You know, the hard thing is not to do that shake."

When Billie praised Stafford by saying that she also sang like a horn, she seems to have had a different and more modest sense of what hornlike singing could be, and at the same time she calls our attention again to how vague and confusing musical labels can be. Stafford's lustrous voice, her carefully controlled approach in live performance, fine diction, minimalist musical gestures, and faultless pitch and technique were admired by many singers. (Frank Sinatra, who sang with Stafford in the Pied Pipers, once said she could hold a note for sixteen bars.)

Stafford is not usually considered a jazz singer because her hits were typically pop oriented, but she did record a number of jazz albums, such as *Swingin' Down Broadway* (1958) and *Jo+Jazz* (1960), the latter backed by Johnny Hodges, Harry Carney, and Ben Webster, musicians from Duke Ellington's band who also accompanied Billie on records in the thirties and forties. Stafford also recorded more blues than Holiday (including *Ballad of the Blues*, a 1959 concept album), found her way into bebop scatting on a couple of recordings, and wasn't averse to altering conventional harmonies or dropping a flatted fifth here and there, especially at the end of a tune.

Though music journalists and critics were generally among Holiday's biggest fans, some had doubts about her. In 1942 Roger Pryor Dodge wrote in the magazine *Jazz* that she could have been a good blues singer if "hot and sweet" singing had not replaced the blues. After her death he was even more damning: "The changes in blues intonation, through the unhealthy influence of Billy Eckstine and Billy Holiday, resulted in a whining intimacy, a merging of blues with the torch song." Their kind of singing, he added, was similar to what beboppers such as Miles Davis and Dizzy Gillespie were playing at slow tempos, a music that he regretted to have to call decadent.

Holiday herself insisted that she wasn't a good singer, and her accompanists testified to her surprising sense of insecurity. In a 1956 interview Mike Wallace asked her about the performers, actors, and singers she said she most admired—Tallulah Bankhead, Ethel Barrymore, and Helen Forrest—and what she had in common with them:

BH: Why, they're actresses, they're artists. I look at them, like, Wow.

MW: And you don't consider yourself in the same league?

BH: No, my God, no!

MW: Why not? You've worked as hard. You've thought as much about it. You've developed a style and technique, just as much as they have done. You've pleased just as many people, so why aren't you just as much of an artiste as any one of them?

BH: Maybe I am in my little way . . . but my God, they make me cry, they make me happy. I don't know if I've ever done that to people, not really.

Not many singers could, in fact, make listeners cry. Abbey Lincoln said that people sobbed every time Billy Eckstine sang "Sophisticated Lady," Duke Ellington's sad story of an elegant woman who hid the pain of a lost great love affair behind "smoking, drinking, never thinking of tomorrow." And despite Billie's demurrals, Frank Schiffman, owner of the Apollo Theater, said that he saw young girls weep whenever she was onstage.

A home recording exists of Billie at a rehearsal talking to musicians between songs, joking, laughing, remarking on any number of subjects, including her own singing: "I'm telling you, me and my old voice, it just go up a little bit and come down a little bit. It's not legit. I do not got a legitimate voice. This voice of mine is a mess, a cat got to know what he's doing when he plays with me."

Untrained, with no ambition to be a vocalist, she insisted that she had literally stumbled into singing. At fifteen, desperate to help her mother find money for the rent before they were put out onto the streets of Harlem, she auditioned as a dancer at a tiny nightclub, only to fail, but then at the last moment was offered a chance to sing. She was an instant success, with a cabaret audience weeping at the passion in her song and throwing money at her. It was a standard show business success story told by so many, but where others had stressed how hard it had been for them to get a break, Billie claimed hers was an accident.

. . . . .

Holiday began her singing career before microphones were widely used, as they were not considered necessary in small bars and cabarets. She related to her audience in a direct and personal manner, holding eye contact, moving from table to table, adjusting her performance in accord with how she was being received. After the microphone became more widely available in 1933, some singers, Holiday among them, were afraid to sing into them for fear their voices would be distorted or too loud. But as the technology improved and its potential was understood, audiences were introduced to a quieter, more intimate use of the microphone—intimate in that it enabled singers to create the illusion that they were closer, singing to each member of the audience even outside the nightclub setting. When the mic was used for radio broadcasts or for making recordings, listeners at home could experience that intimacy, a completely new musical experience. Some singers took this as a cue to whisper words, in an attempt to create a false intimacy. But Holiday found that the level of her everyday speaking voice was where she wanted to be.

The microphone had begun to function like a close-up lens in motion pictures, focusing and amplifying emotions and small vocal gestures, making histrionics, high volume, and grand stagecraft unnecessary. With a microphone, a singer could join the new naturalistic stage methods that were developed following the Russian director Stanislavsky's plea that actors cease portraying emotions to the audience and instead begin communicating with them directly; that the performance was not in the words that were spoken or sung, but in the character that was developed, and character began with basics such as breathing. The mic could set the singer free, and audiences became used to closer and more revealing looks at actors and singers on film and the bandstand.

Singers quickly learned that with amplification they could phrase conversationally, closely, at moderate volume, emphasizing words and syllables as well as melody. They could stretch vowels or deemphasize consonants, and allow musical phrases to extend beyond their normal length. Holiday, along with Frank Sinatra, was one of the first to use a microphone creatively.

Part of the difficulty describing Holiday's voice is that she had so many. In the upper register she had a bright but nasal sound; she sounded clearer, perhaps even younger, in the middle; and at the bottom, there was a rougher voice, sometimes a rasp or a growl. But even these voices were varied or might change depending on the song she was singing.

Singing is a dramatic art, the singer always an interpreter, even if her eyes are closed and she stands motionless. When Billie sang in cabarets without a microphone, her acting was presentational, singing directly to the audience, strolling between tables, showing them what she meant. In later years, before larger and larger audiences, she seemed to erect a fourth wall onstage and sang to herself, assuming the character she sang about and allowing the audience to become voyeurs in a life they imagined. For Holiday, this meant deadpan understatement, the mask of the cool—a blink, a silent snapping of the fingers, her arms slightly raised and moving with the rhythm, one eyebrow arching, maybe a tilt of the head in response to a chord. Her minimal gestures hinted at a rhythmic knowledge that was wiser, hipper, and deeper than could be humanly expressed.

She had a point of view in her songs, a way of positioning herself that went beyond merely getting the words and music right. (Compare Marlene Dietrich's "Falling in Love Again" to Billie Holiday's recording of the same song.) Her ability to communicate strong and painful emotions through singing led many to believe that she was suffering and in pain. But real suffering is not necessary for great singing, only the ability to communicate it in song. There are those who simulate emotions by a catch in the throat, upper-register pyrotechnics, or the exaggerated vibrato (vibrato itself being a means of expressing authenticity of one or another emotion). For singers such as Judy Garland this could mean facial and gestural excesses, and a vibrato that sometimes crossed the line into hysteria. Holiday developed an acting style, not by merely deciding who she should be in various songs, but by a kind of American Method acting—finding the motivation for a song, asking why the song says what it does, drawing on her own experiences and on memories of emotions. For her the question was, how do I relate this song to my life:

> If you find a tune and it's got something to do with you, you don't have to evolve anything. You just feel it, and when you sing it other people can feel something too. With me, it's got nothing to do with working or arranging or rehearsing. Give me a song I can feel, and it's never work. There are a few songs I feel so much I can't stand to sing them, but that's something else again.

To achieve this, a singer has to develop a dramatic sensibility that goes well beyond her own backstory to convey an interpretation exceeding a literal reading of the lyrics. How an audience receives such a performance is another matter—the way they understand the lyrics, how they are being interpreted, what emotions are evoked, and whether or not there is a relationship to her or their own biographies. A singer obviously cannot control all of those perceptions and emotions, and in Holiday's case there was a great variety of strong and deeply felt reactions to her performances:

—Composer Ned Rorem, a devoted follower of Billie's from his youth, was moved by the way she approached a song: She was a romantic, he said, and it came from the inside out. She was all content, not form. It was pure theater, not real life, for art is a concentration of life. She made you accept her song on her premises, and then you got caught up in her content.

—Linda Kuehl, Holiday's would-be first biographer, never saw her perform, but she had surrendered to Billie's singing, and as her research deepened she began to take it all personally, and bitterly came to think of her as a great singer who had abandoned her art for artifice.

—She was a great actress, said jazz critic Martin Williams, one who drew on her own feelings and presented them with an honest directness to a listener. She never fully became what she portrayed, though, but seemed to stand aside from it. "A great actress but one who never had an act."

—Studs Terkel and Nelson Algren saw Holiday at a South Side Chicago club performance in 1956, and Studs reported that "Billie's voice was shot, though the gardenia in her hair was as fresh as usual. Ben Webster, for so long big man on tenor, was backing her. He was having it rough, too. Yet they transcended. There were perhaps 15, 20 patrons in the house. At most. Awful sad. Still, when Lady sang 'Fine and Mellow,' you felt that way. And when she went into 'Willow, Weep for Me,' you wept. You looked about and saw that the few other customers were also crying in their beer and shot glasses. Nor were they that drunk. Something was still there, that something that distinguishes an artist from a performer: the revealing of self. Here I be. Not for long, but here I be. In sensing her mortality, we sensed our own."

—Novelist Elizabeth Hardwick said that "you can listen to opera by yourself, but not certain kinds of jazz. You had to have someone with you when you listened to Billie Holiday, for instance. Otherwise, you might kill yourself."

—Billie could sing words and make them mean something else, according to bassist Charles Mingus, in the way she punctuated a song. She'd perform "Them There Eyes," for example, as if she'd be asking a question. At other times it would be an exclamation. She said the words differently with each interpretation.

—She sang like an instrument, a whole orchestra, according to Baron Timme Rosenkrantz, who first saw her after he arrived in New York from Denmark. "Sometimes there was the soft wail of a saxophone, then the piercing, sharply defined blast of a trumpet. Her voice crept under your skin and stayed there. I've never heard anyone else sing like Billie. Her phrasing was a heart-to-heart conversation with the world out there, so personal it gave one the feeling of being taken into strictest confidence by someone who had such a desperate need to 'tell it all,' that it seemed somehow sacred. . . . When she finished there was a small mound of money at her feet. She didn't even glance at it."

—Paul Bowles, novelist, composer, and student of North African music, wrote of Holiday's 1946 Town Hall concert that her voice was "like modern Greek song, Balkan song, conto jondo . . . Her vocalization is actually nearer to North Africa than to West Africa."

—Carl Van Vechten, photographer, novelist, and Harlem Renaissance promoter, saw her at Carnegie Hall in March 1948, just after she was released from a ten-month stay in a federal prison: "She was nervous and perspiring freely, but her first tones were reassuring and rewarded with a whoop . . . [She sang] with that seesaw motion of the arms, fingers always turned in, that swanlike twitching of the thighs, that tortured posture of the head, those inquiring eyes, a little frightened at first and then, as applause increased, they became grateful. The voice was the same, in and out between tones, unbearably poignant, that blue voice." The next day, however, Van Vechten wrote to himself that her singing had very little variation, especially as she failed to sing the songs as written, sang off the beat, and most were sung in the same key. What's more, her body movements were all the same.

Billie Holiday has not always been well served by writers in their quest to examine the tragedy of her life and its reflection in her art. They assemble dossiers on the slings and arrows she suffered from the music business, Hollywood, nightclub owners, nuns, husbands, drug dealers, her father, police, prisons, doctors, and all of it is more or less true. They note the crack in her voice as a failure that signals pain, the changes in her photographed images as if they were something to be entered into evidence. Her hagiographers with diverse interests find points of identity in her suffering and match them to their own. Her stage imitators model themselves on her worst performances and stage them with embellished hurts and vulnerabilities.

The singers we see in performance are not the real persons. Like actors, singers create their identities as artists through words and music. Singers *act* as singers when they perform, but behave differently in daily life. Trying to have a unified onstage/offstage self like a Liberace, a Johnny Lydon, or a Miles Davis can be enormously stressful and even fraught with danger. The public face that must be maintained requires serious effort, and carries with it moral demands that are difficult to meet, whether it be a diva face, guitar face, or no face. The emotions that are expressed in performance need not be authentic, but only have to appear to be so, and can never be assessed via a backstage view of the performer. All we can know for certain is the performance itself. We expect to see a performer maintain a consistent face or front in performance, and only when drugs, health issues, and personal problems make their way onto the stage and affect the performance are we forced to question the performer's identity. We should not be shocked, then, to learn that, whereas onstage Billie Holiday projected a ladylike distance and grace, offstage her manner was sometimes rough, profane, caustic, and vengeful; she could be violent with racists, call Marilyn Monroe a stupid bitch and throw her out of her dressing room, hang out in men's gay bars (often accompanied by friends who were "female impersonators"), carry a razor blade with her wherever she went, and become involved with men who beat her, robbed her, and drove away her friends. Nor should we be surprised that she could be witty, kind, and perceptive; she could charm intellectuals, artists, and wealthy patrons, help younger singers with their careers, buy drinks for fans who could scarcely afford to see her perform, and dream of a house in the country with a white picket fence, children, and a dog.

In Holiday's lifetime, those who had seen her perform live were a very small number compared with those who knew her only from the radio, television, or recordings. Even then, people who heard her in a small Harlem cabaret would have had a completely different impression from those who had seen her in Carnegie Hall, just as would those who heard only "Strange Fruit" but not a playful number like "I've Got My

Love to Keep Me Warm." Her audiences were part of her performances and helped shape her performing identity. This is not to say that she had no aspirations or control over how she was received, for she surely had specific intentions for how she wanted to present herself—that much is clear from her autobiography. Mediation and mutual reception is the nature of performance, and part of the construction of a performer. If she were alive today, it would not be much different, for performers of note are now surrounded by even more artificial performance spaces—lip-synching, guest appearances that demand a certain persona, reality shows that are scripted and rehearsed, a press that follows them relentlessly, and the lonely bloggers' deep well of imagination.

Today all that we know of her is determined by what we hear in her music—the way it was shaped by recording companies, mixed, edited, packaged, and sold—and by the reviews of and writing about her by those who never actually saw her perform. But audiences still have a role to play in determining how she is perceived, depending on how and where they encounter her voice—in a chic coffeehouse or restaurant, in an ad for an expensive auto, on a movie soundtrack, or heard completely alone through earbuds.

Bessie and Louis

Billie often said that her models were Louis Armstrong and Bessie Smith. More precisely, she said that she wanted to achieve the *style* of Louis Armstrong and the *feeling* of Bessie Smith, style perhaps meaning the way Armstrong sang, his technique, and feeling being the emotions awakened by Smith's singing. Once, when she was speaking critically of singers who imitated other singers, she remarked, "Sure, I copied Bessie Smith and Louis Armstrong—but not note for note; they *inspired* me." "Inspired" was an apt description for how she approached Armstrong and Smith as models for reimagining songs. Bessie Smith and Armstrong were quintessential blues singers who had fully developed their styles before the microphone was invented, and both possessed distinctive voices that could cut through the noisiest crowds. To succeed with her voice, sensibilities, and aspirations, Billie would have to adapt and revise what they had shown her.

Both Smith and Holiday were contraltos, the lowest-pitched voice type of female singers, and both had a narrow range—Billie's was little more than an octave, Bessie's even less—but Smith had a big and powerful voice. Her singing was anything but subtle. Whether she was singing about death, love, pain, ghosts, sex, or money, her point was made quickly and bluntly. Often from the first line of a song it was clear where she was going: "Looka here, daddy, I wanna tell you, please get outa my sight"; "Lovin' is the thing I crave"; "Gee, it's hard to love someone when that someone doesn't love you." Her voice was matched by an imposing physical presence that drew the crowds to the tents and theaters where she performed even after she grew older and her record sales slowed. She paused or took breaths in unusual places, and used a variety of vocal effects—hums, growls, moans, rising and falling volume, and powerfully accented notes. Her voice could be teasing or mournful, but also threatening. When she sang the blues, the repeated lines were always sung differently.

Billie sometimes said it was Bessie's volume she admired. But Holiday rarely employed bursts of volume or emphatically accented notes. Instead she varied volume on single notes, compressed or simplified a song's melody, and seemed focused on nuance. (Compare Holiday's and Smith's recordings of "St. Louis Blues" or "Gimme a Pigfoot.") Billie was not a blues singer, as she always insisted, and in fact recorded only a handful of songs that could strictly be called blues. It was not unusual for an African American singer of that period to choose not to sing blues; Ella Fitzgerald, for example, had no particularly strong feeling for that form. Still, Holiday had some of the rougher vernacular vocal characteristics that made for a good blues singer, and those helped carry her past the swing era into bebop and beyond, when crooners and sweet-toned singers faded. She also could bring a blues sensibility to whatever she was singing, especially when she bent or lightly changed notes to increase their intensity or the expressivity of the music. (Contrast Holiday's "Stormy Weather" to Fitzgerald's recording of the same song.)

A more important difference between Holiday and Smith derived from the difference in their ages. Bessie Smith sang a number of traditional songs and folk or quasi-folk songs attributed to particular composers, and at least until nearly the end of her career, most of them were African Americans. Holiday's career began with the rise of Tin Pan Alley's corporate songwriters, and most of the composers of her songs were white. This doesn't mean that either artist could not change what she was singing to suit herself, but each began with fundamentally different material and also reached different audiences.

Billie was perhaps closer to Louis Armstrong in style, as she suggested, but more to his style of singing than to that of his trumpet playing. Both had immediately recognizable voices, and like Armstrong she sang jazz songs and Broadway and movie music favorites as well as Tin Pan Alley pop tunes, and felt free to shift the phrasing of a song and create suspensions of rhythm not expected by typical fans of those songs. (Compare Holiday's "I Got a Right to Sing the Blues" and "Pennies from Heaven" to Armstrong's versions of those to hear what she borrowed from Armstrong's singing.) Neither Armstrong nor Holiday sang bel canto: no "beautiful" singing, no theatrical flourishes, and no grand endings. (Armstrong's trumpet playing was another story, however.)

Billie recalls her impressions on first hearing Armstrong's "West End Blues":

> It was the first time I ever heard anybody sing without using any words. I didn't know he was singing whatever came into his head when he forgot the lyrics. Ba-ba-ba-ba-ba-ba-ba and the rest of it had plenty of meaning for me—just as much meaning as some of the other words that I didn't always understand. But the meaning used to change, depending on how I felt. Sometimes the record

would make me so sad I'd cry up a storm. Other times the same
damn record would make me so happy . . .

These are not the thoughts of a singer whose greatest strength is simply
making banal pop songs sound better, but those of one who doesn't view
songs as having fixed meanings or, for that matter, fixed rhythms and
melodies. She feels them in ways that depend on her in-the-moment
reading or recall of them.

Truth be told, published sheet music for pop or jazz songs has never
been more than a sketch: basic chords are provided for amateur pianists,
words are written out in Standard English and sometimes in stereotyped
dialect, and rhythms indicated that, if played as written, would sound as
strictly regimented as a march. Only a beginner would ever sing them
literally as written. Accomplished singers may adhere to the texts, but
the way they are phrased, stressed, faded, pitched, and shifted gives the
music startling new shape.

Louis Armstrong made singing in the vernacular acceptable. There
were dialect singers before him, either mocking or imitating others, or
singers who sang in some form of vernacular that was their only language. Rural or folk blues singers, for example, bent or distorted words
because that was the way they spoke, or because they had not been
trained to divide the musical or verbal line into equal units, so that each
line or verse might be a different length. Some might take a breath in the
middle of a word because they'd run out of air. But their records or radio
broadcasts had limited distribution, and the better-known blues singers,
like Mamie Smith and Ethel Waters, sang largely in Standard English
with clear diction. The words Holiday chose to alter or remake, mostly
verbs and nouns, seemed not predetermined, but casually chosen to
suddenly grab the audience's attention.

A singer who chooses to perform within the jazz tradition faces a
challenge that an instrumentalist never encounters. Jazz instrumentalists may keep the words of a song in mind when they solo, staying close
to them in phrasing or mood, or they may ignore the words entirely. But

if a singer adheres to the original lyrics of a popular song, she is limited in how far she can depart from the original melody without garbling the words. One of the solutions to this constraint is to abandon the words entirely by scatting—that is, imitating horns by singing syllables that are often onomatopoeic but not necessarily with obvious meaning, and improvising freely by using any rhythmic values or melody that she chooses. Another possibility is the use of vocalese—composing lyrics to already existing instrumental jazz variations or improvisations of a song—but this solution is much closer to a kind of jazz poetry than it is to jazz singing per se. Existing songs can also be changed without using the words, turning only to vocal acrobatics that impress the laity, but this moves them into an area in which instrumentalists are already dominant. This problem of words vs. improvisation is never quite resolved, even in the best singer's work, and many singers compromise by choosing to retain the original words and melody of a song, counting on small but significant variations to capture an audience's interest.

What's most striking about Holiday's improvisations is that when she makes changes in the rhythm or the melody it is always in service to the words, not the other way around. And yet she still manages to reach the highest standards of the rhythmic feeling that jazz musicians call swinging.

The Music of Speech and Verse

When Gunther Schuller noted that many of the characteristics of Holiday's style are mysteriously impossible to describe in standard musical notation, he suggested that a poet might better be able to express what she was achieving. Holiday's singing might indeed be best described in terms of poetic devices, and possibly even grasped by those more attuned to poetics than those trained strictly in music.

The difference between speech and song is probably much exaggerated, especially since little serious attention has been paid to the matter by musicologists and linguists. A different approach would ask what the two forms have in common. If we look at verse as a form of speech, it's clear that there is musicality in verse itself. For that matter, there is a kind of musicality in all speech. Rhythm, so obvious in poetry, is not so often acknowledged in speech, but the rhythms of speech are far more regular and fixed than we normally think, perhaps because they are so basic that they remain out of awareness. Most of the English spoken in the United States and Britain is a stress-timed language. Syllables may be longer or shorter and last different amounts of time, but the time between consecutively stressed vowels is relatively constant regardless of how slowly or quickly one speaks. Put another way, there is a regular beat to English. How this works out in song, where notes may be held for a time longer or shorter than the rules for speech allow, is not always clear, but it does show that there is room for composers and singers to change the feel of language in song. The possibilities expand even further when songs are written or sung by speakers of different dialects of English—such as that spoken in South Africa, the West Indies, and to some degree in regional and older forms of African American English—in which there is a different pattern of timing, syllable timing, where stresses fall on syllables, many of which are of different lengths, unlike the brief length of all vowels.

The musical nature of verse offers the singer the option of following the curve of the written melody and letting it direct the flow of sound, or of using a flatter, more speechlike voice to call attention to the words' own musicality. In the bridge or middle section of "Foolin' Myself," for example, Holiday sings:

And ev'ry time I pass
And see my face in a looking glass
I tip my hat and say

There is the rhythmic repetition of going from *t* to *t* in "tip my hat," or in the movement from "pass" to "see" to "face" to "glass" to "say" that sets up a pattern of *s*'s and *s*-sounding consonants. While music of verse may already be present in the lyrics of the song, it is not given as much attention by other singers as it is by Holiday, who imparts it with her characteristically lucid diction and idiosyncratic stress.

Holiday virtually recomposed popular songs to such an extent that she invited critics to compare her to some of the most esteemed names in English literary history, poets like John Donne or Gerard Manley Hopkins. Such leaps into comparative prosody may have left bemused fans shaking their heads, but there was more than mere hyperbole (or hype) involved. John Donne, a British poet born less than ten years after Shakespeare, brought a highly personal poetry into existence, using irregular rhythms that were closer to speech than those used in typical Elizabethan versification. Hopkins, a nineteenth-century British poet, experimented with what he called sprung rhythm, a more natural form of verse that he believed was closer to patterns of speech, spoken poetry, folk ballads, and nursery rhymes. When Holiday altered rhythm patterns to free up the sheet music of pop songs, she was following the same impulse driving those earlier poets, and certainly later writers who initiated free verse. None of this is that far from the practice of jazz musicians who alter written song rhythms, turning them toward the jazz vernacular. When Holiday was working at Café Society in the late 1930s, there was a craze for "jazzing the classics," retrofitting the old masters' works with hip rhythmic clothing. It was all part of jazz tradition that is sometimes called "signifyin(g)"—a concept and a word borrowed from literary and spoken language to indicate improvisatory play on and around a subject.

CHAPTER SIX

The Singer II

A lot of singers try to sing like Billie, but just the act of playing behind the beat doesn't make it soulful.

Miles Davis

She could just tear you up with the way she could say a lyric.

Bobby Henderson

*M*uch of Holiday's own sense of drama and emotion was relocated from the lyrics to her use of rhythm and time, and her very modern sense of swing. She could enter a phrase two or three beats late, then seemingly catch up at the end of a phrase, and drop back again into the band's rhythm at the start of the next phrase. (Compare Holiday's "lagging" vocal against a fixed beat in "St. Louis Blues" with Bessie Smith's relatively straightforward rhythm on the same song.) She sometimes seems to be lingering so far behind the beat that it appears that she will still be singing after the musicians have reached the end of the song. Yet it never happens. By extending vowels, clipping notes, stressing syllables, and taking rests along the way, she stays out of the band's rhythm at the same time that she emphasizes the words' meaning. In the bridge, or middle section, of "Foolin' Myself" (1937), every syllable is well off the beat established by the rhythm section, especially in the second line:

And ev'ry time I pass
And see my face in a looking glass
I tip my hat and say

When she reaches the next two lines in the song, she gives stress to most of the syllables, which enables her to return to the band's rhythm and at the same time emphasize the self-disdain in the song:

/ / / / / /
How do you do, you fool

/   /   / / /
You're throwing your life away

On "Billie's Blues" (aka "I Love My Man"), a song she composed, she stresses almost every syllable.

All this might seem to be a prosaic matter, just a function of the way we naturally talk. But in English the normal pattern of writing and speaking consists of stressed syllables alternating with unstressed, so putting words together in a song in a manner in which any syllable or vowel can be stressed, and still making it sound natural, is not all that easy. Add to that the varying rhythmic pulse set up by accompanying drums, bass, and piano, and the possibilities and complexities multiply rapidly. Jazz is an interactive music, one of the most complex of all human musical interactions. When saxophonist Ornette Coleman said that the difference between rock and jazz was that in rock everyone is playing with the drummer whereas in jazz the drummer is playing with everyone else, he struck at the heart of what is special about interaction in jazz. There is a pulse, a rhythm, a subdivision of time at work in well-played jazz, but one that can be manipulated and adjusted by each player such that the rhythmic expectations of both musicians and audience are surprised. Jazz is the sound of surprise.

Though her approach to rhythm seemed new and daring at the time, and may still seem so, much of it was common among instrumentalists in swing music. Regardless of what some textbooks may say about the consistency of swing rhythm, the great players frequently shifted from syncopated to straight time during the same solo. Playing or singing behind or ahead of the beat is one of the most common distinguishing features of jazz, though, granted, no one uses it with the frequency and skill of Holiday.

Her use of delay or retard may have been one of the rare occasions on which a singer was an inspiration for jazz instrumentalists, especially those players of the style known as cool. (Listen, for example, to the first statement of the melody on Lennie Tristano's version of "Foolin' Myself," titled "Love Lines" on the Atlantic album *The New Tristano*.)

What is truly singular about Holiday among vocalists is that in spite of her typically delayed approach to syllables, words, and phrases, she does not always sing behind the beat (or, for that matter, ahead of it), though it certainly may sound as if she is doing so. Whitney Balliett, in a *New Yorker* profile of Teddy Wilson, gave a hint at how this musical phenomenon works when he wrote, "Part of the appeal of the Wilson-Holiday Brunswick [recordings] is the contrast—not to say struggle—between his rhythmic rectitude and her alarming and irresistible rhythmic liberties. She sometimes sang entire vocals outside the beat while Wilson, in his accompanying solo, effortlessly gave her a reading of her exact location."

Johnny Guarnieri, the pianist with Artie Shaw's band when Billie was one of its singers, gives us a sense of what it was like to try to accompany Billie if one didn't know her approach to rhythm:

The first night she handed me some tattered lead sheets, and said, "Give me four bars." I played four bars. But she didn't come in. Figuring she hadn't heard me, or just missed her cue, I started over again. Suddenly I felt a tap on the back of my head and I heard her say, "Don't worry 'bout me—I'll be there." She added that she liked to come in behind the beat, as I discovered, and that I didn't have to bother to make her look good. Looking back, I'd say that few performers had such a solid judgment about tempi as she did, particularly when it came to doing certain tunes in a very slow tempo . . . Billie was the greatest tempo singer that ever lived.

But how did she sing independently of the pianist's or the band's beat, give different rhythmic values to the original song's notes along the way, and still manage to remain faithful to the lyrics? Close listening, and the work of some astute musicians and scholars, provide us with another insight into her style.

What Holiday achieves does not involve what classical musicians call "rubato," a manipulation of rhythm in which the singer and the accompanist both briefly move out of the existing tempo and then return to it. As early as her first recordings with Teddy Wilson, the band stays in a fixed tempo while Holiday's melody line does not strictly follow that tempo but remains unsynchronized with it. One way to think about this kind of differentiated rhythm—which Hao Huang and Rachel V. Huang call "dual-track time"—is to grasp that "there are two beat systems functioning simultaneously, one governing the accompaniment and the other regulating the vocal line." These "two parallel strands organizing the passage of time might be irreconcilable, yet they have to be grasped simultaneously" because that "is the profound conceptual challenge of Billie's art." (See the placement of beats in Holiday's singing, the band's accompaniment, and Cole Porter's words in the transcription of "What Is This Thing Called Love?") Another way to view this technique is to look outside the European musical tradition for a source or precedent. (There are European prototypes of dual-track time in eighteenth-century Italian music and later in Chopin's piano performances of his own compositions where the bass and treble lines each have their own beat system, but they are not typical of European classical music.) Holiday's use of rhythm and time is closer to the cross rhythms of West African music, to Cuban and other Afro-Latin musics, to early blues singer-guitarists' recordings like Charlie Patton's "Pea Vine Blues" and to jazz pianists' recordings such as Jelly

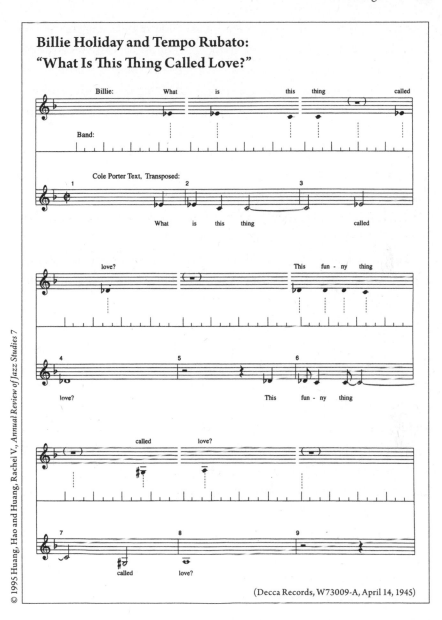

**Billie Holiday and Tempo Rubato:
"What Is This Thing Called Love?"**

(Decca Records, W73009-A, April 14, 1945)

Roll Morton's "New Orleans Blues" and James P. Johnson's "Keep Off the Grass."

Singing is sometimes described as a heightened form of speech, a form of communication that carries messages that can't be communicated in speech. But Holiday's accompanists insisted that Holiday sang like she talked, a style that becomes even more apparent in her later recordings. The idea that instrumental jazz is a speech-inflected music has been noted for years by jazz scholars, and some see it as a defining feature of the music. During an interview she did with talk show host Tex McCrary for Du-Mont TV in November 1956, Billie was asked to recite the lyrics of some of her songs without instrumental accompaniment, and she chose "God Bless the Child," "Don't Explain," and "Fine and Mellow." Her singing and speaking voices were in the same tonal range, and many of the same pitch patterns and the glides that occur between words or syllables were also very similar in both forms of communication.

Her diction was exceptional, whatever she sang. She avoided contractions and melisma (singing a single syllable across several different notes) wherever she could, and made each word count. She was very aware of the importance of phrasing in her songs, the grouping of notes and words in ways that would make musical and verbal sense of them or give them emotional weight. Her performances "live phrase to phrase," as her biographer John Chilton put it. Once, while she was singing in Chicago and Frank Sinatra was there with the Harry James band, she and Frank went out on the town, and she was later asked by columnist Earl Wilson what it was that she had taught Frank that later led him to say how much she had influenced his singing: "I told him that he didn't phrase right. He should bend certain notes. He says, 'Lady, you aren't commercial.' But I told him certain notes at the end he could bend, and later he said I inspired him. Bending those notes—that's all I helped Frankie with."

The poet Robert Creeley once wondered in admiration how jazz musicians were able to rephrase songs written by others so that they seemed different from the original without recomposing them in advance. He might better have wondered about jazz singers, who reshape those same phrases into something intensely personal without ever altering the actual words.

Holiday's songs get much of their affective and emotional power from her ability to create the feel of simultaneously speaking and singing. She developed a kind of speech-song in which sliding pitches that convey emotions like surprise, happiness, or sorrow occur as they do in speech. This use of pitch doesn't appear as often in music, where sustained pitches typically change to other sustained pitches by steps. Holiday's approach allows us to hear the melody of speech while she never completely abandons the melody of the song. She also pauses between phrases, allowing her to realign the difference between the band's rhythm and hers and to prepare for the beginning of the next phrase, which she often starts at a faster tempo. ("What Is This Thing Called Love?" from April 14, 1945, with the Bob Haggart Orchestra and "All of Me" from March 21, 1941, with the Billie Holiday Orchestra are good examples of these techniques in Holiday's dual-track singing.)

A kind of speech-song can also be found in diseuse (literally, "talking" or "storytelling"), a turn-of-the-twentieth-century style that French cabaret singers such as Yvette Guilbert developed for their story songs (many French songs then were essentially cast in the form of stories), where the singer breaks in and out of speech, often with the rhythm section stopped. Others talked over the melody, only occasionally dropping back into song. Édith Piaf, for example, sometimes stops singing completely, speaks several lines of the song, turning the lyric into pure verse, and then returns to singing.

It might be tempting to look for the source of Holiday's style in Parisian cabaret diseuse, since she sang several well-known French chansons, but as with so many other efforts to trace African American creativity to Europe alone, it would be inaccurate.

There are in fact many distinctive examples of speech-music relationships among African-derived peoples of the Americas. In the United States, sermons often begin in prose and then move into intonational verse and are combined with music. Religious songs likewise frequently include short spoken lessons or sermonettes that are accompanied by a choir. Some blues songs contain spoken passages, occasionally based on personal experiences or folktales (whereas in European folk traditions the song is usually *within* the story). Early black pop vocal groups used similar music-speech techniques. In this case a song usually is first sung solo by a tenor with precise diction, and is then followed by a middle chorus spoken in vernacular speech by a different singer. (Listen, for example, to the Ink Spots' "I Don't Want to Set the World on Fire.") Some radio DJs delivered their entire programs in rhymed and highly pitched speech. Gospel singers and soul singers often use spoken phrases or longer spoken passages in the midst of songs that blur the line between music and speech. (Singer Howard Tate is a good example.) The most recent African American use of this tradition is rap, in which the melody of speech *is* the song, often set to rhythms that are similar to children's game rhymes or jump rope verse.

The soft but declarative quality that Holiday brought to many of her songs was also part of the rhythmic irregularity that is so often noted in discussions of her work. It enabled her to find something valuable in melodies of otherwise weak song lyrics by shifting accents around and eliminating melodic excess. From 1939 on she sometimes sang so slowly and with enough emotional detachment that the rhythmic intentions of the original songs became lost. On the other hand, in "Strange Fruit" the horrors she describes benefit from the sense of shocked immobility that this approach can provide. Critic Margo Jefferson suggests that this emotional distance allowed her to refashion "all of the ordinary elements [of song], somewhat realigned and reproportioned, but recognizable and perfectly shaped . . . like a cubist painting . . . a musical cubism."

Billie Holiday and Lester Young: The Romance of Obbligato

In the four years between 1937 and 1941, Holiday and tenor saxophonist Lester Young appeared on a number of recordings together under pianist Teddy Wilson's name. Later, when she was better known, they also performed on recordings under her name. The records were made cheaply, with only sketches of the music to play and no rehearsals, and were aimed at the newly developed jukeboxes that were beginning to be installed in African American bars and restaurants across the country. Yet many of these three-minute recordings are now acclaimed as among the best that either of them made in their lifetimes. Together they were finding a new way for vocalists and musicians to relate to each other. Margo Jefferson once wryly observed that Holiday and Young had the kind of musical collaboration that Louis Armstrong had with himself as a singer and a trumpet player.

Lester Young was a quiet man with a taste for beauty in music who shunned the strutting instrumental theatrics and rough overstatement of many of his contemporaries on the tenor saxophone. Instead, he played softly, with slight vibrato, much the way Holiday sang, and his long, liquid lines were intended to convey what he insisted was a kind of storytelling. Billie wrote that "Lester sings with his horn. You listen to him and can almost hear the words." Telling a story was what Lester Young believed a jazz musician was expected to do. Even if words were not involved in that story, the instrumental solo had to have some sort of narrative line to it, with a coherent flow of sound throughout that was resolved at the end. This was a view widely shared by many horn players of that generation, even if they played in very different styles from Young. Tenor saxophonist Dexter Gordon sometimes spoke a few lines of a song before he played it, and spoke them with carefully pitched words and a rhythm that suggested where he was going to take his improvisation on the horn. Holiday and Young each chose to avoid playing the melody of songs as written, and instead sought to create new melodies close enough to the originals to paraphrase and evoke them, but not be bound by them.

Lester and Billie were very different in manner and character, but when it came to music they both found themselves in the same aesthetic zone. Young declared Billie his favorite singer and called her "Lady Day," a title that acknowledged her dignity. The irony of the name was that at the time no black women could be ladies in the eyes of white people. They could not be addressed in any way that raised their status—not even be recognized as "Miss" or "Mrs.," with the more significant consequence that even marriage could not be fully acknowledged. The further irony is that in much of her public behavior Billie was hardly "ladylike." Her manner was street-hardened, and stories abounded about her temper when wronged, her willingness to be violent when called for. She took no stuff from nobody. But as a singer, as a musician, her stage persona was one of grace in every sense of the word; her poise could freeze a noisy room into shocked silence. She returned Lester Young's compliment by saying there was no musician she'd rather work with, and named him "Prez," the president of the saxophonists.

Holiday's and Young's shared musical affinity is often understood as evidence of their being soul mates, if not star-crossed lovers. (A 2002 Sony CD compilation of some of these recordings was titled *A Musical Romance*.) A video from the 1957 CBS television special "The Sound of Jazz" features the two of them in their last days, and is often pointed to as proof of a special relationship. The actual circumstances were that both of them were ill—Lester too weak to play with the Count Basie band earlier in the show, and Billie not only in bad health but annoyed that she had bought an expensive dress for the show only to learn that the producer wanted the musicians to dress informally. Then, on the day of the live broadcast, a sponsor attempted to have her removed as undesirable for a family audience. But the producers resisted, and she stayed in the show.

It was decided that one of the last numbers that night would be "Fine and Mellow," with Holiday accompanied by a small group of musicians including saxophonists Young, Ben Webster, Coleman Hawkins, and Gerry Mulligan along with trumpeter Doc Cheatham and trombonist Vic Dickenson. To everyone's surprise, Billie sang better than she had in years, and Young's brief solo was a brilliant example of blues minimalism. Many who've seen the video of the program speak of the love and affection that is evident between the two of them during the performance, even though they had actually not spoken for several years following an argument of some sort. Billie's smiles and nods during Lester's brief solo have been read as a sign of their enduring relationship, but for his part Lester shows no acknowledgment of her presence, and she can also be seen nodding in approval at the other soloists.

What in fact made the two of them seem such natural partners were the similarities in their approaches to improvisation on ballads. Lester had a jazz singer's approach to a song: follow the melody, maybe paraphrase it, and create a new one in a horizontal fashion, never constructing one exclusively from the harmonic or vertical structure of a song. And when he and Billie came together they wove mutual melodic lines and in a sense "sang" together. The name for that sort of musical relationship in the Western classical tradition is "obbligato," where one musical line accompanies another, typically with a secondary melody that is independent but that seems necessary to what is heard as the principal melody. But Holiday and Young are far more creative and daring in their understanding of the different possibilities in this relationship. On both the 1937 master recording and alternate take of "Me, Myself, and I," for instance, in the second chorus she improvises lightly but stays close to the melody of the song as written by its composer. Meanwhile, Lester is playing a fully improvised, freshly created solo alongside her, based on the same tune. Both of them are soloing at the same time; that is to say, they are collectively improvising on a common theme without any harmonic clashes, something that Young would have certainly understood, as it was a basic organizing device in the jazz of New Orleans, the town where he was born. On "Who Wants Love?," recorded three months later, they perform together, again in the second chorus, but now it is Young who stays closer to the melody as written, while Holiday improvises behind him. On "He Ain't Got Rhythm," recorded even earlier in 1937, clarinetist Benny Goodman and pianist Teddy Wilson each play different lines as she sings around the melody, again with no clashes, despite there having been no arrangements or rehearsals before they recorded. When the three of them finish, Lester Young comes in on tenor and constructs a different melody.

Billie Holiday once said that "the only ones who can take a solo while I'm singing and still not interfere with me are Lester Young and Teddy Wilson."

This approach to obbligato is something more than the call-and-response so common in African American music. It's more akin to what Zora Neale Hurston heard in preachers' prayers that were embedded within the hymns of the congregants of rural Southern black churches: "The prayer is an obbligato," she said, "over and above the harmony of the assembly." Hurston goes on to say that they are different lines of music, but each is essential and mutual, and together ritually affirm spiritual harmony.

The Four Billies

Most fans and writers agree that in her twenty-six years as a singer on record, Holiday had three distinct stylistic periods. But her last two recorded albums are different enough that they would seem to constitute a fourth. From 1933 to 1942 she recorded for Columbia-affiliated companies, where she was promoted by John Hammond Jr. He took the risky path of casting her as a jazz musician, surrounding her with first-rate players in jam session–like settings, often without arrangements, in which she took her brief vocal solos in line with the instrumental soloists.

When she moved to Commodore Records in 1942, a small jazz company founded by producer Milt Gabler and Jack Crystal (the father of Billy Crystal), she continued her trajectory as a straight jazz singer. But once she agreed to record "Strange Fruit," the first openly political song sung by an African American singer on a pop recording, she announced herself as something more than an entertainer. After Gabler became a producer for Decca Records and signed Billie with them, she began to record more show tunes, and took on torch songs with greater emotional content and fuller musical settings. Meanwhile, as swing moved beyond black communities and was on its way to becoming a national craze driven by white teenagers (John Hammond called it "the Children's crusade"), she faced the choice of becoming commercial or remaining on the edges of pop music.

On "Lover Man," a song written for her, she was accompanied by strings, a more audacious move than it might seem, as very few pop song singers had ever been given such plush surroundings and certainly no jazz singers (or jazz musicians). It helped her expand her pop audience, though some of her jazz fans felt left behind. The cruel joke was that just as she began exploring a new approach to song, she was also drifting into drugs and heavy alcohol use.

In Holiday's third period, the 1950s, jazz itself was very different from when she'd made her earlier records. The conventions of swing were becoming exhausted, and jazz had become self-consciously revolutionary and culturally important in ways never anticipated. Her 1930s records were starting to seem quaint in the wake of bebop singers like Sarah Vaughan, who were threatening to replace her, except that Holiday, older and developing a different character, had begun to replace herself.

In the last decade of her life, her voice beginning to coarsen and her range narrowing, she crossed over to Norman Granz's Clef and, later, Verve Records, the premier sources of mainstream jazz in the 1950s. She and Granz began reexamining her repertoire in a new light that would give her the courage to rerecord them. Unlike older black singers, she had never been completely relegated to "race" records, those intended exclusively for an African American audience. Being marketed to a national audience was an enormous advantage to her, but it also meant that she would have to avoid current pop songs that were sometimes ill-suited to her, and she would not be able to depend on the near-blues songs that were still in favor in the black community. Granz encouraged her to stick with jazz standards and to revisit her best songs. Her work over the next few years was enhanced by the arrival of high-fidelity recording with extended recording limits, and by being surrounded by some of the finest younger jazz musicians. There were few surprises and no innovations in this period, but her popularity spread to a worldwide audience.

By 1958 her health worsened, and her voice had changed so much that she relied on little more than a bare recitative in which only her phrasing, her timing, and a few of her vocal characteristics remained intact. At her request, Columbia nonetheless agreed to record her with a forty-piece orchestra with arrangements by Ray Ellis, the star of a music style that would soon become known as easy listening. To some listeners, the album *Lady in Satin*, which she recorded that year, was unbearable, the death throes of a once great singer. To others, it was a revelation, Holiday at her purest, a distillation and a highly nuanced presentation of all that her music had been about. It's an argument that still persists today, with all sorts of interpretations attempting to explain what is conveyed on this record. (Novelist Haruki Murakami, for example, recently claimed that what he hears in this late music is forgiveness.)

It might not seem surprising that a singer would change her interpretations over the course of a twenty-six-year career, but the demands of aging fans who expected her to sing the same songs in the same way are often abided by, though sometimes with disastrous results. In Holiday's career, this issue was even more obvious since she rerecorded many of her biggest songs an extraordinary number of times: "Billie's Blues," twenty-two times; "My Man," thirteen; "All of Me," ten; and another nineteen of her other songs were rerecorded at least eight times or more. These multiple versions allow us to see that her approach did change over the years—tempos generally became faster, and the keys changed to allow her to lower her voice. But there was still great continuity in the general features of her style: She continued to improvise on the melody in very consistent ways, if anything taking greater risks with pitch as she grew older. Her timing never abandoned her, and she continued to find her way free from the constraints of her accompaniment. (Compare the versions of "All of Me" as recorded on January 21, 1941, April 22, 1946, and January 2, 1954; or those of "Yesterdays" recorded April 20, 1939,

July 27, 1952, and November 10, 1956; or of "My Man" recorded November 1, 1937, December 10, 1948, July 27, 1952, and July 6, 1957.) But her voice had been so much a facet of her biography, so emblematic of her life, for so long, that to most listeners the changes in it were just the latest phase of the mise-en-scène of her suffering.

CHAPTER SEVEN

The Songs I

*S*ongs occur in work, love, death, war, recreation, and any number of other important social events and gatherings. As far as we can tell, they've been a part of every known culture since the beginning of time and would seem to be one of the few cultural universals. Their words and melodies, and the manner in which they're sung and performed, are cultural indicators, a summary of societal features. While tempo, volume, pitch, rhythm, timbre, breathing, and phrasing all occur in everyday speech, usually at a low level of awareness, they are emphasized in singing, which may give song the peculiar power it has to evoke memories and emotions even without words.

Song is effectively an extension and elaboration of speech, engaging the body and mind in a way that speech can never do. One of the distinctive features of song is the repetition of its messages again and again at different levels: the recurrence of words, the redundancy of melody, the fixity of rhythm, the persistence of musical forms, the reiteration of musical traits (such as phrasing and taking breaths)—none of which are acceptable in speech, except among children, the mad, and lovers.

In classical songs the emphasis is on the words, but in the best jazz singing it's primarily about the way they are performed. Billie Holiday said she sang like jazz musicians played, but, unlike jazz musicians, she didn't first voice the melody in its standard form and then vary it by improvisation. From the very first note she improvised, and she continued doing so throughout the entire song. In using her voice instrumentally, she was faced with the problem of how to keep the words of songs from interfering with the effects she was aiming for with her singing. Gunther Schuller says that she "instrumental[ized] the material at hand . . . by alchemizing words and music into a new alloy in which the parts were no longer separable." Perhaps what is so powerful and affecting in the best of Holiday's art is her ability to let us listen behind the words and to hear their nonverbal antecedents in the evolution of speech, whether in the form of cries, shouts, laughter, sighs, gasps, or emotional outbursts—in short, all the pain and the joy of being human.

The songs a singer chooses to sing are an element of her style, and one of the most important elements, since these choices help determine the musical and physical demands that will be placed on her voice, the roles she will play as a performer, the gestures she makes, whether the songs will have to be introduced or explained, and perhaps even the clothing required. Billie Holiday's repertoire was extraordinarily wide-ranging. A representative sample from her twenty-seven-year career might include "My Man," a tune associated with Fanny Brice and the Ziegfeld Follies of the 1920s; songs by the Gershwins from Fred Astaire and Ginger Rogers's 1937 Shall We Dance; "Big Stuff," written for her by Leonard Bernstein, to be heard at the beginning of his ballet Fancy Free; "Yesterdays," from Jerome Kern's 1933 musical Roberta; four of Bessie Smith's songs; three that were sung by Bing Crosby in the 1936 film Pennies from Heaven; Duke Ellington's "Solitude"; "Speak Low," with music by Kurt Weill and lyrics by Ogden Nash; "I Wished on the Moon," with words by Dorothy Parker; "Gloomy Sunday," a Hungarian song translated into English; and "Mandy Is Two," a tune written by Johnny Mercer in praise of his young daughter.

Holiday's most often recorded songs in the studio and live are "Billie's Blues" (aka "I Love My Man"), "Them There Eyes," "My Man," "Lover, Come Back to Me," "Fine and Mellow," "I Cover the Waterfront," "Strange Fruit," "God Bless the Child," "What a Little Moonlight Can Do," "Lover Man," "No More," "Don't Explain," and "Willow, Weep for Me." When asked what her favorites were among those she had recorded, Holiday responded, at different times, "No More," "Things Are Looking Up," "Deep Song," "Fine and Mellow," and "Gloomy Sunday."

A poem can be treated as a single piece of writing that stands on its own, and may be read without knowledge of who wrote it, where or when or why it was written, who published it, or who has read it previously. In contrast, the singer may not have written the lyric, and if she did, another person may have composed the melody. The melody may or may not have been written to fit the words. A particular singer's interpretation of the song may change its meaning (or even its words and melody) as originally written. There may be different takes from one recording session, or rerecordings at a later time. Musicians, arrangers, producers, recording engineers, and the studio location can also influence the creation of a recorded song. Songs are often written to fit a particular need—a show, a concert, a means of creating a singer's identity, and any number of other possibilities. To understand a particular singer's interpretation of a given song, we can ask about its origins, how and where it was presented, how she came to sing it, and what it meant to her, if not to the listener. In Billie Holiday's case, where there is such a diverse variety of songs in her repertoire, it helps to know more, and not assume more than we need to.

In those days 133rd Street was the real swing street, like 52nd Street later tried to be.

Billie Holiday

The idea of cabaret could mean different things in different parts of black America. In some cities, like Philadelphia, it involved the modest presentation of a singer or an exotic dancing group, a pianist or small band, or, in later years, a DJ. Such cabarets were presented only occasionally, were usually held above a bar or in an unrented building, and were advertised in the local neighborhood with handmade signs. During Prohibition, bootleg liquor was served, and after the repeal of the Eighteenth Amendment they operated without a liquor license, the spirits having been bought at state liquor stores at full price and sold at even higher prices than those of local bars. The attraction was a community gathering in a relaxed atmosphere that avoided rougher crowds and the cold draft of a white nightclub or bar. In Harlem the impulse for cabarets was similar, but there it meant full-time clubs housed mostly in basements of brownstone residences that generally opened around midnight. The neighborhood also had a number of large nightclubs like Connie's Inn and the Cotton Club, which presented the stars of black entertainment and which were owned by whites and "catered to the white trade."

The block of 133rd Street between Lenox and Seventh Avenues was the center of the uptown cabaret district. Places like the Nest, Tillie Fripp's restaurant, the Clam House, Mexico's, Basement Brownie's, and Pod's and Jerry's offered an after-hours and literally underground basis for an alternative and more inclusive culture of freedom than that of the respectability proposed by the black middle class. Cabarets were welcoming gathering places for women, gays, those at different economic levels, as well as the people who lived close to the color line on either side, or crossed it. These nightspots and the way of life they represented and encouraged have been described as the other side of the Harlem Renaissance, another kind of racial uplift. It's hard to imagine that such small venues could have significant influence beyond their neighborhoods, but through novels, poetry, music, newspapers, recordings, and occasional radio broadcasts of floor shows they presented a new kind of social and cultural reality, one that offered a forum for idiosyncratic people of great artistic and intellectual abilities who might otherwise never have found an audience or been able to influence the larger society. The cabarets were also points of attraction for white musicians, actors, literati, and high-society folk, many of whom became regulars and something more than mere slumming tourists and curiosity seekers. (Jazz trombonist Dickie Wells once said that the city could be divided into night people and day people. The difference between them was that the day people all wished they could be night people.) At the very least these white regulars could be a source of amusement (and money), and for some they even represented a hopeful sign that whites might be learning something from their visits.

John Hammond Jr. was one of those regulars at the Harlem clubs and cabarets, often accompanied by his friends the Harlem painters Charles Alston and Romare Bearden. Hammond was a New York blue blood whose mother was a Vanderbilt and whose father was a successful business executive and a descendant of Civil War general John Henry Hammond. John Junior was an early convert and true believer in African American music and saw in it the potential to break the hold that race had on American life. He had the sort of bona fides that almost no other whites could claim: He was a member of the board of the NAACP; as a journalist, he had written about the injustices visited on black Americans in the courts, in work, and in music; and he regularly made donations to organizations that worked for social change, as well as to artists and musicians in need. He was also a man known to annoy some with his imperious, proprietorial manner, a tendency to at times take more credit than was warranted, and to presume to offer advice when it was not asked for. At the same time, his wealth and social position were often unfairly used against him, even though he devoted his life to music and gave up many of the privileges he could have had given his heritage (beginning with his removal from the social register for marrying beneath his level). He was one of the most important figures in the development of American music and perhaps did more than any other white individual in bringing African American music and musicians before the public.

Hammond first heard Billie Holiday at Monette Moore's club, a short-lived but well-attended spot named for its owner, a popular singer who had performed downtown and uptown and who at that time was an understudy for Ethel Waters. Hammond had located most of the places that sponsored black entertainment in New York City in his quest to find the best jazz musicians and blues singers. But when he first saw Billie perform at Monette's, his whole horizon was widened: He declared her the best jazz singer he'd ever heard, raved about her to everyone he knew, hauled friends up to Harlem to hear her, and wrote about her in his column in the British music magazine *Melody Maker*.

The young Benny Goodman was one of those Hammond took to see Billie, and her first recording, "Your Mother's Son-in-Law," was made under Goodman's name with Hammond's urging, and was produced by Hammond. Benny was still a freelance musician at the time, and it would be a few years before he led the swing band that made him famous. The recording session took place on November 27, 1933, only three days after Bessie Smith's final recordings, another session arranged by Hammond, in Smith's case to revive the career of his favorite blues singer. Billie was already nervous about working with a group of white musicians she didn't know and facing a microphone for the first time, when she learned that her session followed one with Ethel Waters held in the studio that same day, and that she was being backed by the same band that had played for Waters. She performed "Your Mother's Son-in-Law," a novelty tune that was to appear shortly in *Lew Leslie's Blackbirds of 1934*, with a busy arrangement that was too fast and in a key that pitched her voice so high that it forced her to virtually shout over the band. Hammond continued to urge Benny to use her again, and she recorded with him almost a month later, this time on "Riffin' the Scotch," another novelty, a song based on a sort of musical pun, with the name of the liquor worked against some bagpipe clichés and a story line of a woman who has gotten rid of one bad man only to wind up with another. Most listeners don't take this recording seriously, as it sounds as if it was thrown together that day in the studio by session musicians Goodman, Dick McDonough, and Buck Washington, with words added by Johnny Mercer, and was something Billie had to make the best of to be able to move on to a recording career. Yet it does show her at only eighteen already using what would become her signature sense of independent rhythm to find her way around the rigidity of the band. She was a swing singer among mostly white musicians who were yet finding their way into this new style of black music.

In the depths of the Depression, the record business had shut down almost completely, so it was a year and a half before Hammond could find a way to get Billie back into the studio, and when he did it was with small bands under the leadership of pianist Teddy Wilson, another musician Hammond had been promoting. These recordings exist only because Hammond convinced the Brunswick Record Company that the newly perfected jukeboxes then being installed in neighborhood bars and restaurants featured no pop music that blacks wanted to hear. To guarantee that the records paid for themselves and that the company made at least some money, he organized recording sessions that cost no more than two hundred fifty to three hundred dollars by using only six or seven musicians and a singer, working without the cost of arrangements and rehearsals. From 1935 to 1942 this small-group business plan would produce some of the finest music that jazz has ever offered.

While the recordings were made on the cheap, they were not jam sessions, if "jamming" meant musicians coming together to play something easy, or music that was somehow "natural" to them. The groups that Wilson put together were made up of some of the most accomplished jazz musicians of their time. The lineups varied from session to session, depending on who was in town, but the musicians all knew one another and shared a common musical vocabulary. Because all of them were already a part of an established musical tradition, they had a sense of form and procedure that allowed for the creation of "head" arrangements, something they could perform together without sheet music, advance preparation, or discussion.

Wilson described these musicians as being aware of the importance of these sessions:

> The Teddy Wilson small group sessions were the only chance these men had to play with their peers instead of being the best of the whole band...The music that was produced was a rare monthly event—art for art's sake...As far as Billie Holiday was concerned, she was very popular with musicians. You might call her a musicians' singer, and she was in the company of soloists who were on a par with herself.

In retrospect, the pairing of Teddy Wilson and Billie Holiday seems like an act of divine casting. Wilson's elegance at the piano was not then the norm in jazz. His clean melodic lines and perfectly chosen and executed arpeggios complemented Billie's lean song lines. He under-stood how to match his countermelodies to what she was singing and to fill in between her vocal lines to enhance the texture of the song. There was nothing facile or obvious about their interaction, and there was never a miscue. Wilson may have preferred a different quality of voice than Holiday's, but that is never reflected in his playing. Within a year he would be accompanying Ella Fitzgerald and Helen Forrest.

The critical and popular response to these recordings was largely positive, especially in Europe, where some of the most effusive praise for them was first published. (Hammond himself wrote his first apprecia-tion of Holiday in Britain.) There were a few critics, however, who thought that Wilson and Holiday were a match only in that what they were creating was not *hot* jazz—bold, fast, impassioned music. Hugues Panassié, Europe's most important jazz writer, said that Wilson had a finger style, with intelligent and well-exercised fingers, but that it was not a style of the heart. He had no respect at all for what he thought were Holiday's strange melodic twists.

Music publishers in the United States were likewise dissatisfied with Holiday's singing, which posed a potential problem. In those days the source of most new songs for recording was the publishers, who brought them to record companies. For their purposes, vocals that departed too far from the written melody would be harder to sell, both because they could sound too strange for popular taste and because the recorded version of the songs would be different from that provided in the sheet music, which was then a big source of money from sales to amateur mu-sicians and singers.

It's commonly believed that Billie Holiday was forced to sing songs that were not up to the level of her artistry, that she recorded whatever she could just to survive, or that as an African American singer she was given only the leftovers, the lightweight material, with the best songs going to white singers. But a survey of her entire output of recordings doesn't support any of these beliefs. "A Sailboat in the Moonlight," for example, was one of her songs that was considered fluff that had been rejected by the better singers. Written by John Jacob Loeb and Carmen Lombardo, the song was first recorded by Guy Lombardo and His Royal Canadians and reached number one on the *Billboard* Hit Parade by August 1937. Billie Holiday and Teddy Wilson went into the studio with it less than a month after Lombardo, and saxophonist Johnny Hodges also recorded it with Buddy Clark as the singer and members of the Duke Ellington band (including Ellington himself on piano) in the same month. The song itself may have been fluff, but rather than being a left-over, it seems to have been an obvious choice for those seeking at least some portion of commercial success. Listening to Lombardo's hit version is essential to understanding what Holiday does with the song. She makes no concession to popular taste, departing far from the original melody, though she does keep the lyrics intact and understandable, silly though they may be. In fact, the clarity and precision of her enunciation of them is basic to what makes the piece work for her. She stresses the words "just" and "two," makes the rhymes "setting" and "letting" and "drift" and "lift" ring against each other, and extends the "A" in "A chance to sail away" in the first chorus. Then, after putting stresses between the beats during her second appearance in the song, she hammers every syllable but the first on the beat in "A chance to drift for you to lift," and then shouts the last line as if she were her own band taking the song out. Meanwhile, Lester Young has been constructing a tenor saxophone countermelody that enhances her singing and offers her touch points for response and new variations.

If anything, most of the great singers have recorded weaker and more trivial songs than Holiday: Consider Frank Sinatra's "Mama Will Bark," Rosemary Clooney's "Botch-a-Me," Jo Stafford's "Shrimp Boats," or Ella Fitzgerald's "My Wubba Dolly." In fact, it was Ella, a more popular singer than Billie, who often had success with cheerful nonsense songs and juvenilia. "A-Tisket, A-Tasket," her 1938 hit with the Chick Webb band, was not even a pop composition, but a rural African American girls' game song. Yet she had the look, the spirit of youth, that these pieces needed. Ella was the ingénue to Billie's worldly sophisticate. She was the band singer the swing era folks wanted, even if Billie might have been the one they needed.

"Good" jazz songs do not always make for great jazz. As Jelly Roll Morton, the man who claimed he invented jazz, put it, jazz is not in the songs themselves, but in how they are played or sung. When it was suggested to Morton that Scott Joplin's "Maple Leaf Rag" was not the sort of material that was suitable for jazz, he objected: "You see, jazz is applied to the tune, and the quality must be in the operator . . ." Jazz was not a thing, in other words, but a method, a way of styling music. Nor was jazz about making trite or poor songs better. All jazz musicians work at making whatever music they are playing better, but they do so through recomposition, variation, invention, improvisation, and always aim for a new creation. Their approach is very different from that of classical singers or musicians, for whom the written score is paramount. The goal of classical musicians is to perform that score as well as possible in their own interpretation of it, but the score is always respected. Bad compositions, even those written by great composers, are not greatly improved by good musicians, and most classical musicians are not likely to try to improve them.

Billie Holiday, like all great jazz musicians, was first and foremost an improviser and secondly an interpreter, and when a tune like "What a Little Moonlight Can Do" offered her little in the way of melody or lyrics, she compensated by detuning the melody, shifting the rhythmic accents around, and ignoring the moderato tempo indicated on the song's original sheet music, taking it instead at a stompingly immoderate presto. "It's Like Reaching for the Moon" is likewise a minor piece of songwriting, but a modest exercise in metaphysical pop poetry, a reaching for love. Holiday sings it in a key high enough to make her figuratively look upward, and lets words like "stars" fall while she extends the word "reach" out into musical space. She is accompanied by Johnny Hodges and Harry Carney, two of Ellington's long-term colleagues, musicians who improvise contrasting flurries of notes behind her elongated and spatial lines. It's a vocal that is also interesting for her rare use of intense vibrato, here stretched to the point of the tremulous.

In July 1936 John Hammond's role as producer of the Wilson-Holiday recordings passed in large part to Bernie Hanighen, a young man from Nebraska and a graduate of Harvard, where he had led his own band, written songs and musicals, and, like Hammond when he was attending Yale, spent his weekends in the cabarets of Harlem. Under Hanighen, Holiday continued in much the same musical context but she was now recording for Vocalion Records, one of the many subsidiaries that the American Record Corporation (later to become Columbia Records) owned or leased. But he gave Billie more time to sing on each record, bringing her vocal in earlier on each track, followed by the musician's solos, then having her return to reprise the song just before the ending. He doubled her pay and put her name on the record as a leader for the first time, even though her role in picking songs and musicians remained the same.

"No Regrets," recorded at their first session together on July 10, 1936, showed her work continuing at the same high level under her new producer. This song was almost a cheerful farewell to a love affair, their education being worth the price it cost. Billie projects the image of a woman leaving in broad daylight, sashaying out the door with nothing broken, pride intact. Artie Shaw and Bunny Berigan play brilliantly alongside her, clarinet and trumpet winding together in a duo with the joyous spirit of young white musicians discovering black jazz. ("No Regrets" makes for a fascinating parallel with Édith Piaf's "Non, je ne regrette rien." The Little Sparrow's interpretation is in the spirit of an MGM production, more appropriate to a scene of her riding out of Algeria with the French Foreign Legion, defeated, but her arm raised in a salute of both farewell and independence.)

That same initial session with Hanighen is also notable for producing the first nonoperatic recording of a song from George Gershwin's *Porgy and Bess*, a show that had closed on Broadway only a few months earlier and was still mired in controversy. An opera about rural black people, written by a Southern aristocrat and two songwriters with ties to Tin Pan Alley, staged entirely by white people, was slated from the start for trouble. No one could be entirely dispassionate about it unless he or she was not an American. The lines of dissension were not drawn so neatly as white vs. black. There were those on either side of the racial divide who liked it or argued vehemently against it, and there was a high vs. low cultural split as well. George Gershwin described it as a folk opera, but it did not feature any folk songs. Some people didn't even consider it an opera: How could a pop songwriter compose an opera? What could a white man know about black folks? And that degrading libretto in dialect!

The fact remained that *Porgy and Bess* contained excellent songs, and everyone seemed to have recognized that. There were calls for the opera to be boycotted by black performers, but no one suggested that the songs should go. Duke Ellington, an urbane man who avoided public conflict wherever he could, said that "it does not use the Negro idiom. It was not the music of Catfish Row or any other kind of Negroes." But Ellington recorded songs from *Porgy and Bess*, as did hundreds of jazz musicians of every color.

People may have argued about how Gershwin got the idea for "Summertime," the lullaby that opened the opera—did it come from the old Negro spiritual "Sometimes I Feel Like a Motherless Child," or from a Ukrainian Yiddish lullaby?—but they knew it was significant: It has become one of the most recorded songs in music history, with some thirty thousand versions, and a jazz standard. Billie's recording of it on July 10, 1936, reached the hit charts, but what's most fascinating about her version is that she turns the opera's plaintive lullaby into something aggressive and vaguely ominous, reminiscent of one of Duke Ellington's early Cotton Club "jungle" themes, with Artie Shaw's clarinet dancing around Bunny Berigan's growling trumpet to the rhythm of Cozy Cole's tom-toms.

When Billie recorded a second number from *Porgy and Bess* on December 10, 1948, her pianist, Bobby Tucker, said that he had never before played "I Loves You, Porgy" (or the other song recorded on that date, "My Man"). Both were improvised at the session with Billie. The version of "Porgy" she sang was extracted from the opera's duet between

Bess and Porgy, dropping Porgy's part and the verse to the song, and editing out some of the stanzas and the choral part. While she recast the folk dialect of the lyrics (singing, "I love you, Porgy" instead of "I loves you, Porgy" and "I want to stay with you" in lieu of "I wants to stay with you," etc.), she sang the pieces stylistically as close to the blues as one could and still recognize the song. In a radio interview she gave in late December 1948 on the *Curfew Club* from San Francisco, Billie acknowledged that she had altered the song from the original opera score:

> I just made some records for Decca. I made "Porgy." It's from *Porgy and Bess*, but you won't recognize it because I don't sing it anything like they do in the play, and I also put a middle to it [laughs] . . . I hope Gershwin doesn't mind [chuckles].

Billie's sometime producer Greer Johnson thought "Porgy" was the most beautiful song Billie had ever done, and he asked her why she didn't sing it more often. She said that she didn't think that "*Porgy and Bess* had done much for the race." But she did own records by Gershwin, including *Rhapsody in Blue* and an album of selections from *Porgy and Bess*. Singer Thelma Carpenter said that she and Billie would often take the parts of Porgy and Bess and sing their music along with the recordings.

Journalist Al Aronowitz, a colleague of Bill Dufty's at the *New York Post*, recalled the night he and his wife, the Duftys, and Billie went out for an evening, first to Birdland to see the Miles Davis Quintet, then to Hell's Kitchen to hear a Beat poetry reading. At one point Aronowitz asked Billie why she had never recorded "My Man's Gone Now" from *Porgy and Bess*: "I know! I know!!" she answered. "He asked me to sing that song when they opened that show. He asked me to play the part of the girl who sings that song." "Who asked you?" Aronowitz questioned. "George Gershwin," she replied, and explained:

> No, I couldn't sing that song night after night after night. It's too sad. It's the saddest song ever sung. That song breaks your heart.

It would've killed me. It killed the girl who got the part. She sang it night after night after night after night and she dies. It broke her heart. Singing that song would've killed me, too.

The part of Serena, the character who performed that song, was played by Ruby Elzy in the 1935 production of *Porgy and Bess*. She died at age thirty-five, just a week after her last performance. Though he auditioned over one thousand singers for *Porgy*, it seems unlikely that Gershwin would have offered Holiday the role when he was casting in 1934–1935 because all of the performers he eventually chose (with the exception of John Bubbles, who played Sportin' Life) had been classically trained. Later, James Baldwin, in a review of Otto Preminger's 1959 film version of *Porgy and Bess* starring Dorothy Dandridge and Sidney Poitier, noted Billie Holiday's recent passing and suggested that she would have made "a splendid, if somewhat overwhelming Bess."

Of all the songs that Holiday recomposed as she sang, none is more radically reconceived than "I'll Get By" (recorded May 11, 1937). The original melody (stated loosely by Johnny Hodges's saxophone at the beginning of the record and at the end by Buck Clayton on trumpet) is interesting on its own, rising and falling and yet moving with the inevitability of the pull of musical gravity. While it's not surprising that she decides to flatten the song out, given her customary musical methodology, as Gunther Schuller points out, when she reduces the melody's range by repeating the same note (A) twenty-six times, she "performs major surgery" on the song, to the point that it becomes overbearing. It is an extreme example of her mode of operation, and made to seem all the more so when Teddy Wilson follows her with a graceful and shapely melodic invention of his own. But the British trumpeter and jazz writer Humphrey Lyttelton hears something different in her invention. He quotes the jazz trombonist Benny Morton as noting that Billie is "turning the melody line upside down." Instead of starting on the lower F of the song ("I'll") and rising to a high A ("I"), she starts on the high A and drops downward. On the repetition of the original chorus she does the same with the word "poverty," only dropping from the A to an E on the third syllable instead of an F, which would be expected in the written original of the song, which was set in the key of F major. While she admittedly limits herself to a six-note range and does repeat a single note twenty-six times, she does so in the context of a daring and fascinating reinvention of the song. (For a "straight" rendering of the original, hear the Ink Spots' 1944 version, which was released during World War II and became a hit.)

"Things Are Looking Up" (November 1, 1937) is another of Holiday's favorites among her own recordings, and rightly so. The original version of the Gershwins' song from the 1937 film *A Damsel in Distress* as sung by Fred Astaire (or even Ella Fitzgerald's later recording from 1959) seems lackluster and unconvincing, even at its jaunty tempos, in comparison to Billie's version. Singing at a more relaxed tempo, she reworks the melody throughout the song and produces one of her most optimistic (though perhaps guardedly so) recordings.

"Back in Your Own Backyard" (January 12, 1938) was a 1928 song associated with Al Jolson and Billy Rose, a sentimental piece that could have been written in the late nineteenth century. Despite its positive message, its melody tilts toward the melancholy, and most of the singers who recorded it performed it that way. For the Holiday up-tempo version, Buck Clayton bugles the introduction, which leads to a dead stop, at which point Billie picks up his lead and floats into the words. She avoids the birdcall-like dips in the original melody and focuses on small touches that subtly change the rhythm: the stresses on the second syllables of "feather," "waiting," and "under," or her pointed emphasis on "back" in the final lines of the song. All the while she is phrasing across the beat, resisting the obvious, until she reaches the bridge, where she stresses every word of "weary at heart" directly on the beat, engaging briefly with the swing of the rhythm section. Lester Young's solo that follows is one of his best, and, despite its brevity, full of surprises.

With Count Basie

When John Hammond first heard the Count Basie band, it was a revelation. The Basie players were very different from Eastern jazz bands: Much of their music was based on the blues, and they had a remarkable singer in Jimmy Rushing, though Hammond thought the vocals were secondary to the remarkable dance music they brought with them from the Midwest. Their rhythm section had a lighter, more even, and propulsive feel that was the envy of every band that heard them (Benny Goodman, especially, favored the swing they generated); the ensemble was strong and brassy; they had the ability to create spontaneous arrangements based on collective experience; and their use of riffs and call-and-response was state of the art. It was music of urban sophistication that still retained a feel for the blues.

Hammond immediately wanted to sign the Basie band to a recording contract, but discovered they had already been signed by Decca. He did, however, manage to get part of the band recorded in 1936 (under the name Jones-Smith Incorporated) a few months before Decca could get the full outfit's records out. When the Basie band came to New York in 1937, Hammond acted as their adviser, working closely with their manager Willard Alexander.

Hammond brought Holiday and Count Basie together, knowing that she had already recorded with Basie's rhythm section and his star musicians Lester Young, Buck Clayton, and Herschel Evans on some of the Teddy Wilson sessions, and that she preferred to work with them, especially with Lester Young. Basie later added her as a band singer, but performing very different material from Jimmy Rushing's blues. When Basie played the Apollo Theater, it was his two vocalists who caught the audience's fancy.

Billie fit in just fine as "one of the boys," gambling, cursing, drinking, and laughing with them, but there was more to her than that. She was the rare singer who didn't need arrangements and could find her way through whatever they were playing. Since much of what they did play was worked out collectively, sometimes in the moment, they appreciated her good ear as well as her voice. Saxophonist Preston Love said that she always listened closely to the band and inspired them when she'd turn away from the mic, partly facing them, and compliment individual musicians on their solos. It was a Lady-like thing to do, and very different from the behavior of a typical band's trophy singers.

As the Basie group's reputation grew in New York, so did Holiday's, and it was ordained that they would have to compete sooner or later with the Savoy Ballroom's house favorite, the Chick Webb band and their singer, Ella Fitzgerald. The showdown came on January 16, 1938, when the Savoy sponsored a battle of the bands. The ballroom was packed with celebrities, especially those from the music world, which included most of Benny Goodman's band, Duke Ellington, a dozen other bandleaders, and singers such as Mildred Bailey and Ivie Anderson. The *New York Amsterdam News* described it pugilistically: "Ella Fitzgerald, entering the microphonic arena in white fighting togs, held a 'Bei Mir Bist du Schoen' advantage over the blue-clad Billie, and unlike her boss, the Chick, played a confident defensive game. On the other hand, Billie, the Holiday girl, in the pink throughout the battle, threw her notes at Queen Ella in grand fashion." Ella sang "Loch Lomond" and Billie sang "My Man." When the ballots were counted, Ella had won the audience by three to one. Even so, the publicity the event received earned the Basie group and Billie new opportunities to record. But Holiday was now under contract to Vocalion Records, and that prevented her from recording together with the band on Decca.

Only three songs exist from her days with Basie, live recordings from two dance halls in 1937, the Savoy in New York and the Meadowbrook in New Jersey. "They Can't Take That Away from Me" shows how quickly she adapted comfortably to big band accompaniment, gliding over rhythm suspensions and finding her own way over the glassine 4/4 of a great swing rhythm section. What impresses most, though, is the way she changes the emphases on the simplest words—"you," "hold," "never"—as if she's phrasing from word to word. On the up-tempo "Swing, Brother, Swing" she rides high over the band like a lead trumpet player, aggressively punctuating and echoing the rhythm below. "I Can't Get Started with You" is the least successful, a very popular song of the day with which she never quite seemed comfortable, perhaps because of its wordiness. What saves this recording are the moments when she and Lester Young's tenor saxophone are both staying true to the melody, not really improvising but each interpreting it in his or her own way simultaneously.

It was at this moment of its peaking popularity that Billie left the band. Her explanation was that there were too many managers running the band, so she quit. Others said that she was fired for refusing to sing the blues, and that John Hammond had asked Basie to drop her. That seems unlikely, as Hammond was the person who had asked Basie to hire her, and he knew she seldom sang blues; in any case, Jimmy Rushing was the established star blues singer with the band. Basie said Billie quit because she could make more money on her own. The final account of her departure came from Willard Alexander, who said that Hammond had not been responsible for her firing, and in fact if it hadn't been for his intervention on her behalf, she would have been gone six months earlier. "The reason for her dismissal," he said, "was strictly one of deportment, which was unsatisfactory, and a distinctly wrong attitude toward her work. Billie sang fine when she felt like it. . . . We just couldn't count on her for consistent performance." Basie replaced her with Helen Humes, a lively and cheerful singer, closer in style to Ethel Waters, Mildred Bailey, and Ella Fitzgerald, but Jimmy Rushing continued to get most of the blues songs, leaving Humes with the ballads.

With Artie Shaw

When he arrived in New York, Artie Shaw was a saxophonist and clarinetist with a good reputation and great ambition. He had established himself in the Midwest but was now ready for bigger things, though he was obliged to wait for six months before he could get his Musicians Union card to be able to work. To while away the time, he began wandering in Harlem in search of the kind of black jazz he had heard only on records. While standing outside the door of Pod's and Jerry's one night, he heard piano playing that was so alien to what he knew, and yet so appealing in its mix of freedom and sense of form, that he began returning to stand in front and listen night after night. On one of his trips back to the same spot, he met the pianist at the door—Willie "The Lion" Smith—and the two of them struck up a friendship. They toured the Harlem nightspots, meeting people, sitting in, swapping ideas, and Artie joined Smith to play at Pod's and Jerry's every night for free as his apprentice. (Shaw wrote a short story about that experience called "Snow White in Harlem," and the Lion wrote about Artie in his book *Music on My Mind*.)

The club was in the process of evolving from a place of half-empty seats and candlelight (when management couldn't pay the electric bills) to a first-stop-after-midnight gathering place for musicians and celebrities from the theater. The regulars among the musicians were Benny Goodman, Duke Ellington, the Dorsey Brothers, and Tiny Bradshaw, and the celebrities included Mae West, Joan Crawford, Jack Dempsey, Gene Tunney, naughty singer Gladys Bentley, Moms Mabley, and Mayor Jimmy Walker. It was there that Shaw first saw Billie. Timme Rosenkrantz was present one night and described the fried chicken and biscuits, the bad whiskey, the customers (Paul Whiteman, Mildred Bailey, and Joe Venuti), and his own discovery of Billie:

> In a corner sat a distinguished-looking fellow with a big cigar clenched solidly between his teeth, flailing the hell out of an upright piano. Willie "the Lion" Smith! . . . Then came the copper-colored beauty, Billie Holiday, wearing a white gardenia in her hair to frame her lovely face. Instantly the room fell as quiet as falling snow, as Billie lifted a voice that was the embodiment of her strange beauty . . . Willie "the Lion" was a knowing and

masterful accompanist. He offset the lush brutality of Billie's songs that night with his happy stride piano.

Shaw soon found a job playing behind her in a group put together by her new producer, Bernie Hanighen. Artie had no interest in "girl singers" or "boy singers," as they were then known, and regarded them as commercial necessities at best, but Holiday was clearly something special. He told her he would have a band one day and she would sing with him when he did. She took it as just more flattery, which she had heard plenty of from white guys even before she was known outside of Harlem.

But Shaw would not become a typical bandleader. He was exceedingly well self-educated, an intellectual with no interest in doing the same thing night after night, the first prerequisite of popular stardom. In fact, over the years he seemed to be trying to do everything he could to avoid what he had to do to be a commercial success. He began playing classical music, which brought both the jazz and classical fans down on him (each for different reasons), had musical arrangements written for him by the African American classical composer William Grant Still, flirted with bebop, and briefly crossed into Cuban and Mexican popular music. He also had a wicked sense of musical humor that usually passed over the heads of his audiences: Shaw's recording of "Dancing in the Dark" ended over the closing chords of Stravinsky's "The Firebird." His faux classical "Concerto for Clarinet" had a *doina* slipped into the middle, and whether his source for this folk dance music was Béla Bartók's Romanian field recordings or Lower East Side weddings he had witnessed in his youth, it was a daring ploy.

Shaw wanted to launch a new band with Billie because he believed she was better than any singer he had ever heard. When he learned that she had left Count Basie's band, he immediately drove through the night from Boston to her mother's place in New York to ask her to join his outfit. Artie knew how fine she sang, but when he told others about her he didn't point to her recordings to prove it. Instead, like Professor Ralph Kirkpatrick, he said, "I gave her a record of Debussy's 'L'après-midi d'un faune.' She could sing the whole thing, the top line: 'Da, da-da-da-da-da-da dee—She could *do* the whole thing. Didn't have the range for it—but she had a *very* good ear." (It must have meant as much to her as it did to him: She still had the recording until she died, and often played it for guests.)

Shaw's was not the first white band to use a black singer—Jimmy Dorsey's band had June Richmond, and Claude Thornhill recorded with Maxine Sullivan. But Shaw meant to tour with her not just as a band singer, or an equal to the other band members, but as a star, and soon his picture and hers were together at the front of theaters and dance halls. He knew she wouldn't want to sing the latest hits, what the dancers wanted to hear, and that he would be under pressure to get someone who would. If the singer to be dispensed with was black, it could be all the easier if it was worked right, so nasty rumors were spread by song publishers to force him to drop her. *Down Beat* ran an editorial denouncing what it called a whisper campaign. Shaw resisted and then took the band on a tour of the South, a crazed freedom ride before its time, with Billie being escorted into hotels and restaurants by the toughest members of the band, demanding she be accommodated. Billie never hesitated to take on drunks and belligerent bigots, either, resulting in the band's having some late-night escapes from Southern law enforcement across county lines. Artie took musical chances, too, sometimes departing from dance tunes and pop songs to let the band loose to jam on the blues for a half hour late in their sets, with Billie coming in and out with bits of her own made-up blues lyrics while the baffled dancers just stood around.

The band barely survived, even by playing New England boys' prep schools that wouldn't allow girl singers on the campus, and girls' schools where a Cuban arrangement of "Jungle Drums" created ecstatic upheavals among the students. As things got tougher financially and the future of the group was in doubt, compromises were made. When Billie gave her notice that she would be leaving, Artie hired Helen Forrest to be a second singer for a month while she learned the tunes. To keep Billie with the band, Artie and the musicians quietly lowered their own salaries to pay her. Forrest's account of the month she traveled with Billie and the band suggests that both Holiday and Shaw were modest in the few words that each wrote about what were in fact their rather heroic efforts on the road:

> She treated me well. The band's vocal arrangements were written for her, so I sat around. She'd say to Artie, "Why don't you let this child sing?" He'd say, "She hasn't got any arrangements yet." And she'd say, "Well, let her use mine. But don't let her sit there doing nothing all night." But we sang in different keys and her arrangements didn't fit me.
>
> Lots of times she wasn't allowed to sit on the bandstand with me. She had to use the back entrance and wait backstage to go on. Artie used to say she had to sit on the stage or the band would walk off, but she'd beg him not to get into trouble because of her, and he'd give in. If I didn't want to sit on the stand without her she'd tell me not to cause trouble for myself, and I'd give in. The funny thing is that everyone says that she finally gave up when the band got to New York for its big opening at the Lincoln Hotel and she wasn't allowed to sit on the stand, but the fact is there wasn't any room for any singers on the bandstand and we both waited at a table up front for our turn. Maybe the fuss was because we sat together.
>
> I used to tell her I didn't want her to leave, that the thought of her leaving made me feel bad, and I hoped it wasn't because of me. She said, "Sweetheart, it's not your fault. The band's got the greatest singer in the world and it doesn't need me anymore. I don't want to be a band singer and the life I've been living is not for me. I got to go and I'm going."

Once again Billie had signed a contract with a recording company other than the band leader's, so she was not able to make recordings with Shaw's band. The only evidence that remains on record of the Shaw-Holiday social and musical experiment is a single song, "Any Old Time" from 1938, written for her by Shaw.

Though well sung with a pleasant arrangement, it gives only a hint of what this inspired meeting of talents must have sounded like. It was recorded at the same session that produced "Begin the Beguine," the Cole Porter piece that launched Artie Shaw into fame, but by then Billie had already left the band, having grown sick of what she called "major NAACP-type productions" that it took for her to get something to eat, a place to stay, or even a bathroom in the South. There were debates over whether she should sit on the bandstand or just appear for her songs, the usual separate-but-unequal routine for a mixed-race stage performance, in the North or South. But it was in the North where she was finally pushed too far. While playing in the Blue Room in the Hotel Lincoln in New York, famous for its radio broadcasts of swing bands, the owner Maria de Ramirez Kramer asked Billie to use a freight elevator so that customers would not think that people of color were welcome there as guests (or possibly as prostitutes). Columnist Walter Winchell called the hotel out for its treatment, and John Hammond was quoted as noting the irony that "it was in the Hotel *Lincoln*!"

When she left Shaw's band in 1938, Billie was back at work in three weeks as the star attraction at the opening of Café Society, and two weeks later she was on the *Camel Caravan* radio show singing with the Benny Goodman band. Meanwhile, in 1940, Lena Horne was hired to sing with the Charlie Barnet band, a rival of Shaw's, and she later said that it was Billie that Barnet really wanted, but Billie wasn't interested. In an interview, Billie said she would never sing with a big band again. She and Shaw exchanged some acrimonious remarks in the press about each other's role in her departure, but they later spoke favorably of each other for the rest of their lives. Shaw, after reaching a level of success that few ever achieve in recordings, radio, and film, withdrew from swing, the music he had helped create, and went on to study higher math, produce movies, and work on a two-thousand-page novel.

Café Society

Holiday was fortunate to have done most of her recording with four producers who were among the most important in the history of jazz in the United States: John Hammond, Milt Gabler, Norman Granz, and Barney Josephson, all of whom had the insight and courage to introduce jazz to the country and the world by changing the way the music was heard, creating new conditions for hearing it, and breaking down barriers to those who would get to hear it.

Josephson, a shoe salesman from New Jersey, seemed an unlikely person to change the social and cultural life of Manhattan. Raised in a socially conscious and committed leftist family with modest resources, he was one of the non-elite whites who went up to Harlem to hear jazz. He had also traveled to Europe, where he visited political cabarets that inspired him to open a similar club in New York, though his would be built around jazz, with the twist that they would feature and welcome people of color. It would not be the first New York City nightspot without racial barriers, as many Harlem clubs were open to whites, but this was to be a downtown club that would make a point of welcoming black audiences as well as presenting whites and blacks together on the same stage. Josephson had a fever for jazz, and saw the music not as a form of crude good-time music or as part of a cultural underground, but rather as the quintessentially high art of America that had reached its apogee through the creative efforts of African Americans. All it needed was the proper exposure.

Josephson gave his club, with its basement location, affordable prices, doorman in a ragged tuxedo, and *New Yorker*–esque cartoon murals of blue bloods, the name Café Society as a mockery of uptown society. The performers stood on the same level as and close to the audience, and were theatrically lit. Despite its Depression high-low shtick, the club nonetheless had a culturally elegant aura, created by the brilliance and originality of the performers and the presence of people of color mixing with like-minded individuals onstage and in the audience. Clare Boothe Luce called it the wrong place for the right people.

Josephson had been excited by the daring concept behind John Hammond's most significant effort, the "From Spirituals to Swing" concerts he produced at Carnegie Hall in 1938 and 1939, which attempted to trace the musical history of African American folk, religious, and jazz music. When Barney saw the oversold house and the wild enthusiasm of the audience for these events, he attempted to re-create them by using some of the same performers from that concert and extending the concept even further with a wider variety of singers, modern dancers, and comedians. He would feature the likes of singers Sarah Vaughan, Lena Horne, Lead Belly, Sister Rosetta Tharpe, the Golden Gate Quartet, and Hazel Scott; dancer Pearl Primus; musicians Albert Ammons, Meade "Lux" Lewis, Pete Johnson, Big Joe Turner, Lester Young, Django Reinhardt, Buck Clayton, Big Sid Catlett, James P. Johnson, Red Allen, and Mary Lou Williams; comedians Zero Mostel, Imogene Coca, Jack Gilford, Sid Caesar, Carol Channing, and Danny Kaye; and actors/singers Judy Holliday, Betty Comden, and Adolph Green.

The audiences at the Café were an odd mix of left-wing intellectuals, the wealthy, black and white show business people, jazz musicians, and Greenwich Village locals. One might find among them Edward R. Murrow, Lillian Hellman, Dashiell Hammett, Martha Graham, Ezio Pinza, Leopold Stokowski, Gypsy Rose Lee, Cole Porter, Dorothy Parker, Noël Coward, the Duke and Duchess of Windsor, Fiorello La Guardia, and even, once, Eleanor Roosevelt.

Today, it might be easy to mock the degree to which whites in the audiences were moved by songs about the toil and suffering of black folks, and to regard some of the performances as merely protest on demand. But whatever their politics, audiences were being exposed to performers they had never seen in uptown nightspots and were seated alongside people they had never been close to anywhere else in the city.

Despite full houses every night, Josephson was so inexperienced at management that he ran out of money within weeks, and was kept in business only through a loan from Hammond, Benny Goodman, and Willard Alexander. But within a year the club was such a success that he opened a second nightery, Café Society Uptown, in a cavernous, high-ceilinged space that seated 350 people.

The first Café Society opened on the night before New Year's Eve in 1938, with Billie Holiday as the star attraction. This venue presented her with new faces in the audience, a different political ambience, and a fresh take on cabaret culture. Instead of strolling from table to table, directing her songs to different individuals, or bantering with them, she remained in the stage area. There was now a book of music arrangements with formal introductions and dramatic endings, a house band, rehearsals, and songs focusing on her as a soloist rather than as a band singer. All this created a distinct break between singer and audience; shouts or comments from the audience, whether supportive or antagonistic, were tolerated but not encouraged, and the relaxed atmosphere that had made the Harlem cabaret a home away from home was gone.

She did three sets a night of six songs each. The modes of performance were now those of Eastern Europe and Paris as much as they were African American. Despite the grumbling of some in the past about her professionalism, Josephson never had any complaints about Billie's work:

> I always looked on Billie as a finished performer, a pro. I never had to tell her to change her numbers, whereas I had to tell everyone else. I had to tell Lena Horne when she was just starting out. But you don't tell professionals how to work. . . . You'd be out of your mind to tell her anything. Billie was meticulous about her work. She would come down and raise hell with the orchestra. She was tough! If Frankie Newton played a note that disturbed her while she was singing, he heard about it. If the pianist was one note behind or too fast, she picked it up. The four-letter words you'd hear! Well, she would let out a tirade and they'd be scared to death of her. The respect I had for her, they had, and I think even more

so because they were musicians. It was always Lady Day, and when they said "Lady," it was like Lady Montgomery of Great Britain.

Billie Holiday's recording of "Strange Fruit" was released in 1939, the same year that *Gone with the Wind* was breaking box office records and Marian Anderson was barred from singing in Constitution Hall by the Daughters of the American Revolution. Race, then as now, haunted America, and entertainment media mirrored its anxieties through carefully controlled means. If it was possible to sell images of race to a broad population without losing the white South and a significant portion of the North, or violating the unwritten codes of racial interaction, Hollywood would do so, regardless of the bending of history that it took to tell a story. So it was that no black crime or black criminals were shown in the 1940s movies that ironically became known as film noir. African Americans could be drafted and sent overseas to serve in the military, but they were never shown to be part of the war effort except as cooks and orderlies. There was no portrayal of interracial love, no shared meals, not even a handshake, and no black person was called "Mr.," "Miss," or "Mrs." There was no chance, then, that the lynching of blacks would ever appear in a film in the thirties and forties, no matter how often it was reported in newspapers. This was the vision of America into which Billie Holiday's recording of "Strange Fruit" would intrude.

It was not the first song about lynching. Some earlier pieces, such as Bessie Smith's "Haunted House Blues" and Lead Belly's "Hangman's Blues" and "The Gallis Pole," had veiled allusions to lynching, but the first published song was "Sistren an' Brethren," an African American folk song collected by Lawrence Gellert, published in the *New Masses* in January 1931, and reprinted in various places thereafter. The next published, and more widely known, piece was Irving Berlin's "Supper Time," sung by Ethel Waters in the 1933 stage production of *As Thousands Cheer*. In the scene in which the song is featured, a mother sits in her kitchen thinking about how she should tell her children that their father is dead. A large newspaper headline about lynching is spread across the back wall of the stage. It was a shocking song to see in the context of a Manhattan revue, but those who heard it only as a song apart from its theatrical setting might have understood it as just another "my man done gone" bluesy tune.

Abel Meeropol, a New York City high school teacher who wrote under the name Lewis Allan, published a poem titled "Bitter Fruit" in the union magazine *New York Teacher* in January 1937. For years there had been efforts to make lynching a federal crime, but Congress and the president had refused to act on the matter. (Franklin Delano Roosevelt failed to support the only bill that stood a chance of passing.) Meeropol wanted to do something to raise public awareness of these acts of violence, and in late 1938 he set the poem to music. After his wife and others sang it publicly, the New Theatre League published it under the title "Strange Fruit" in 1939. A choral arrangement was then made by Earl Robinson (the composer of "The House I Live In," a song that Frank Sinatra later made famous), with alterations in the melody and harmony and with a line added from the Negro spiritual "Go Down, Moses." It went through further musical changes by the Edward B. Marks Music Company when Allan published it with them in 1939.

The newly hired floor show director of Café Society, Robert Gordon, had heard it sung at a union meeting and showed it to Barney Josephson and Billie Holiday. Josephson claimed that she was initially not enthusiastic about adding it to her songlist, and when he heard her sing it with little emotion in one of its first performances, he assumed she didn't comprehend its meaning. Later, when she cried during one of her renditions of it, he concluded that she had finally come to understand it. It seems very strange that he assumed that any person of color in the United States in 1939 would not know the song's meaning. Billie certainly understood it on the night in 1958 that she sang it for Maya

Angelou and her little son, and then explained its lyrics graphically to the child, upsetting the boy and Angelou. In *Lady Sings the Blues* Billie wrote that when she was first shown the song, she "dug it right off. It seemed to spell out all the things that had killed Pop," drawing attention to the death of her father, Clarence Holiday, whom she believed had died when he returned from World War I and was refused treatment at a white veterans hospital in Dallas. She undoubtedly also knew the widely told account of Bessie Smith, who was believed at the time to have died under similar circumstances. Billie's only concern about the song, she said, was that audiences might hate it.

She had reason to worry, as nothing like this piece had ever been attempted in popular music. It was an adult song, one that could not be counted on to appeal to the key demographic of teenage fans, or even to most mature audiences. The genre that was to be called protest songs was not recognized until the late 1950s, so the shock of hearing such words and sentiments in pop ballad form was all the greater when she sang it in 1939. As Ralph Ellison wrote in *Going to the Territory* in 1986, "The ultimate goal of lynchers is that of achieving ritual purification through destroying the lynchers' identification with the basic humanity of their victims. Hence their deafness to cries of pain, their stoniness before the sight and stench of burning flesh . . ." Holiday's intention was to disrupt that ritual, but she also feared that if she interpreted a song in too emotional a manner, she would be accused of sentimentality, or worse. (A few years later James Baldwin would write, "It is only in his music, which Americans are able to admire because protective sentimentality limits their understanding of it, that the Negro in America has been able to tell his story.") She was changing the rules by which songs were presented to audiences, and more pointedly breaking the pop social contract, such as it was, between black singers and white audiences. She would not just be entertaining them, but instead bringing to light a subject scarcely even mentioned in song before, and one that could evoke powerful emotions. Café Society was one of the few nightclubs, white or black, where a song like this could be performed without potential for trouble.

Josephson made very sure that the audience got it. He programmed "Strange Fruit" at the end of every one of the three nightly sets, ensuring that it would be the final encore; he ordered the club's entire staff to cease activities while Billie sang; and he turned out all the house lights, with the exception of a small spotlight on her face. When the song ended, there was always a long silence, followed by a huge ovation. She then left the room without comment or acknowledgment, after which the musicians began playing in a lighter mood to help the audience resume normal club behavior.

The usual reaction to the song was sheer shock. Some in the audience were confused by the song, thinking in some way or another that it was a love song. Others, understanding it all too well, found it too painful to contemplate. Then there were those who walked out in disgust. Some clubs she later performed in asked her not to sing it. At times she chose to withhold it from the audience. "It has a way of separating the straight people from the squares and the cripples," she remarked.

There were songs before and after this one that protested many things, but if they lacked memorable or singable melodies they were quickly forgotten. The melody of "Strange Fruit" is not especially distinguished, but the shock of its words and its imagery make up for any deficiencies in the tune. The song even drew the attention of the FBI, who wanted to know if the Communist Party had prompted Lewis Allan to write it.

When Allan read an interview that Holiday gave to *PM* newspaper in 1945 in which she said that he had suggested that Sonny White, her piano accompanist boyfriend, "turn it into music," and that with the help of music arranger Danny Mendelsohn they finished it in three weeks, he wrote a letter to the editor attempting to publicly claim his role as composer and lyricist, the first of many he would submit to publications for years to come. Allan always received royalties for both the words and the music, but what he was objecting to was what he considered the public slighting of his role as composer because Holiday claimed a contribution to the song. *PM*'s editors printed a response from Billie in which she explained that what she was talking about in the interview "was the interpretation of the song that she had worked on . . ."

When *Lady Sings the Blues* was published eleven years later and the same words from the *PM* interview appeared again, Allan demanded that Doubleday change the misattribution of "Strange Fruit" or he might take legal action. His claim was that when he proposed that Billie sing the song, the only thing she asked him about it was the meaning of the word "pastoral" (not a bad question, given the ambiguity of the term). Barney Josephson further supported Allan's claim when he repeated that at first Billie didn't understand the meaning of the song. When Arthur Herzog Jr., a publicist and writer of song lyrics who had shared copyrights with Billie for "Don't Explain" and "God Bless the Child," also began to ask for more credit for *his* work, Doubleday's lawyers feared the possibility of even more litigation. Although it was not an uncommon practice at the time for songwriters to give singers and bandleaders publishing credits to get them to record their songs, the lawyers were still concerned about these new claims.

At this point Bill Dufty rose in defense of his cowriter. First, he told the lawyers that songwriters were always offering her their songs, and when she agreed to sing them she and her musicians altered lyrics and/or music to suit her style. "Holiday doesn't sing Cole Porter, or George Gershwin or anybody else's melodies like they wrote them. She does her own variations. If Allan wants to come into court with his sheet music, I'll bet we could play the Holiday record and if the melody was the same I'd eat the record. . . . The point . . . is that nothing happened until Miss Holiday did the song, and did it her way, applying her own very formidable talents to it. Holiday doesn't sing songs; she transforms them."

The question of the ownership of jazz musicians' variations on copyrighted melodies is part of a long-running debate. But at the time, there were other questions about the originality of "Strange Fruit." Some saw similarities to "Sistren an' Brethren," a song that had some currency in leftist circles:

When black face is lifted, Lord turnin' way . . .
Yo' Head 'tain' no apple fo' danglin' from a tree
Yo' Head 'tain' no apple fo' danglin' from a tree
Yo' body no carcass for barbacuin' on a spree

"Sistren an' Brethren" was published several times between 1931 and 1936, and it had also been sung and played by Sonny Terry in Jane Dudley's solo dance performance of *Harmonica Breakdown* in the mid-1930s. French listeners thought they heard other sources for "Strange Fruit" in the fifteenth-century poet François Villon's best-known work, "La ballade des pendus" (The Ballad of the Hanged) or in Théodore de Banville's nineteenth-century "Le verger du Roi Louis" (The Orchard of King Louis).

But Dufty felt there was something bigger and more malevolent at work in the questioning of Billie Holiday's role in the shaping of her recording of "Strange Fruit":

> For years both American fellow travelers and the FBI have been agreed on the myth that Allan wrote a song about lynching and Miss Holiday was Svengalied into singing it by certain operators. Herzog gets at this with most frankness when he says . . . that he heard that Josephson tried to get Holiday to do the song and "she didn't want to." I have even heard it said that she sang this song for about a year before she really understood what she was doing.
>
> This is what they seem to be getting at, one and all. And this is what enrages me. It gets to the point of the book (*Lady Sings the Blues*), and disputes all of it and its reason for being written—to bury exactly this kind of picture of her as a simple little barefoot girl.
>
> Billie Holiday has been kicked around and harassed for years by the authorities. One of the reasons is that this song "Strange Fruit" made her well known and politically controversial. . . . It would have been so easy for Billie to please the authorities by telling them she didn't know what she had been doing, drop the song from her repertoire . . . and start folding her hands in prayer and

singing one of Marian Anderson's non controversial hymns. She might even have gotten her police card . . .

But she didn't. She wouldn't. She knew more about lynching in her bones than any Communist could tell her from any books. She knew all about it and knew how a song about it should be sung. That's why I believe her version of the episode as it appears in the book. . . .

I know of no law which requires that a singer give any writer credit for holding the copyright on any song she sings or mentions.

Yet at the urging of Doubleday's attorneys on July 22, 1957, Billie and Dufty signed a cautiously worded statement that may have at least partially satisfied all parties:

We give this statement to clarify the facts about "Strange Fruit." "Strange Fruit" is an original composition by Lewis Allan who is the sole author of "Strange Fruit."

It was introduced to Miss Holiday by Barney Josephson and Mr. Allan in February of 1939. This is the first time she had heard it or seen it. She introduced it later at Café Society.

Aggrieved though Allan was about what he saw as Holiday's claims, he was also backhandedly sympathetic later on: "I can understand the psychological reasons why the peripheral truths and actual facts surrounding her life were unimportant to her and why she took liberties with them or invented some of them out of whole cloth. . . . I did not hold any empathy toward Billie Holiday for her lapses into fancy nor would I want the fact that she made untrue statements bruited about now that she is dead."

The idea of recording "Strange Fruit" was raised by Billie at a recording session for Vocalion Records in 1939 when they found they still had time left over after they'd finished the planned songs. But the producer felt the song was too radical, and allowed the musicians to leave the session early rather than record it. John Hammond has also been blamed for turning the song down, but he would never have objected to the subject as such, especially since as a reporter for the *New Masses* he had gone to Alabama to cover the infamous Scottsboro Boys trial that involved fabricated accusations of rape against a group of young black men. He did, however, think the poem the song was based on was third-rate, and that the song itself was wrong for Billie. Later he said that, though its success had helped her reach a white audience, it had turned her from a jazz singer into a mannered chanteuse.

It was that rejection that led her to drop by the Commodore Music Shop after the recording session and complain to Milt Gabler, the store's owner. Gabler was well known among jazz musicians who regularly gathered at the store to talk and listen to new recordings. (*Time* magazine called them "loafers.") Gabler had set up his own small recording company, Commodore Records, while he was running the music shop. Later he was hired by Decca Records, where he produced a long list of hits by Lionel Hampton, the Andrews Sisters, Red Foley, the Weavers, Peggy Lee, the Ink Spots, Sammy Davis Jr., Louis Jordan, and Bill Haley. But his passion was always jazz, and he had seen Billie many times at Café Society. When she told him that Vocalion had declined "Strange Fruit," he offered to record it for his own company. His decision was not based on making a social statement; it was about getting a rising star on his own label: "I did it for kicks. . . . It was exciting." Hammond got permission from Vocalion for Gabler to record her, because Gabler was a good customer of their record-pressing plant and presumably because Hammond approved it. Gabler hired the same musicians who backed her nightly at Café Society to accompany her.

There is no question that the Commodore recording of "Strange Fruit" predictably stunned listeners, in part because it fell outside the standard pop paradigm. But some also argued that, whatever the emotional and political edge of the words, it was not a jazz song, maybe not even a song sung in a black American style. Yet throughout the record there are downward arcs of notes and slight bendings of pitch characteristic of the blues, especially on the words "Southern," "South," "sweet and fresh," "of burning flesh," and others. The recording begins with a certain formality that confirms that considerable thought and preparation with her pianist and arranger had been involved, but that same formality might also suggest that the song was not intended to be either jazz or pop. The vocal is withheld for seventy seconds, a fourth of the song's length, while Frankie Newton's quietly floating trumpet introduces Sonny White's stark outline of the melody on piano, accompanied by muted drumrolls much like those heard at New Orleans funerals. When Holiday comes in, she seems to be bearing witness to what she is describing, her vocal a near recitative, flattening the melody, approximating speech. The melody slowly rises through the second and third verses and widens, reaching an abrupt leap near the end. This kind of dramatic structure is not unknown in jazz improvisations; Coleman Hawkins's "Body and Soul" follows a similar pattern, but somehow it seems more surprising when employed by a vocalist, especially this vocalist. The melody she creates is quite different from the original composition, different enough that she might well have claimed composition of the music; her continuous variation makes the melody seem through composed, not repeating and recycling like most pop songs.

It is not unusual for a singer to become strongly identified with a song. But the identification of Billie Holiday with this particular song made it especially difficult for many to believe that it had been written by a white man. If anything, this identity with her continued to grow, and by the time the movie *Lady Sings the Blues* appeared, Billie was portrayed as witnessing a lynching while she was on tour with a band in the South.

Once she had realized how important the song was to audiences and to her career, she became angry when she heard that the folksinger Josh White was singing it at Café Society after she left, and she demanded he stop performing it. A strong claim on a song made famous by a certain singer is common among those who make a living from songs written for them or given to them. Billie had learned this early on, when Ethel Waters came onstage to forbid her from singing "Underneath the Harlem Moon," which Waters considered her own. White had never met Billie, however, and when they both turned up at photographer Gjon Mili's loft for a "*Life* Goes to a Party" session for *Life* magazine, he backed her on guitar while she sang some blues, a rarity for her. He managed to convince her, he said, that more people needed to hear "Strange Fruit" because it was more than just a song. The *Washington Afro-American* called it a sermon of democracy.

Holiday's recording initially sold some twenty thousand copies, but it has been reissued again and again and shows no sign of slackening. It's been recorded by dozens of singers over the years, though usually in far more dramatic form than Holiday's (Nina Simone's highly cinematic version, for example), and sometimes with some of the stronger words omitted. On the other hand, there were those who disliked the song—Paul Robeson, Albert Murray, and Billie's mother; others, like Lena Horne and Eartha Kitt, for many years found it too painful to sing. The song was formally and informally banned from airplay in several countries. Though few reviews of the record were openly hostile, some were perverse. An article titled "Strange Song" in *Time* led with: "Billie Holiday is a roly-poly young colored woman with a hump in her voice.... She does not care enough about her figure to watch her diet, but she loves to sing." The song, *Time* said, "provided the National Association for the Advancement of Colored People a prime piece of musical propaganda," and "Billie liked its dirge-like blues melody, was not so much interested in the song's social content." The African American press was far more sympathetic to the song's content, but a headline from the *Atlanta Daily World* could still read like something from *Variety*: "Billie Holiday Records First Song About Lynching Evils: Buxom Singer Chirps It Nightly at Café Society."

When Lillian Smith's *Strange Fruit,* a novel about Southern intolerance of racial and sexual difference, appeared in 1944, she acknowledged that her first title, *Jordan Is So Chilly,* was not acceptable to her publisher. It was suggested she change it to the title of Holiday's song. Writer Harvey Breit tried to bring Billie and Lillian together to talk, and though he made two appointments for them, Billie failed to show. Breit later wrote in a review of Billie's autobiography that at the time he was annoyed, but after reading her book he knew why she hadn't appeared: "Miss Holiday was in a whole lot of trouble."

At the "Strange Fruit" session, Gabler made two 78-rpm records with four songs. "Strange Fruit" was shrewdly coupled with "Fine and Mellow," a blues that became Commodore Records' first hit, which Billie had written in the folk tradition of linking together small portions of other blues with some lines of her own (and if Milt Gabler is to be believed, also one of his own: "He's got high-draped pants . . . ," etc.). The last line of the song, the clincher, "Love is like a faucet, it turns off and on," most likely came from Ethel Waters's 1923 recording "Ethel Sings 'Em," as did the stop-time chorus of the song. "It was one of the first modern blues," said Gabler. "It wasn't with an old-time piano player and a muted trumpet. We had an arrangement." When Meeropol heard about the planned recording of "his" song, he insisted on being paid in advance, which was not the practice in the record business. Lawyers were consulted and warnings issued, but Gabler went ahead with the recording and Meeropol received royalties in the usual manner.

These songs plus the two others she recorded at that session, "Yesterdays" and "I Got a Right to Sing the Blues," became part of her core repertoire for the rest of her life. She had earlier asked Hammond if she could be backed by a string section, something only a very few top singers had been granted, none of them jazz artists. Strings meant extra expense and added a touch of class that ran against the grain of jazz orthodoxy. But Billie's request made sense to Gabler, who viewed her as a ballad singer, and maybe even a torch singer, who could become widely popular in that genre. That was the music she told him she wanted to sing and the career she wanted to have.

Apparently they were both correct, for some of her best and certainly most popular work was later recorded with Gabler after he became a producer at Decca Records, where he set her against violins and in elaborate arrangements by Toots Camarata, Gordon Jenkins, and others. With these recordings she found new audiences, who most likely had never heard "Strange Fruit." At the same time, she lost favor with some jazz fans who thought that such Euro-trappings were a betrayal. A decade later, Charlie Parker's recording with strings would likewise not find much acceptance with hard-core jazz fans. The esteemed jazz producer George Avakian was still bothered by that Parker session when he chose to pass on a chance to produce Holiday's 1958 Columbia LP *Lady in Satin* album, which also featured strings, in spite of his love for classical music.

There had also been complaints about a few very slow-tempo records she had made between 1939 and 1942, and now such recordings by her were growing in number. (Her March 25, 1944, recording of "How Am I to Know?" on Commodore Records is a good example of state-of-the-art slow.) One night in 1941 Teddy Wilson visited Café Society to see Billie, and when they talked between sets she told him that she had finally found her voice. This was the way she wanted to sing.

"Gloomy Sunday," a Holiday recording that gained notoriety to the point of becoming a world-wide legend, is often passed over by Holiday's chroniclers. Yet she said that this song, a grim and painfully slow account of a lost lover and the rituals involved in preparation for suicide, was one of her best recordings. The second of her "storytelling songs," recorded for Columbia-affiliated OKeh Records on August 7, 1941, it followed "God Bless the Child" and preceded "Strange Fruit." The song rapidly became internationally known and was alleged to have been banned on a few radio stations when claims spread about listeners becoming so depressed by it that they killed themselves. Scant evidence exists to prove such assertions, and even though it may not have been widely banned, the legend persists as strongly as ever. (This song along with "Strange Fruit," "I Cover the Waterfront," and "Love for Sale" were the four Holiday songs banned by some radio stations.)

The original version of "Gloomy Sunday," a 1933 Hungarian song by Rezső Seress with lyrics by László Jávor, is very different from what was heard by most people outside of Hungary. That earlier version was set in the Great Depression during the rise of fascism in Hungary, possibly predicting the coming of World War II in Europe:

> Cities are being wiped out, shrapnel is making music
> Meadows are colored red with human blood

The first recordings of "Gloomy Sunday" in English were all made within a month of each other in 1936, but by then the British lyricist Desmond Carter had reset the song as a message from the grave by a departed lover:

> They bore me to church and I left you behind me
> My eyes could not see one I wanted to love me

It was this version on a recording by Paul Robeson that was initially banned in the UK. But then, in a strange act of aesthetic nationalism, the BBC's director of music declared that it could be sung on radio—but only by a British singer. It could also be played by an orchestra, but never by a dance band.

The first American recording was made in 1936 by Bob Allen, a singer with the Hal Kemp Orchestra, a band certainly not known for songs with heavy subjects. It was also recorded that year in a swing dance tempo by the Paul Whiteman Orchestra with the singer Johnny Hauser, as well as, in a sober salon mood, by Hildegard, a supper club singer who, though born and raised in Adell, Wisconsin, styled herself as a worldly chanteuse and was a favorite of Eleanor Roosevelt and Liberace. Four years later Artie Shaw recorded it with Pauline Byrne as a bluesy dance tune whose final chorus has the orchestra sounding like Cab Calloway's in a *Betty Boop* cartoon.

By the time Billie Holiday released her version of it in 1941 (perhaps prompted by Shaw's recording), the song had been simplified and restructured by lyricist Sam M. Lewis. Like all the previous versions, it was in a minor key:

> Gloomy is Sunday, with shadows I spend it all
> My heart and I have decided to end it all

It was sung at a funereal pace with the addition of five new lines and a change of key from minor to major that softened the song with a 1940s B-movie finale in which the survivor says that she or he was only dreaming, and the loved one is still alive and only sleeping.

The Holiday recording became the source for at least sixty or more versions by everyone from Ricky Nelson to Jimmy Smith (with a funky organ treatment), Ray Charles to Elvis Costello, Sinéad O'Connor to Björk, who first recorded it with a Miles Davis soundalike solo by Mark Isham, and later sang it dressed as an angel at designer Alexander McQueen's funeral at St. Paul's Cathedral in London following his suicide.

Two recent films have reactivated the legend surrounding the song: *Gloomy Sunday* (Germany, 1999), in which a doomed love affair is connected to the Holocaust (perhaps inspired by the use of "God Bless the Child" on the soundtrack of *Schindler's List*) and uses the original version of the song; and *The Kovak Box* (U.S., 2006), a thriller/fantasy film in which the Holiday recording is used to drive victims to their deaths when played over the telephone.

CHAPTER EIGHT

The Songs II

*I*t is usually assumed that it was Billie Holiday's move from Vocalion to Commodore and Decca Records that led to a change in her singing style and in her choice of songs. But it was clear even in her last recordings with Columbia-associated labels that she was already headed in a new direction. Just before "Gloomy Sunday," she had recorded "God Bless the Child," "Am I Blue?," "Jim" (with its reference to carrying a torch), and "Until the Real Thing Comes Along" (her last session with the several different record labels owned by Columbia), on which she is reunited with Teddy Wilson. She was already a different singer than she had been in their earlier recordings.

"God Bless the Child" has of late been turning up in numerous films and at funerals and national events, and is rapidly becoming a secular hymn, much like John Lennon's "Imagine." It's safe to say, though, that virtually no one knows exactly what this song is about. For years guesses have been made at the meaning of both the title and the lyrics. While Billie claimed it was based on a passage in the Bible, the relevant verse has not yet been found. Matthew 25:29, sometimes called "The Parable of the Talents," has been suggested: "For everyone who has will be given more and he will have abundance. Whoever does not have, even what he has will be taken from him." But as is true of much biblical exegesis, that passage has been subject to many different interpretations, none of which, however, seems to fit the song. More puzzling is the title, which is also the key line of the song. Assuming that the song speaks of disparities between those who have and those who don't, and that children are always dependent on adults "who have," why would God bless the child who "has"? The title of the song, which was supplied by Holiday, may be better read as "God *Blessed* the Child (That's Got Its Own)," and a notation on the original sheet music supports that interpretation: " 'God Bless' the Child,' a swing Spiritual, is based on the authentic proverb 'God Blessed the Child That's Got His Own.' " But no proverb similar to the song's title has yet been discovered, either.

Use of the apostrophe in "bless' " and the subtitle with "blessed" makes better sense of the song and suggests that perhaps it may have been either dialect usage or a mishearing of Holiday by the song's composer, Arthur Herzog Jr., later corrected, with both titles left on the cover. Herzog said that the song was rushed together in order to take advantage of a boycott by NBC and CBS of the American Society of Composers, Authors and Publishers (ASCAP), which was seeking higher royalty rates for music played on the radio. For ten months radio stations could not play anything or anyone ASCAP represented, and were forced to come up with folk songs, marches, or any music so old that it had never been copyrighted. Herzog saw this situation as an opportunity for new songs not yet registered with ASCAP to get heavy airplay, and so he asked Billie to help him create one. He said he wanted her to give him "an old-fashioned Southern expression" that could be turned into a song; she suggested "God bless' the child." When he asked her what it meant, she replied that when the adults in a family all had money and a child had none, "God bless' the child that's got his own." The song took twenty minutes to write, he said, and he wrote both the words and music. Billie contributed only the key line and asked to have one note moved down a half step. But then he contradicted himself by adding, "She has never written a line of words or music."

Holiday recalled the moment differently. The title of the song was, in her description, something she had said to her mother after she had turned

Billie down when she asked for money. Billie resented being denied because she had been keeping her mother's restaurant solvent by underwriting it. She had been angry about the incident for three weeks, until one day, while reliving it, that phrase came back to her and "the whole damn song fell into place in my head." She then called Herzog, and the two of them sat at the piano in Café Society while she sang it and he picked it out on the piano. "We changed the lyrics in a couple of spots, but not much."

Neither of these accounts seems quite right. There are certainly African American songs built on proverbs, biblical passages, and folk expressions, such as "I've been down three times" (in "Drowning in the Sea of Love"), "Knock on Wood," "Only the Strong Survive," and the like. It seems unlikely, however, that Herzog would have asked her to choose a "Southern" phrase as a basis for a song, or that he or they could have composed an entire song, words and music, from that kernel in twenty minutes. The original sheet music for the piece credits both Herzog and Holiday, but the composer is not identified. (BMI—a rival performing rights organization to ASCAP—does cite both Herzog and Holiday as composers and lyricists.) On other occasions, Herzog would say that Billie brought in a sheet of finished music, but that neither of them knew who had written it. Both of them were apparently willing to give the other only the smallest amount of credit for his or her respective work.

Billie makes a point of describing the origin of "Don't Explain" in *Lady Sings the Blues*. It arose, she wrote, from a particular moment at the end of her relationship with her husband Jimmy Monroe. She typically situated songs she had written or cowritten in her own experience.

Herzog, though, says that he wrote two versions of the lyrics, the first with some "blue" material in it, and that when Decca did not want to issue it, they rerecorded it using the second version. He claimed that Billie briefly mixed up the two versions. No recording of the song with objectionable material is known to exist, but the first, a 1944 recording, has in the second stanza the line "You mixed with some dame," and in the 1945 recording it is replaced with "What is there to gain" and a few other minor variations. The 1945 recording is much slower and contains repeats of some of the stanzas, but otherwise it's unclear why Decca would rerecord the same song within a year.

Herzog was also annoyed with her for recording "Tell Me More and More and Then Some" in 1940 and claiming credit for writing both music and words. She had come up with the tune and was excited to record it until Danny Mendelsohn told her it was too similar to "St. James Infirmary," a song with roots in the eighteenth-century broadside ballad "The Unfortunate Rake," and was known in all sorts of variations, such as "Streets of Laredo," "The Bad Girl's Lament," and as a blues. No problem, said Billie, and told Danny to change it a bit. Whatever her original version sounded like, the one she recorded was different enough to justify copyrighting it as an original song.

In 1942 Capitol Records was created in Hollywood by songwriters Johnny Mercer and Buddy DeSylva, along with Glenn Wallichs, an executive in an electronics firm. In spite of their slim chances of competing with the three biggest record companies, Victor, Decca, and Columbia, they became hugely successful and signed some of the biggest stars in the music business. The first few singles they produced featured the Paul Whiteman Orchestra, a once powerful group in the music world but still a big enough name, if a dated one, that they hoped would help launch them nationally. Whiteman and Holiday seem like an unlikely pairing: His name and the PR slogan hung on him, "the King of Jazz," didn't sit well with jazz fans after the 1930s. But his deep involvement with George Gershwin, his excellent choice of singers and musicians (including Bing Crosby and Bix Beiderbecke), his employment of African American arrangers, and his recording with Paul Robeson suggest that he was not quite what his reputation suggested.

"Trav'lin' Light" was an instrumental tune by trombonist Trummy Young that he played with the Earl Hines band in the 1930s with no name and no arrangement. When Young learned that his old friend Jimmy Munday was arranging music for Paul Whiteman, he asked Jimmy to make an arrangement of it and suggested that Whiteman record it. Johnny Mercer heard the band rehearsing it and added words and a title, and since Billie was in Los Angeles at the time, Whiteman wanted to have her record it with him. Since she was still technically under contract to Columbia, she was listed as "Lady Day" on the record label.

Billie had come to LA because her husband, Jimmy Monroe, had been arrested for drug smuggling, and while he was on trial she found work at the Trouville Club. When he was found guilty and sentenced to a year in jail, she stayed on at the club. By the time she and Whiteman recorded "Trav'lin' Light," she was on the verge of being put out of her hotel for not paying her bills. Afterward the matter was made right, she and Trummy went out to celebrate, and she wired her mother to send her money to return to New York.

This onetime performance on record with Paul Whiteman's Orchestra on June 12, 1942, seemed to have made little impression when it first appeared. She did not sing "Trav'lin' Light" very often, but it grew in popularity and significance over the years until it seemed to become one of her signature pieces. It also offers a very clear and vivid example of Billie's improvisational ability.

The recording is spare and pensive, and begins abruptly, with no introduction, the melody played straight by Skip Layton on a muted trombone. (Layton is given credit on the record label as a soloist, a very unusual gesture, especially for such a short performance.) The arrangement uniquely frames Holiday between the brief opening solo and a closing one also played by Layton, and allows the listener to hear how she paraphrases the melody and makes subtle changes in its rhythm, never quite following but only suggesting what was written by Young or played by the trombonist. Holiday's improvisational artistry is so compelling here that most people who remember the song recall her revision of it as the way it was actually written. (A very different performance of the song from Paris in 1959 can also be seen on YouTube.)

Just after it was recorded, the American Federation of Musicians banned all recording activity by its union members because the record companies would not agree to the union's demand that their discs not be played on jukeboxes or the radio without compensation. When no agreement was reached, there were no recordings made until 1944, so "Trav'lin' Light" was Billie's last studio recording for almost two years, with the exception of a few V-Discs recorded for use on military bases.

"I'll Be Seeing You" was written for a short-lived 1938 Broadway show and was first recorded soon after its closing by the supper club singer Hildegard. When her recording was rereleased in 1943, perhaps in an attempt to recast it as a wartime letter from home, a number of other singers also quickly made their own versions. Bing Crosby was the first, going into the studio in the second week of January 1944. He promoted the song on his weekly NBC *Kraft Music Hall*, and the record reached the *Billboard* charts three months later, becoming the number one seller by July, remaining in that position for four weeks. Holiday recorded the song on April 1, 1944, and though it never reached the charts, it sold a respectable number of records. Frank Sinatra's up-tempo version reached number four in May 1944 and stayed on the charts for seventeen weeks. It was the last song he recorded with the Tommy Dorsey Orchestra, so it may also have been heard as a parting song to the band.

The seldom sung verse that starts the song places it in Paris in April, and as with "April in Paris," it's the magic of the city that drives the song. The "I" and "you" of it are viewed through locales and settings as if two people who merely passed on the street might have caught each other's eye for only a second, and in the spirit of Baudelaire's poem "À une passante," they nonetheless knew they could be lovers. But since none of the popular recordings included the verse, it left the personae and their relationship up to the imagination of the listeners. (Some also say they can hear the origins of this song in the final movement of Mahler's Third Symphony, which Mahler had originally titled "What Love Tells Me.")

Since "I'll Be Seeing You" was very short, even when sung as slowly as Holiday chose to do, she repeated the second eight lines of the lyric to fill out a three-and-a-half-minute recording, but when she sang it live she usually kept to the original sixteen lines.

It is a song that has had a long life, recorded by vocalists as diverse as country singer Brenda Lee, Gene Pitney, the Carpenters, Rickie Lee Jones, doo-wop groups such as the Five Satins, and most notably in a duet by French chanteuse Françoise Hardy and Iggy Pop. It was the basis for a movie of the same name, in which a soldier suffering from battle fatigue meets and falls in love with a young woman who is on furlough for the Christmas holidays. It also appeared in the final episode of *Star Trek: Deep Space Nine*, and in an episode of *Beavis and Butthead*. Despite not having been one of the hit versions in its time, Holiday's recording is the one most often heard seventy years later.

Fifty-second Street

The cluster of jazz clubs on West Fifty-second Street between Fifth and Sixth Avenues and spilling over toward Seventh in New York City was a midtown Manhattan parallel to the Harlem cabarets. The clubs came about as part of a shift in spending and investment in entertainment once Prohibition was repealed at the end of 1933 and later again when the Depression began to ease. They were small, maybe fifteen feet by sixty feet, and were located in the basements of brownstone residences. They featured miniature tables for a few dozen people, little space for dancing, and no air-conditioning. Small-band jazz was born and raised here: music without amplification, with sonic qualities that suited the spaces in which it emerged. Sitting so close to a band and a singer, one could hear the sizzle and rattle of cymbals, the deep thump of a bass drum, the mix of air and sound coming from the horns, the depth and resonance of the piano, the breathing of a singer, all features that recordings never manage to capture. It was the musical equivalent of the deep blacks and silvery whites of 1950s photography, an acoustic reality lost to us as musicians and listeners, dependent as we all are on amplification, mixing, filtering, recording, the dry ice of digitization, and monster video screens.

It was a time and place for experimentation, and small bands were often assembled for a single night. There was no clear musical orthodoxy in these clubs, none of the constraints on age, era, or musical politics that we have seen in our own times. It was possible to move from club to club cheaply and with ease, hear musics of different styles and eras, and see musicians of different persuasions working together. The whole history of jazz was on display. Both fans and musicians moved freely on this street congested with music, some visiting their colleagues on their break, others trying to squeeze as much playing or listening as possible into a single night. Sometimes bands ended their sets by marching through the audience and out onto the street. Even the clubs moved, some as many as five times within a block or two, jockeying for advantage. It was the kind of organic aesthetic that could be found only in Manhattan and New Orleans, the mix that no city planners or arts czars have since been able or willing to create. Not that it was heaven for all. A few clubs actively discouraged black customers unless they were famous, and some ugly scenes involving soldiers and musicians occasionally erupted.

The excitement these places generated was in part the result of a semi-legal post-Prohibition atmosphere, and in the mid-1940s by some lurid accounts that began to be circulated in newspapers and magazines about the addictions of jazz musicians, the horrors of heroin, and mobsters using the clubs as fronts. Bebop made its first full appearance in 1944 when it began to move from Harlem to these midtown clubs, and it threatened to became known as the soundtrack of a drug culture. Addiction was something of an occupational hazard because of the heavy circulation of drugs by dealers through the clubs and streets, and the ease of use by customers and performers alike. Some musicians seemed to wear their addiction like uniforms at the home front, or medals from the American Campaign. Their use of narcotics made them part of an elite of sorts, binding them together as artistes. But drug use was not necessarily something done under the weight of suffering, pain, or failure. It could also be celebratory, enhancing the best moments of life, intensifying peak events.

If Billie Holiday (along with drummer Gene Krupa) was one of the most publicly acknowledged addicts in jazz, she was always ambivalent about discussing the subject. Her openness about addiction was to a certain extent forced on her; her jail sentences and struggles with the police were common knowledge. Whatever private feelings she may have had about her drug use, her autobiography portrayed her as hurt by her image as a user, and as one who held a quite conventional morality concerning addiction.

Even though she had built up a large following by this point in her career, Billie frequently worked these Fifty-second Street clubs, as she would never have been asked to perform at the large elite nightclubs of Manhattan like the Stork Club, the Plaza, or the Blue Angel.

When Milt Gabler first heard Billie sing "Lover Man" in one of the clubs, they both felt it could be a pop hit, so he signed her to Decca Records for a one-year, twelve-song recording contract, moving her away from his low-distribution (and low-pay) boutique Commodore label. For the first time, she would receive royalties on sales, and would be given the support of an orchestra with a string section. The two-year Musicians Union strike against the record companies was ending, and this was the first chance that Decca had to record Holiday.

"Lover Man" is another song with unclear history and authorship. Although in *Lady Sings the Blues* Billie seems to imply that it had been written for her by Jimmy Davis and that pianist Roger "Ram" Ramirez had little to do with its composition, it had been copyrighted in 1941, several years before her session on October 4, 1944, with Ramirez listed as composer along with Jimmy Davis and James Sherman as lyricists. Gabler had already recorded it on Commodore Records with pianist Eddie Heywood, and then had him record it again for Decca. The song on the other side of the Decca single was an instrumental version of "Begin the Beguine" played with a boogie-woogie bass line that became a minor hit after Artie Shaw's recording, and so managed to draw attention to "Lover Man."

The song alternates between minor and major, and Holiday's dreamy, mesmerizing performance makes it seem as if nothing—the orchestra, the composer, the studio—matters but her singing. She sings it as slowly as a song can be sung without the flow of the melody coming apart, and yet her rhythm was steady. And after her passionate phrasing of "Huggin' and a kissin' / Oh, what we've been missing," she owned this song. Though it was clearly aimed at a pop market and jukebox play, "Lover Man" would become a favorite of jazz musicians, especially after Sarah Vaughan and Charlie Parker later recorded it.

At the same session she recorded "No More," a now forgotten song by composer Toots Camarata and lyricist Bob Russell. Camarata had a long and broad career as a musician, arranger, and composer working in every type of media, and Russell had written lyrics and music for numerous singers, bands, and films. Billie recorded two other songs with Russell's lyrics, "Do Nothing Till You Hear from Me," set to Duke Ellington's music, and "Crazy He Calls Me," written for Billie (with its famous office poster lines, "The difficult I'll do right now / The impossible will take a little while"). "No More" is an odd song, strikingly irregular in harmony and heavy with vernacular lyrics.

> You ain't gonna bother me no more, no how
> Love just goes so far, no more

It may or may not impress on first hearing, but singing it is quite difficult, and even the tune alone is hard to remember. While it has a fairly conventional chord structure, it's a minefield for a vocalist: a melody with notes outside the expected scales scattered throughout that produce an angular, restless, and chromatic feeling. Performing "No More" requires an ear finely tuned enough to know how the individual notes fit in the overall structure of the piece and the vocal assurance to resist the temptation to sing the expected notes in the melody instead of the dissonant notes called for, and still stay in tune. Only a few singers have recorded the song, and they were surely tempted by Holiday's success with it. If anyone thought that her being an untrained singer meant that Holiday was prone to inaccuracy, he need only listen to this performance, one that she thought was among her best.

A month later Holiday recorded another difficult song, Leonard Bernstein's "Big Stuff," the prologue to the ballet *Fancy Free*, which he created with choreographer Jerome Robbins. Instead of an orchestra performing an overture in the pit for the premiere at the old Metropolitan Opera House, the audience heard the recording of a song coming out of a radio onstage, an incredibly radical start to a ballet that brought Afro-inflected music and a tale of three sailors on leave in New York cruising for women into the whitest of all Euro-American art forms. Bernstein had seen Billie at Café Society (where he had also performed), and Robbins had choreographed and danced "Strange Fruit" in 1940, and they wanted her voice to set the tone for the evening. But because of lack of money, Bernstein's sister Shirley was heard on the record that was used that night in April. The ballet was an instant success and had an extended run, and Broadway and movie adaptations (under the title *On the Town*) followed. As he was readying the music to *Fancy Free* for a recording by Decca later that year, Bernstein was able to get Billie to sing the opening song, an abstraction of a blues with an ancient rolling bass figure, odd intervals and phrasings, and some explicit, if awkward, lyrics:

Let's take a ride in my gravy train
The door's open wide,

Holiday recorded it four times over the next year and a half, first with a dance band, then with an orchestra, with the arrangers and conductors changing, and each time she made the melody more believable, interesting, and rhythmically flexible than it read on paper, and hit all the notes, even though it lay out of her normal range. The rerecordings were made at Bernstein's request, though his reasons for rejecting the first two recordings are not known. Milt Gabler said the problem with the third version was that Bernstein objected to Holiday's adding an extra note to the piece. If so, it would not be an unreasonable objection within the classical tradition, but then why would he have asked Billie Holiday, of all people, to record it, known as she was for changing notes in virtually everything she sang? It should be said, though, that she stayed close to his composed melody in every recording she did. The last version, which required three and a half hours and five jazz musicians to complete, was finally approved by Bernstein and was used for some future performances of the ballet.

Singers sometimes develop relationships with songwriters who tailor works to fit them. Holiday had several such partners, Arthur Herzog Jr., most notably, and though it appeared to be a contentious partnership, the difficulties seem to have arisen only after their collaboration had ended and Billie's fame was spreading. George Cory and Douglass Cross were two songwriters that she met through Mabel Mercer, and their song "I'll Look Around" was one Billie recorded after she'd heard Mercer's version. Cory and Cross (better known for "I Left My Heart in San Francisco") were entranced by her, following her about, running errands, waking her for performances, and wrote "Deep Song" for her, a torch number that threatens to turn into a horror blues à la Robert Johnson's "Hellhound on My Trail":

The blues crawl in my door
To lick my heart once more

In 1939 and 1940 Billie recorded songs by Irene Wilson (later known as Irene Kitchings), a pianist and bandleader who was married to Teddy Wilson when Billie recorded with him. When Teddy left Irene for a showgirl, she and Billie became close. Bandleader Benny Carter encouraged Irene to compose songs, and Billie steered her to Arthur Herzog. Together Wilson and Herzog wrote four numbers that Billie recorded:

"Some Other Spring" (July 5, 1939), "I'm Pulling Through" (June 7, 1940), "Ghost of Yesterday," and "What Is This Going to Get Us?" (both February 29, 1940). They were pieces that Irene said expressed her feelings after Teddy left her. (Irene Wilson is not to be confused—as she always is—with Irene Higginbotham, another songwriter, who composed "Good Morning Heartache" and "No Good Man," both recorded by Billie on January 22, 1946.) Producer Bernie Hanighen also wrote songs that Billie recorded: "Yankee Doodle Never Went to Town" (October 25, 1936), "When a Woman Loves a Man" (January 12, 1938), and "If the Moon Turns Green" (May or June 1952).

"My Man" was so strongly identified with Holiday that eighteen versions of it by her exist on record. The song's two-part, major-minor, verse-refrain structure betrays its French origins, and its alternating sung and spoken passages were stock in trade for chanteuses who communicated a sense of confession and authenticity to Parisian audiences. The song was originally written in French as "Mon homme" by Jacques Charles for a 1920 revue and was first sung by Mistinguett, the great music hall diva. Charles's inspiration for the song was Francis Carco's play *Mon homme* and the recent death of singer Gaby Deslys, whose husband, Harry Pilcher, was having an affair with Mistinguett. Since Pilcher was also desired by Jacques Charles, the song, then, may speak of a real or fantasized obsessive and violent relationship between two men, which would change the emotional weight of the song, if not in degree then in kind.

It was introduced in America by Fanny Brice in the *Ziegfeld Follies* during a time in which Brice had lost everything she had, trying (and failing) to keep her gangster husband, Nicky Arnstein, out of prison. Audiences at the time read her performance as autobiographical as she sang it absolutely motionless, costumed in a torn dress like an apache girl under a bridge in Paris. She paused frequently throughout the song to heighten the drama, the song's structure was simplified by the

Ziegfeld people, who also added new lines, and it was performed by both acting and singing it.

That was the way Holiday presented it, much to the chagrin of those who preferred the jazz singer of a few years before. Her recording with the Teddy Wilson Orchestra on November 1, 1937, was a lively dance tune with abbreviated lyrics and some misplaced band work, which made it feel like a movie in which none of the actors quite knew what the film was about. Eleven years later, on December 10, 1948, she radically reconceived the song for Decca, slowing it to a crawl, rich with recitative, dramatic pauses, and especially memorable now for the addition of the original descending spoken lines "He isn't true / He beats me, too / What can I do?" Even though these words are often apologized for or edited out completely (as in the *Glee Songbook*), much like some of the lyrics to "Gloomy Sunday," those who heard it when she first sang it may have read it as Billie's revealing the pain of her sacrifice for love. Some of today's listeners may also interpret it as Holiday's offering herself to save other women from the pain she had endured.

In July 1952 she recorded it in the studio again for Clef Records (later Verve Records), surrounded by a small group of jazz musicians in an effort to duplicate her 1937 recording. Though she remained in a torch mode that was not entirely satisfactory in the jazz setting, she maintained her pauses, with the same tortured effect.

Town Hall Concert, February 16, 1946

Greer Johnson, who knew Billie from the days he and Elizabeth Hardwick had followed Holiday from club to club, had become a publicist and done some concert promotion, and continued to stay close to Billie. He thought she was far too important to be treated as just a nightclub singer and should be presented in concert as the equal to a Lotte Lehmann, the greatest German lieder singer of the 1930s and 1940s, and be billed as America's Jazz *Artist*. In a moment of wild enthusiasm he even imagined her singing the cycles of Schubert and Schumann lieder, arranged just for her voice. Though he failed to convince her of *that*, he did get her to agree to perform a cycle of her best songs, structuring an entire concert around a single theme or mood, and arranged so the songs flowed together.

New York's Town Hall was hired for a concert, and Johnson went to work publicizing it as a serious event. Photographers from *Look* magazine were scheduled to be present that night, and testimonials were printed in the program from classical and jazz performers such as Leonard Bernstein and Ella Fitzgerald. To round out the career-changing move he had in mind, Johnson invited no jazz critics at all, and instead sent requests for reviews to people like Paul Bowles of the *Herald Tribune* and Mark Schubert of the *Times*. Robert Coleman of the *Daily Mirror* reported that Johnson had said, "In a sense it is a jazz lieder program, and not a jam session. So that's that, you jitterbuggers."

The whole idea was risky: Jazz singers didn't perform solo concerts, and classical music writers didn't attend jazz shows. The concert was scheduled for a late Saturday afternoon, and Billie had by then established a reputation for not showing up for performances before midnight. Although she had agreed to the whole concept, as the date drew near she became uncomfortable. She didn't want to pose for photographers. She had never heard of the concept of picking out songs beforehand and listing them in a program. Greer assured her that Lotte Lenya, the Austrian actress and storytelling singer and wife of Kurt Weill, programmed *her* songs that way for her appearances at Town Hall. Billie didn't know Lotte Lenya, but in any case she didn't want to program a performance in advance when she might not feel like singing those songs when the day came.

The hall was sold out, room was made onstage to seat hundreds more, and even then a thousand were turned away. Holiday sang nineteen songs, mostly in the same tempo and mood, eleven of them from the Commodore and Decca recordings that may have suggested the idea of a song cycle in the first place. It was a songlist that she would return to repeatedly for years to come. Reviews of the concert were very appreciative, though there were quibbles about the program needing a few up-tempo numbers mixed in with the slow ballads. But it was such a success overall that afterward Billie wanted to do concerts exclusively: "It seems if people pay a whole lot more for a ticket they'll sit quiet and listen."

If one were buying Billie Holiday records as they were appearing in the late 1940s, there were several surprising changes of direction and gaps along the way. Following the very successful session on February 8, 1947, that resulted in "Deep Song," "There Is No Greater Love," "Easy Living," and "Solitude," there were no new records available from her until December 1948. When she did finally return to the studio, the choice of repertoire seemed bizarre. From the same session that produced the new and definitive versions of "My Man" and "I Loves You, Porgy" came "Weep No More" and "Girls Were Made to Take Care of Boys," surely the weakest songs and recordings ever sold under her name. Gordon Jenkins's "Weep No More" seemed to have been written to take advantage of the publicity surrounding Holiday's by then very public private life, amounting to what Holiday biographer Chris Ingham called a post-prison press release:

> I've drunk the bitter cup
> I've downed the bitter pill

Both songs were lyrically insipid, the recordings made even worse by the presence of the Stardusters, a wordless singing group of the type that producers of pop songs during that period used because they thought it enriched the song (or doubted the singer could carry it by herself). Seven months later she would begin recording several songs associated with Bessie Smith—"Tain't Nobody's Business if I Do," "Keeps On A-Rainin,'" "Do Your Duty," and "Gimme a Pigfoot" (all together suggesting an album of Bessie's songs was in the works, though Gabler denied it)—followed by two vaudeville-like duets with Louis Armstrong, and at the end of the decade, a return to form with "You're My Thrill," "Crazy He Calls Me," and "God Bless the Child."

Decca was casting about for some new direction in her career: from torch singer to pop singer to retro blues singer back to torch singer. During this two-and-a-half-year recording period, she spent several weeks in detox, followed by three more weeks in the solitude of the New Jersey countryside; she failed to show up for a recording session for which she was fined the costs; she escaped a drug arrest in Philadelphia in a rain of police gunfire, only to be arrested on a separate instance of possession in New York, for which she pled guilty, hoping to be put into drug treatment, but instead was sentenced to a year and a day in a federal prison, where she picked vegetables, slopped hogs, and washed dishes but never sang a note for nine and a half months. When she was released on parole she immediately performed two successful concerts at Carnegie Hall, appeared for five nights in *Holiday on Broadway*, did several months of nightclub appearances, and spent six weeks at the Strand Theatre along with the Count Basie Orchestra. She was arrested for assault with a deadly weapon in Hollywood, though the charges were dropped ten days later. Charged with possession nine days afterward, but later acquitted, she then spent a week at the Apollo and appeared on several TV programs over three nights.

This sequence of events certainly was not what Decca had in mind when they were changing their ideas about how Billie should be produced. It is astonishing, however, that she could continue to work at this pace in such chaotic personal circumstances, all the while adapting to a constantly shifting musical environment.

Billie Holiday, Norman Granz, and Verve Records

Billie first visited Los Angeles back in October 1941 to open Café Society, a new club run by the actor and comedian Jerry Colonna, who was attempting to copy (without authorization) the two New York clubs. Although the venue folded within a few weeks, while she was there she was introduced to dozens of Hollywood stars and executives. She also met Norman Granz, a student at UCLA and a film editor at MGM, who was hanging out at jazz clubs with his girlfriend, Marie Bryant, a dancer and singer who had worked with Louis Armstrong, Lionel Hampton, and Duke Ellington and was rising fast in LA. When Billie returned a year later to work at Billy Berg's Trouville Club, Granz chatted with her between sets; one night she broke into tears as she told him that some of her friends of color had been turned away when they came to see her perform. Granz and Marie had already experienced something similar as an interracial couple; her story moved him to go straight to Berg. Because Granz knew that Berg would tell him he would lose business if he integrated the club, Granz approached him with an offer to stage low-cost Sunday jam sessions with the best of Los Angeles's musicians if he could be assured there would be no discrimination against anyone. Berg bought the idea, presumably because he was not doing any business in the afternoon as it was, and whatever happened, it wouldn't affect his evening events. But when the Sunday sessions became overwhelmingly successful, he desegregated all of his club's performances. Granz took that as a sign that more could be done, and he developed a series of public jam sessions at nonsegregated venues that succeeded better than he imagined.

Yet this was a city where, over the next two years, racial strife intensified with the infamous Sleepy Lagoon gang murder case and the Zoot Suit Riots, events that lumped together Mexican Americans, African Americans, jazz musicians, and miscellaneous hipsters. Granz staged a jazz fund-raiser for the defense of those arrested at the Philharmonic Auditorium. "Jazz at the Philharmonic" was the title of the event, and it was too good a name to lose, so for years afterward he presented jazz events that filled concert halls across the country, producing recordings, putting musicians up in the best hotels, and paying them well. He was breaking social and musical rules left and right, and becoming something of a hero to those who knew and worked with him.

But not everyone in jazz was happy with Granz as impresario. He liked to put musicians of different styles and generations together on-stage and encouraged heated competition between them that thrilled audiences and had them cheering and stomping. It resulted in a circus atmosphere, some said. Others were not in favor of putting musicians in large halls where they often had to change what they played to fit the space.

Singers were a different story with Granz. He had always been a fan of Ella Fitzgerald, and paid dearly to get her away from Decca so that he could manage her career and produce her records on his own label. Like Billie, Ella had recorded extensively for Milt Gabler, and Granz followed Gabler's lead with album-oriented productions, concept albums, and richly arranged songs. Where he excelled was carefully thought-out live recordings and her many songbook albums, monuments to the greatest American composers of popular song.

After a couple of JATP concerts with Holiday as a guest in the mid-1940s, he signed her as well, and from 1952 to 1957 produced a long se-ries of albums that broke with Gabler's softer approach. Granz attempted to return to the glories of her 1930s small-group sessions by surround-ing her with some of the best musicians of the time—Oscar Peterson, Jimmy Rowles, Charlie Shavers, Harry "Sweets" Edison, Ben Webster, Paul Quinichette, Benny Carter—and most of the songs on her records with him were proven standards. They ranged over a wide variety of sub-jects in diverse moods, though the album covers, which typically fea-tured darkly lit photos and David Stone Martin's spidery, stark line drawings, implied a troubled story inside.

Granz wanted her to try songs she hadn't done before, and "Every-thing Happens to Me," "Tenderly," "Stormy Weather," "East of the Sun," and "Autumn in New York" were choices welcomed by fans who found it hard to believe that she hadn't done them before. Only a few of the num-bers she recorded, such as "P.S. I Love You," seem ill-conceived. With Billie, Granz was also willing to take some chances in the studio. Some-times there were arrangements, but more often she and he decided on songs at the last minute. At times they recorded on the fly. Pianist

Oscar Peterson recalled that she could launch into a song without naming it or waiting for something to be planned:

> She'd walk over, say, "I used to do this," and begin singing . . . but the way she sang it, we could hear the key and just begin playing behind her. It would automatically become a run-through and as soon as it was over, she'd go over to the mike and say, "All right, let's try this one now." I'd say, "Wait a minute, Billie—" but she was off and running. I didn't always have time to work out a written introduction for her, but she didn't care. She'd just say, "Play those little things you play, and I'll come in."

When Jimmy Rowles was a pianist on a Granz recording, he was uncomfortable with Norman's last-minute choices of songs, and on his own rehearsed with Billie beforehand to pick out some material:

> We never had time to get together on chords, Barney Kessel, the bassist, and me. Now that's really difficult, especially when Norman would pull out a tune and say, "Here it is: 'Prelude to a Kiss' . . . go!" Everyone's got their own conception of how to play the tune and so it comes out sounding like a jam session.

Granz sometimes also let her take as long as she wanted to make a record, and to come and go from the sessions as she pleased, though it could be a very expensive process. The results, surprisingly, were consistently good, and the musicianship high. Consistency had worked well with Ella Fitzgerald, where one might never expect to be surprised. But surprise and discovery were the keys to Billie's best 1930s work, and though the results of Granz's approach were more conventional, there were often details to strike the listener. "Love for Sale," a 1952 duo with Billie and Oscar Peterson, is as intimate a recording as she ever made, especially since Granz recorded her voice louder, hiding nothing. Peterson recalled, "[Norman] wanted to display the complete interplay between us, and he wanted her to express the song anyway she felt. . . . He told me 'just go with her'—and so I did." Bringing in musicians from the Basie band for one album, or returning to some of her 1930s triumphs ("I Wished on the Moon," "What a Little Moonlight Can Do"), were also inspired choices, even when they were not as rewarding as he may have wished.

The Last Sessions

Holiday's final two studio recordings, *Lady in Satin* (Columbia, 1958) and *Last Recording* (MGM, 1959), are the most controversial recordings she ever made, and have been argued over endlessly for the past sixty-five years. Her record companies seemed to want to forget them: *Lady in Satin* has not been reissued for seventeen years, and *Last Recording* for twenty-six years. When in 2001 Columbia brought out its big CD boxed set *Lady Day: The Complete Billie Holiday on Columbia, 1933–1944*, it left out her 1958 album. All the stranger because both recordings were rather lavishly produced, especially the first, with its full string section, big band, three women singers backing her up, and some of the best jazz and classical musicians in the country. It was the most expensive production she had ever been given.

It was Billie's idea not to renew her contract with Verve and to move back to Columbia after many years. She was not getting much work and she needed the money just to get by. Ever since she had heard Nelson Riddle's arrangements for Frank Sinatra in the early 1950s, she had wanted Riddle to arrange an album for her. But when she heard Ray Ellis's treatment of "For All We Know" on his 1957 album *Ellis in Wonderland*, she decided she could work with him. Ray Ellis was a journeyman saxophonist who in the mid-1950s began arranging hit songs for the Drifters, Doris Day, Connie Francis, Johnny Mathis, and Bobby Darin, and had become a protégé of Mitch Miller at Columbia. According to her new lawyer, Earle Zaidins, she had been complaining that Joe Glaser never got the right bookings for her, and she was forced to do the same music over and over. Her best audiences had been white, she said, and she wanted regular bookings in the big "white rooms" like the Plaza, the Waldorf, and the Empire Room. When she and Zaidins went to Columbia, they signed her to record with Ellis.

After years of revisiting older material with Norman Granz, Columbia saw her return to the label as a new beginning, and it was agreed that for the record she was to sing only songs that she had never recorded before. That meant learning them and fitting them to arrangements by a man she'd never worked with, yet she failed to show for any meetings or rehearsals to go over the songs with Ellis. The recording sessions were set to start at ten each night, but she never arrived before midnight. She had run through some of the material with her pianist Mal Waldron, but Ellis had put introductory verses into the arrangements for a number of the songs. Since she normally ignored the verses of songs and went right to the refrains, she didn't know the words or the melodies for some of them. Even worse, she seemed unfamiliar with a few of the songs as well.

She was not in good health and was drinking gin from a water pitcher throughout the sessions. When the playbacks were checked by the engineer, she didn't want the musicians to hear them because she was embarrassed by her singing. The word in the studio was that she was setting herself up for failure, and comparisons to Marilyn Monroe were whispered about. Ellis finally lost his patience. The on-the-spot rehearsals, the false starts, retakes, and overdubs began to pile up on the tape reels, and when they discovered they were short one song, Ellis and Holiday had to take a cab at three in the morning to Colony Records on Broadway, where they leafed through sheet music until they found "You've Changed," a song she had in fact recorded once before. They finished the sessions in only three days, but Ellis left in disgust and wanted no part of the remix sessions that followed.

Somehow, though, she had made it work. She was aging prematurely, she was sick and had to be helped on and off the stage, and she was having trouble reading and remembering lyrics. There were missed notes, her voice was husky at times, and her vibrato had become much faster.

The tempos were slower, and there were no improvising musicians for her to converse with musically as she sang, but the arrangements, though lush, were sometimes minimal, and set her voice floating loose on top of them. She counted on the strength of her recitative, the ability to sing out of tempo and not seem lost. Her phrasing was still sensitive to the words, remaking their points of emphasis and shifting meaning by surprising changes of stress as she sang. The essence that Gunther Schuller said lay behind the surface techniques of her singing seemed more obvious now than ever with the loss of some of her other abilities, but her vocal artistry was still there. The musicians were impressed. She was still a star to them.

Billie thought *Lady in Satin* was the best album she ever made (even though she was unhappy about Ray Ellis's insisting on having "those white bitches sing behind me"). She particularly liked "Violets for Your Furs" and told her friends that young singers should listen to it. She also liked "You've Changed," even though she had been crying as she sang it. The strings were a comfort to her: Singing with small jazz groups had been giving her headaches, she said.

When the album appeared in 1958, the lines were drawn hard and fast among her fans. Those used to hearing her in the sparest of jazz bands felt the string arrangements were saccharine and cluttered. She'd abandoned jazz; it was a flawed attempt at a pop record, commerce at its worst. Glen Coulter, the most sensitive writer on Holiday, blamed Ellis entirely: The "ideal accompaniment for a jazz vocal is a many-noted commentary which does not interfere with what the singer is doing, but rather provides a texture of the utmost contrast and is a springboard of rhythm. Ellis provides a sleek, slow, insufficiently subordinated counterpoint that throws Holiday's time off and gives her nothing to brace itself against." Odd that those who thought she was at her best when she overcame inferior songs would think she would not be able to rise above what they considered inferior accompaniment. Others objected to her voice. The album was morbid, and literally a disgrace. She was imitating herself, the curse of the aging artist.

The liner notes were themselves startlingly defensive, as if the buyer was being warned, but too late. A goodly part of producer Irving Townsend's notes for the original LP reminded the listener that Holiday had had a miserable life, though for the material she was performing on the record, that was a benefit, because it made it "so easy to believe what she sings." Is it jazz? he asks. "Yes. It is jazz because Billie Holiday sings jazz, no matter what the accompaniment is . . ." In Ray Ellis's remarks in the liner notes for the CD issue almost forty years later, he wrote that he had been unhappy with her performance when they recorded it, but that he now realized that he was listening musically, rather than emotionally. Michael Brooks's comments for the same CD reissue were outright grim: "An autobiographical study . . . an open wound . . . vocal cords flayed by the acid of racism and commercial indifference . . . the strings did not bring out the best in Billie . . . she tried to divorce herself from her roots."

Still, there were those, including many musicians, who thought *Lady in Satin* was a triumph when it first appeared. Miles Davis, for example: "I'd rather hear her now. She's become much more mature. Sometimes you can sing words every night for five years, and all of a sudden it dawns on you what the song means."

If there were some who thought that recording *Lady in Satin* given her mental and physical state was a mistake, then another record by her a year later must have been seen as madness. *Billie Holiday* (the title was changed to *Last Recording* when she died four months after its issue) is one of the least acknowledged recordings by a major artist, and even her biographers have tried to ignore its existence.

By 1959 Ray Ellis had moved to MGM as an executive, where he would work with Barbra Streisand and later produce his own easy listening albums. One of his first projects was the Holiday recording. In her discussions with Ellis, Billie made it clear that she wanted it to sound more like the albums Sinatra was making at the time—brighter, more confident, maybe using some of Sinatra's songs, and *this* time, no backup singers. Again, all the songs would be ones she had never before recorded.

The accompaniment on *Last Recording* was divided between three ensembles, all smaller than the ones used on *Lady in Satin*: two with strings, one without, along with three soloists—Jimmy Cleveland, trombone, Harry "Sweets" Edison, trumpet, and Gene Quill, alto saxophone. A few of the songs have arrangements close to the sound of the Sinatra/Nelson Riddle albums, with "Sweets" Edison providing muted trumpet fills as he did so often on Sinatra recordings, and "All the Way" and "I'll Never Smile Again" were associated with Sinatra. Two songs were quite old: "There'll Be Some Changes Made," a hit for Ethel Waters the year it was first written, and "Baby, Won't You Please Come Home," identified with Bessie Smith. One, "It's Not for Me to Say," was almost brand new.

Her health was much worse than when she'd recorded the year before, and she was so weak that she often had to be held up in a chair by her secretary, Alice Vrbsky. It was Alice, not Ellis, who now determined how long the sessions could last, and she ended them when Billie was weakening, so most of the songs on the record are first takes. Some of them are faded at the end, suggesting that there might have been problems with her held notes at the conclusions. The orchestra sometimes sounds shallow in the mix, and on several songs Billie's voice is too high. It is most likely that she was not able to sing in the keys in which some of the arrangements were written, and it was too late and too expensive to redo them. The results sound as if the orchestral track was recorded in the key as planned, then slowed down to a lower pitch and tempo. Billie was then recorded separately at the same lower pitch as the revised orchestra track, next overdubbed to the orchestra's track, and then both orchestra and voice were brought together and sped back up to the desired key and tempo. (Ray Ellis at one point conceded that this had been done, but later changed his mind about his answer.) The results may sound a bit weird, but as many said of the album, it was better than it had a right to be. Whatever the troubles in the studio, it still sounded authentically like Billie Holiday, and no one else has been able to get that sound. How ironic, then, that necessity forced a mid-twentieth-century studio to use electronic tricks to complete the project, bringing Billie Holiday into twenty-first-century electronic pitch correction, shape-shifting compression, punched-in edits, and the authenticity of vampire sonic technology.

When she was on her deathbed at the Metropolitan Hospital in Harlem, her lawyer told her that he could arrange yet another recording with MGM, but Billie doubted that she would ever be able to sing again. He was persistent, explaining that the MGM executives were serious businesspeople, that they had already checked with the doctors to see if she would live and were assured that she would. If that was so, Billie suggested, they could bring the recording equipment to the hospital and they could call the record *Lady at the Met*!

Billie Holiday's death on July 17, 1959, and her hospitalization leading up to it were eerie reenactments of much of her life. When she collapsed on May 31, she was taken to Knickerbocker Hospital, where she was signed in as Eleanora McKay. No one in the hospital knew who she was, and, with needle marks on her body, she was left in the hall for hours, since the institution was not allowed to treat drug addicts. A Viennese doctor who was an admirer intervened to have her moved to Metropolitan Hospital in Harlem, where she was treated for heart and liver problems. So began the second-longest engagement of her career—forty-seven days in the hospital.

When heroin was found in her room, she was arrested, fingerprinted, and photographed lying in her bed, her flowers and possessions taken away, as police officers and doctors now vied to be her guards. Meanwhile, it was business as usual: One lawyer got her to sign with another agent, even though Joe Glaser, her current agent, was paying her bills; she signed contracts to be in a new film and to produce a magazine article, and plans were made for another book, to be titled *Bless My Bones*. Her watchdogs and nurses asked for her autograph and played her impounded MGM recording on her record player at the nurses' station.

On the day she died, the *New York Post* ran a full front-page headline and her picture, along with the first of a long string of articles on Holiday by William Dufty. It was that cover that inspired Frank O'Hara's postmodern elegiac poem "The Day Lady Died." The *Post* outsold all other New York papers that day.

I set out to write a book that cast new light on the extraordinary artist who was Billie Holiday. My intention was not to deny or gainsay the tribulations and tragedy of her life, but to shift the focus to her art. The consistency and taste she brought to nearly every performance, even those when her body was failing her, display a discipline, an artist's complete devotion to her work, and a refusal to surrender to the demands of an insatiable world.

She was anything but a self-promoter. She had no lawyer for most of her career except when court appearances demanded it. She had no real publicists, and seldom gave interviews. The pieces about herself that she wrote or collaborated on were few and written to achieve specific ends. Most of her guidance for dealing with the public came from Joe Glaser, a man who himself was a cipher, and whose own dealings with the public often served him poorly.

Making sense of a musician's life can be a precarious undertaking. Music is its own language, and difficult to translate into words. The value in music can seldom be convincingly connected back to individual performers or composers. Yet fans, musicologists, and biographers alike find this an exercise that is hard to resist. No wonder so many of us look to the words of a song to find clues to a singer's life.

Holiday's life is still difficult to fathom; some secrets still linger and contradictions continue. Whatever the source of her failures and vulner-abilities, she fought hard to keep her music out front, and aspired to ever wider audiences. Singers who bravely cross the lines of race, class, nation-alism, and gender do not merely take on the mannerisms and language of others. They create a way to adapt the musical architecture of songs and their key ideas, and reach into a deep structure to make these songs trig-ger social and emotional responses in everyone who hears them.

In the other biographies I've written, I've tried to stay out of the way, avoiding excessive explication of what someone meant when he was quoted, or guessing at his thoughts or feelings, and I have been loath to offer explanations based on knowledge that I didn't have. But with Billie Holiday, I became caught up in the details of her life as she and others had represented it. I found enough new information that I felt I had to share it. But I also found myself wanting to defend her, hoping to give her a new hearing in the court of biographical opinion.

Let her have the last word: "I'm Billie Holiday. Singing's the only thing I know how to do, and they won't let me do it. Do they expect me to go back to scrubbing steps—the way I started?"

Acknowledgments

Writers of biographies build up considerable debts, and authors hope to be able to remember them all to repay them. I live in fear of having missed someone, and I'm sure that I have. If so, I'll owe you even more.

To begin with there is Billie Holiday and William Dufty's *Lady Sings the Blues*, the foundation of all work on Lady Day. Next there are the biographies on Billie Holiday that have shaped her story. I could not have done without them. John Chilton's *Billie's Blues*, Robert O'Meally's *Lady Day: The Many Faces of Billie Holiday*, Farah Jasmine Griffin's *If You Can't Be Free, Be a Mystery: In Search of Billie Holiday*, Stuart Nicholson's *Billie Holiday*, Chris Ingham's *Divas: Billie Holiday*, and Donald Clarke's *Billie Holiday: Wishing on the Moon* are essential reading, as are several others in French and Italian. The late Linda Kuehl's research and her drafts for a never completed book on Holiday have been the basis of several of the more recent books and will be necessary resources for any future work, since some of her material has become available in published books, especially Julia Blackburn's *With Billie*. I owe a special debt to Frances McCullough, Linda Kuehl's editor, who deposited the Kuehl manuscript and notes into the Institute of Jazz Studies library, and also helped me to better understand the circumstances surrounding Ms. Kuehl's work. I've also benefited greatly from Ken Vail's *Lady Day's Diary*, and Phil Schaap, Ben Young, and Matt Herman's *WKCR Billie Holiday Festival Handbook*, an invaluable discography. Two labors of love for which I'm thankful.

I received very special help from H. Dennis Fairchild, William Dufty's partner of many years, who graciously shared with me some of the rarer of Dufty's publications and gave me insight into his work. Also I want to thank Dave Hanna, who recorded in audio Bill Dufty's life history and gave me access to it.

Libraries have been very important to my efforts, especially The Gabe M. Wiener Music and Arts Library of Columbia University, the special Holiday collections at Emory University and the University of Maryland, and the Institute of Jazz Studies at Rutgers University–Newark. I'm so pleased to be able to record my debt to two scholar-librarians who were of immense help to me: James Tad Hershorn at Rutgers University–Newark and Wolfram Knauer of the Jazzinstitut Darmstadt, both of them my personal heroes. The many Web sites and discographies devoted to Holiday were also of great value, and I salute those who painstakingly built and maintain them.

Among my colleagues I thank Robert O'Meally and Farah Jasmine Griffin, both brilliant and generous people. Tad Shull, Susan Stewart, Loren Schoenberg, Gary Giddins, Lewis Porter, J. R. Taylor, Will Friedwald, and Rachel Vetter Huang and Hao Huang were my tutors for various phases of this project, and I feel blessed to have had them share their wisdom with me and I take pleasure in listing their names together. Chris Albertson, George Avakian, and Nat Hentoff, all of whom knew Billie Holiday, were kind enough to let me interview them about their relationships to her.

I want to acknowledge the help given to me by Sara Villa, a woman of boundless abilities who generously helped me with translations, and more than that gave me the benefit of her shrewd readings of the Holiday literature in languages other than English.

Thanks, too, to the many people who have helped keep Holiday's writing and music available to the public, especially Michel Fontanes of France, who has kept the Masters of Jazz CD series of Billie Holiday recordings alive and expanding.

Then there are friends whom I could not do without in writing this book or for anything else: Roger Abrahams, Grey Gundaker, Dan Rose, Nick Spitzer, and Robert Farris Thompson. Each of them in their own idiosyncratic and cool way encouraged and helped me despite my incessant complaining about the difficulties of writing.

This book would not exist without the hard work, care, and truly great knowledge of my agent, Sarah Lazin, and my editor, Rick Kot. Rick is the king of editors and Sarah the queen of agents, long live them both. Diego Nuñez worked hard and carefully as a copyreader, a job deserving the highest praise from everyone but seldom receiving it. Carolyn Coleburn, Ellen Abrams, and Holly Watson are my treasured publicists. Can't live without them.

I dedicate the book to Heather, Matt, and Miles Szwed. I count on them and they never fail. But as always, it's Marilyn (Sue) Szwed who has to suffer most from my anxieties and obsessions, but at the same time manages to help and encourage me without fretting. And for that there is no gratitude great enough.

Introduction

2 **Barack Obama heard in her music** Barack Obama, *Dreams from My Father* (New York: Random House, 1995), p. 138; *The Starr Report* (Washington, D.C.: Government Printing Office, 1998), p. 707.

3 **a columnist in the *Los Angeles Mirror* suggested** Florabel Muir in 1950, quoted in David Brackett, *Interpreting Popular Music* (Cambridge: Cambridge University Press, 1995), p. 53; see also pp. 51–53.

3 **There is a powerful urge** Happy songs do exist, but, as David Bowie once said, if you want to lose an audience, sing them a song about what a happy boy you are.

3 **Our Lady of Sorrows** Francis Davis, "Our Lady of Sorrows," *Atlantic Monthly*, November 2000, pp. 104–8.

3 **As Stanley Crouch put it** Stanley Crouch, "The Invincible Sound of Swing: An Appreciation," in José Muñoz and Carlos Sampayo, *Billie Holiday* (Seattle: Fantagraphics Books, 1993), p. 52.

CHAPTER ONE: The Book I: *Lady Sings the Blues*

13 **a persona of tragedy and sorrow** Robert Belleret, *Piaf: Un mythe français* (Paris: Fayard, 2013).

15 **She had certainly read *Lady Sings the Blues*** Ken Vail, *Lady Day's Diary: The Life of Billie Holiday, 1937–1959* (Surrey, UK: Castle Communications, 1996), p. 176.

16 **Billie was staying with the Duftys** Rhonda B. Sewell, "Biographer Remembers Billie Holiday's Greatness," *Toledo Blade*, April 1, 2001, pp. B1–B3.

17 **She was especially put off** William Dufty, "The Legend of Lady Day, Part 1," *East West Journal*, January 15–30, 1973, p. 8.

17 **It was agreed that "no agent or broker"** August 1, 1955, from the Lester Cowan and Ann Ronell "Trial of Billie Holiday" Collection, Special Collections, University of Maryland Libraries.

18 **"She wouldn't be in the mood and would get angry"** Sewell, "Biographer Remembers Billie Holiday's Greatness," pp. B1–B3.

18 **Dufty discovered that the material in it was rich** Harriott himself later started a novel based on Holiday's life but died before it was finished.

18 **"Mom was 13"** Frank Harriott, "The Hard Life of Billie Holiday," *PM*, September 2, 1945. During the research these numbers were changed but were still not accurate.

19 **"Miss Holiday's explosiveness"** Quoted in "The True Story of Billie Holiday, Part 6," *New York Post*, July, 26, 1959. Twenty-five years later the same paragraph would appear in a "Who Said That?" teaser quiz in a Simon and Schuster ad for *The Intimate Sex Lives of Famous People*.

19 **"We have been working for a week now"** Letter from William Dufty to Norman Granz, June 28, 1955, H. Dennis Fairchild archive.

20 **the weaknesses of the autobiographies** Christopher Harlos, "Jazz Autobiography: Theory, Practice, Politics," in Krin Gabbard, ed., *Representing Jazz* (Durham, NC: Duke University Press, 1995), p. 160.

21 **she had been reading from the book** Letter from Dufty to Granz, H. Dennis Fairchild archive.

21 **"Dear Mr. Barker, Since my meeting"** Ibid.

22 **Even more ominously, McKay insisted** Al Dunmore, "Billie Holiday Book Pulls Some Punches," *Pittsburgh Courier*, December 29, 1956, p. A14.

23 **Dufty reassured him** Norman Granz to William Dufty, August 2, 1955; Dufty to Granz, August 2, 1955, and August 19, 1955, H. Dennis Fairchild archive.

23 **Billie said, "I can't help it"** William Pepper, "Banned Billie OK for Park?," *World Telegraph*, July 30, 1957.

23 **He opened his review by declaring** Saunders Redding, "Book Review," *Baltimore Afro-American*, March 15, 1957, p. A2.

23 **"Well I don't know if you have been digging it"** William Dufty, "The True Story of Billie Holiday, Part 1," *New York Post*, July 20, 1959.

24 **"I never was a child"** Ethel Waters with Charles Samuels, *His Eye Is on the Sparrow* (New York: Doubleday, 1951), p. 1.

CHAPTER TWO: The Book II: The Rest of the Story

27 **she wrote in the margin** William Dufty in the BBC film *Reputations: Billie Holiday—Sensational Lady*, BBC TV 2, December 21, 2008.

29 **four hundred dollars that he gave her** Mezz Mezzrow and Bernard Wolfe, *Really the Blues* (New York: Citadel Underground, Reissue Edition [1946], 2001). Early draft, *Lady Sings the Blues*, Robert O'Meally archive.

30 **"He was supposed to be getting ready to marry"** Robert O'Meally archive.

30 **Kane was a great picture** Billie Holiday with William Dufty, *Lady Sings the Blues* (New York: Harlem Moon, 2006), pp. 106–7.

30 **Holiday and Welles made a striking pair** In 2000 Christine Vachon and Pam Koeffler of Killer Films announced they were developing *Fine and Mellow*, a film to be based on the Welles-Holiday affair; see *Movieline*, September 2000.

31 **I remember the night Orson Welles came into the Onyx** Early draft, *Lady Sings the Blues*, Robert O'Meally archive.

32 **Holman performed the song in tan blackface** Carla Kaplan, *Miss Anne in Harlem: The White Women of the Harlem Renaissance* (New York: Harper, 2013), pp. 40–44.

32 **Holman was first known to Billie** Holiday and Dufty, *Lady Sings the Blues*, pp. 59–60.

33 **As Billie discreetly put it** Ibid., p. 59.

34 **He later claimed to have had an affair** Christopher Wilson, *Dancing with the Devil: The Windsors and Jimmy Donahue* (New York: St. Martin's Griffin, 2000).

35 **she was also deeply wedded to jazz** Tallulah Bankhead, "The World's Greatest Jazz Musician," *Ebony*, December 1952.

35 **two women began sharing their show business miseries** Joel Lowenthal, *Tallulah: The Life and Times of a Leading Lady* (New York: Harper, 2008), p. 409.

36 **"Well, godammit darling"** Robert O'Meally archive.

37 **An account of the three-way phone call** Ibid.

37 **Tallulah followed up the call with a letter to Hoover** FBI file on Billie Holiday. (For a time this file was for sale on Amazon.com!)

38 **she wrote Bankhead** Robert O'Meally, *Lady Day: The Many Faces of Billie Holiday* (New York: Arcade, 1991), p. 124.

39 **"I put in a couple of big words"** George Monteiro, *Conversations with Elizabeth Bishop* (Jackson: University Press of Mississippi, 1996), p. 24.

39 **Kirkpatrick recalled her** Kai Erikson, ed., *Encounters* (New Haven, CT: Yale University Press, 1989), p. ix; Kuehl manuscript, Rutgers University–Newark.

39 **"the most extraordinary gift of phrasing"** Gary Fountain and Peter Brazeau, eds., *Remembering Elizabeth Bishop: An Oral Biography* (Amherst: University of Massachusetts Press, 1994), p. 104.

40 **Louise Crane is not mentioned** Holiday and Dufty, *Lady Sings the Blues*, pp. 97–100.

40 **Crane's fascination with Holiday** Fountain and Brazeau, *Remembering Elizabeth Bishop*, p. 328.

40 **ready to move away from the downtown slummers** Marianne Moore, *Selected Letters* (New York: Penguin, 1998), p. 414.

41 **When he learned that it was his cousin Louise** John Hammond with Irving Townsend, *John Hammond on Record: An Autobiography* (New York: Penguin, 1982 [1977]), pp. 208–9.

41 **Hammond said that Holiday never forgave him** Ibid., p. 209.

42 **wrote of Billie as "the bizarre deity"** Elizabeth Hardwick, *Sleepless Nights*, new edition (New York: New York Review of Books Classics, 2001), p. 35.

42 **"She is very beautiful in a long white dress"** Simone de Beauvoir, *America Day by Day*, Carol Cosman, trans. (Berkeley: University of California Press, 1999), p. 44.

44 **"Ask him to take away that damn mustard"** William Dufty, "The Legend of Lady Day, Part 1," *East West Journal* 2, no. 20, 1973, p. 9.

44 **Billie loved children** Alice Vrbsky, her maid, in the film *The Long Night of Lady Day* (1984).

44 **Billie always asked him to bring his two-year-old son** John Szwed, *So What: The Life of Miles Davis* (New York: Simon and Schuster, 2002), p. 64.

45 **she attempted to adopt a child in Boston** Attorney Earle Warren Zaidins, in the film *The Long Night of Lady Day* (1984).

46 **"These goddamn American doctors"** William Dufty, "The Legend of Lady Day, Part 2," *East West Journal* 2, no. 21, 1973, p. 9.

47 **When the lights went down for the first performance** Gilbert Millstein, liner notes to *The Essential Billie Holiday: Carnegie Hall Concert Recorded Live*, Verve V-8410.

47 **"erect and beautiful; poised and smiling"** Ibid.

47 **heavily edited recording was made from the two concerts** *The Essential Billie Holiday: Carnegie Hall Concert Recorded Live*, Verve V-8410.

47 **Two reels of tape exist** "Billie Holiday—Carnegie Hall Concert Tape with Unreleased Content," http://recordmecca.com/products-page/museum-quality-collectibles/billie-holiday-carnegie-hall-concert-tape-with-unreleased-content/. Many thanks to Jeff Gold of Recordmecca.

48 **"the life and the art had become a kind of voyeuristic tragedy"** Gerald Early, "Pulp and Circumstance: The Story of Jazz in High Places," in Robert G. O'Meally, ed., *The Jazz Cadence of American Culture* (New York: Columbia University Press, 1998), pp. 393–430.

48 **a series of eight articles in the *New York Post*** Letters to the Editor, *New York Post*, July 20, 1959.

49 **articles in *Ebony* were particularly important** *Ebony*, February 1951, pp. 22–24, 26–28.

49 **"When you're writing, straighten them out"** Michael Levin, "Billie Holiday: 'Don't Blame Show Biz,'" *Down Beat*, June 4, 1947, p. 1.

50 **"A lot of the real dicty people with talent"** "Billie Talks About Fish and People," *Los Angeles Mirror-News*, February 1957.

50 **"I hate these East Side clubs"** "Billie Holiday Sounds Off Against Segregation in Gotham Nighteries," *Baltimore Afro-American*, 1942.

50 **"It was slow, this attempt to climb clear"** *Tan*, February, 1953.

50 **"I never felt inferior to anybody"** *Confidential*, October 1959.

51 **"I'm not the suicide type"** Billie Holiday, "Heroin Saved My Life," unedited draft for *Confidential*, 1959, H. Dennis Fairchild archive.

51 **Dufty said that when he visited her room** Dufty in the BBC film *Reputations*.

52 **this meant showing how the stigmatized women** Coretta Pittman, "Black Women and the Trouble with Ethos: Harriet Jacobs, Billie Holiday, and Sister Souljah," *Rhetoric Society Quarterly* 37, no. 1 (Winter 2004),

pp. 56–61; Glen Coulter, "Billie Holiday, The Art of Jazz," *Cambridge Review*, 1957, p. 124; Farah Jasmine Griffin, *If You Can't Be Free, Be a Mystery* (New York: Free Press, 2002); Kim L. Purnell, "Listening to Lady Day: An Exploration of the Creative (Re) Negotiation of Identity Revealed in the Life Narratives and Music Lyrics of Billie Holiday," *Communication Quarterly* 50, nos. 3 and 4 (Summer/Fall 2002), pp. 444–66.

CHAPTER THREE: The Image: Film, Television, and Photography

56 **The song's opening lines** Gunther Schuller, *The Swing Era* (New York: Oxford University Press, 1989), p. 530.

56 **he asked her to play the role** Frank Brady, *Citizen Welles* (New York: Scribner, 1989), pp. 333–34.

57 **It soon becomes a worldwide phenomenon** Elliot Paul, "It's All True," Lily Library, Indiana University Welles Mss. Collection, folder 13-26.

57 **What might have been material for a conventional** Throughout the script there were hints of films and novels of the past and the future: E. L. Doctorow's *Ragtime*, Ishmael Reed's *Mumbo Jumbo*, and the films *The Jazz Singer* and *Paris Blues*.

58 **"Today, I was at your studio and got an earful"** "The Memos Part IX: Dr. Bernstein to Orson Welles," May 21, 2012, www.wellesnet.com/?p=1573.

58 **Filming was halted abruptly** For a glimpse of what some of the film would have looked like, see the DVD *It's All True* (Paramount Pictures, 1993).

59 **plans for the film, now titled *New Orleans*** Sherrie Tucker, "'But This Music Is Mine Already!': White Woman as Jazz Collector in the Film *New Orleans* (1947)," in Nichole Rustin and Sherrie Tucker, eds., *Big Ears: Listening for Gender in Jazz Studies* (Durham, NC: Duke University Press, 2008), pp. 235–66.

60 **Jazz had somehow become a lady** Billie said that the director later remarked to her of the actress playing the opera singer, "You made her look like a hole in the screen." Donald Clarke, *Wishing on the Moon: The Life and Times of Billie Holiday* (New York: Viking, 1994), p. 247.

60 **Holiday arrived late, twelve days** Barney Bigard, *With Louis and the Duke: The Autobiography of a Jazz Clarinetist* (New York: Oxford University Press, 1988).

61 **"I'm just not the maid type"** Murray Kempton, "Lady Day Had a Way with Words," *Newsday*, July 10, 1994, p. A35.

61 **Armstrong played in front of the Woody Herman band** Tucker, "'But This Music Is Mine,'" pp. 235–66.

61 **Biberman was replaced by Arthur Lubin** Elliott Paul quoted in an e-mail from Arnold Goldman to John Szwed; see also Tucker, "'But This Music Is Mine,'" p. 255.

62 **When *New Orleans* opened at the Winter Garden** Harrison Smith, "Lightning Strikes Twice," *Jazz Forum* 5 (Autumn 1947), pp. 16–17.

62 **"all that Uncle Tom stuff in it"** Early draft, *Lady Sings the Blues*, Robert O'Meally archive.

63 **smiling and begowned, exchanged a few words** Leonard Feather, "Billie Holiday Tells a Million Televiewers About the Dope Leeches," *Melody Maker* 29, no. 1050 (1953), pp. 10, 12.

63 **The show aired** Nat Hentoff, "Giants at Play: It's 50 Years Since CBS's Pioneering 'Sound of Jazz,'" *Weekly Standard*, December 10, 2007, p. 40.

64 **The script for *The Trial of Billie Holiday*** The script included quotes from the court transcript used with permission of Holiday's attorney, Jake Ehrlich, and the narcotics agent involved with the case. It was as close to film noir as it was a biopic. Ann Ronell, *The Trial of Billie Holiday*, 1957, Lester Cowan and Ann Ronell "Trial of Billie Holiday" Collection, Special Collections, University of Maryland Libraries.

64 **Dufty wrote her of his good impression of Cowan** Letter to Lady and Louis from William Dufty, undated (c. December 1956), reprinted in Ken Vail, *Lady Day's Diary*, p. 182.

65 **United Artists advanced money for production** Thomas M. Pryor, "Cowan Lists Film on Billie Holiday," *New York Times*, September 11, 1957.

65 **More than that, it would lead to millions** Letter from Lester Cowan to Billie Holiday, undated, from the Lester Cowan and Ann Ronell "Trial of Billie Holiday" Collection, Special Collections, University of Maryland Libraries.

65 **Asked if he had discussed the casting** Pryor, "Cowan Lists Film on Billie Holiday."

65 **"If they change that there's no story"** Pepper, "Banned Billie OK for Park?"; unidentified clipping, Institute of Jazz Studies, Rutgers University–Newark.

65 **Cowan had also considered Lana** Max E. Youngstein (United Artists) to Lester Cowan, February 17, 1958, Lester Cowan and Ann Ronell "Trial of Billie Holiday" Collection, Special Collections, University of Maryland Libraries.

66 **Cross said that Gardner had tried to get Billie** Julia Blackburn, *With Billie* (New York: Pantheon, 2005), p. 148.

66 **"My buddy, Ava Gardner, once asked me"** James Baldwin, "The Devil Finds Work," in *The Price of the Ticket: Collected Nonfiction, 1948–1985* (New York: St. Martin's, 1985), p. 622.

66 **Cowan's film failed to go into production** *Hollywood Reporter*, September 21, 1959, and November 1, 1960.

66 **This time it was announced that the movie** Ibid.

66 **Moreau was the only person who could play Billie** Letter from William Dufty to Ann Ronell, July 29, 1965, Lester Cowan and Ann Ronell "Trial

of Billie Holiday" Collection, Special Collections, University of Maryland Libraries.

67 **Dandridge was playing a Holiday-inspired** "Blues for the Junkman" was also known as *Murder Men* in an expanded theatrical version in an episode of a noirish NBC-TV film series called *Cain's Hundred*, February 20, 1962, season 1, episode 21.

67 *Camera Three* *Camera Three*, CBS-TV, September 9, 1962, season 7, episode 41.

67 **Anticipating that Louis McKay would contest** *Baltimore Afro-American*, September 4, 1971, p. 10; Hollie I. West, "Movies on Billie Holiday," *Washington Post*, July 30, 1971.

69 **Dufty later dismissed the film** "Dufty's Dirty Truth," *East West Journal*, March 1973, p. 4.

69 **"I wanted to make a piece of entertainment"** J. Randi Tarraborelli, *Diana Ross: An Unauthorized Biography* (New York: Citadel, 2007), p. 248.

69 **"Why should we be saddled with it just because we're black?"** Ibid., pp. 249–50.

69 **there were inauthenticities in the film** Though Ross said she did not try to sound like Holiday, she did admit that she tried to imagine what drugs were doing to her voice at various points in her life so as to know how to interpret them. Diana Ross, *Secrets of a Sparrow: Memoirs* (London: Headline, 1994), p. 197.

70 **"Let's face it, you're not my husband"** Andrusier Autographs, http://www.andrusierautographs.com/product/holiday-billie-1915-1959-3/.

71 **re-create Holiday's bedroom and dressing room** Ross, *Secrets of a Sparrow*, p. 201.

72 **images suggest that he might be looking back to the exoticism** Franco Minganti, "Qualcosa sulle immagini in movimento," in Giorgio Rimondi, ed., *Lady Day, Lady Night: Interpretare Billie Holiday* (Milan: Greco and Greco, 2003), pp. 57–72.

72 **Van Vechten later wrote** Carl Van Vechten, "Portraits of the Artists," *Esquire* 58, no. 6 (1962), p. 256; "The Reminiscences of Carl Van Vechten," Columbia Center for Oral History Collection, May 14, 1960, p. 232.

73 **"*Life* Goes to a Party" features** "Jam Session at Mili Studio," *Life*, October 11, 1943, pp. 117–25; http://billieholiday.info/index.php?Magazine#i55d7 654; W. Royal Stokes and Don Peterson, *Swing Era New York: The Jazz Photographs of Charles Peterson* (Philadelphia: Temple University Press, 1994); "Charles Peterson Goes to a Party (1939)," Jazz Lives, December 12, 2009, http://jazzlives.wordpress.com/2009/12/12/charles-peterson-goes-to-a-party-1939/; Ernie Anderson, "Billie Holiday," *Storyville*, March 1993, pp. 95–103.

CHAPTER FOUR: The Prehistory of a Singer

78 **In the 1850s Walt Whitman** J. K. Kinnard, "Who Are Our National Poets?," *Knickerbocker Magazine*, October 1945; Walt Whitman, *An American Primer*, new edition (San Francisco: City Lights, 1970 [1904]).

79 **And second, they were able to use the microphone** Henry Pleasants, *The Great American Popular Singers* (New York: Simon and Schuster, 1974).

80 **Hitler's mistress Eva Braun** Guy Walters, "Hitler's Mistress: Extraordinary Lost Pictures of Eva Braun at Play," *Daily Mail*, October 14, 2014, www.dailymail.co.uk/news/article-1364687/Hitlers-mistress-Eva -Brauns-rare-pictures-party-mode-dressed-Al-Jolson.html.

81 **"By 'coon songs' are meant up-to-date songs"** Quoted in Nick Tosches, *Where Dead Voices Gather* (New York: Little, Brown, 2001), p. 103.

82 **revision and sly appropriation of coon songs** Billie Holiday's mentor Shelton Brooks's composition "Darktown Strutters' Ball" was a revisiting of the coon song, and when it was recorded in 1917 by the Original Dixieland Jazz Band it became one of the first jazz songs.

82 **New York Times in 1895 reported** Quoted in Lynn Abbott and Doug Seroff, eds., *Ragged But Right* (Jackson: University of Mississippi Press, 2007), p. 17.

82 **review of Irwin in Courted into Court** Ibid.

83 **away from the Follies and on her own** Pamela Brown Levitt, "First of the Red Hot Mamas: 'Coon Shouting' and the Jewish Ziegfeld Girl," *American Jewish History* 87, no. 4 (1999), pp. 253–90.

83 **But when a white performer revealed her skin** Abbott and Seroff, *Ragged But Right*, pp. 20–21.

85 **When she sang "Backwater Blues"** Sterling Brown, "Ma Rainey," *The Collected Poems of Sterling A. Brown* (New York: Harper and Row, 1980).

87 **her repertoire openly echoed that of Bessie Smith and Ethel Waters** Peter Antelyes, "Red Hot Mamas: Bessie Smith, Sophie Tucker, and the Ethnic Maternal Voice in American Popular Song," in Leslie C. Dunn and Nancy A. Jones, eds., *Embodied Voices: Representing Female Vocality in Western Culture* (Cambridge: Cambridge University Press, 1994), pp. 212–29; Susan Ecker and Lloyd Ecker, liner notes to *Sophie Tucker: Origins of the Red Hot Mama, 1910–1922*, Archeophone CD 5010, 2009.

87 **they might be called flappers** Fanny Brice mocks the flapper style at the end of a 1930s clip of the song "When a Woman Loves a Man," www.you tube.com/watch?v=cTT2t8w8vw4.

89 **Sophie Tucker once paid Waters to teach her** Donald Bogle, *Heat Wave: The Life and Career of Ethel Waters* (New York: HarperCollins, 2011), p. 135.

92 **Most French singers of these songs were older** Wolfgang Rutkowski, "Cabaret Songs," *Popular Music and Society* 25, nos. 3 and 4 (Fall 2001), pp. 45–71.

92 **singers of torch songs have been called many things** Stacy Holman Jones, *Torch Singing: Performing Resistance and Desire from Billie Holiday to Edith Piaf* (Lanham, MD: Altamira, 2007), p. 24.

93 **Blues lyrics and their melodic characteristics** Michael Taft, *Talkin' to Myself: Blues Lyrics, 1921–1942* (New York: Routledge, 2005), p. xvi.

94 **no one seemed to care how unsavory** David Yaffe, *Fascinatin' Rhythm: Reading Jazz in American Writing* (Princeton, NJ: Princeton University Press, 2006), pp. 155–57; Will Friedwald, *A Biographical Guide to the Great Jazz Singers* (New York: Pantheon, 2010), p. 575.

95 **Helen Morgan was Irish American** I am indebted to the fine article by John Moore, "'The Hieroglyphics of Love': The Torch Singers and Interpretation," *Popular Music* 8, no. 1 (1989).

CHAPTER FIVE: The Singer I

97 **[Holiday's] art transcends the usual categorizations** Schuller, *The Swing Era*, p. 528.

98 **years after she had been acclaimed as a great vocalist** Teddy Wilson interview, September 2, 1979, Smithsonian Jazz Oral History Project, Reel 3.

99 **Stafford was her own favorite singer** Dan Burley, "Song Stylist Jo Stafford Favorite with Harlemites," *New York Amsterdam News*, March 17, 1945, p. A1. Stafford was the most popular singer among black listeners in 1945, leading even Dinah Washington and Ella Fitzgerald.

99 **Compare Stafford's "I'll Be Seeing You"** Adone Brandalise, "La voce come sguardo," in Rimondi, ed., *Lady Day, Lady Night*, pp. 73–78.

99 **"When I got into show business"** Quoted in O'Meally, *Lady Day*, p. 42.

100 **especially at the end of a tune** Stafford also sang Hank Williams tunes and country songs (some of which were hits), released folk song and gospel albums, recorded comedy music albums with her husband Paul Weston (under the adopted personae of "Jonathan and Darlene Edwards") that made fun of lounge singers, and even recorded "I'll Take Tallulah."

100 **Dodge wrote in the magazine *Jazz*** Roger Pryor Dodge, *Hot Jazz and Jazz Dance* (New York: Oxford University Press, 1995), p. 299.

100 **Their kind of singing** Ibid., p. 274.

101 **BH: Why, they're actresses, they're artists** Billie Holiday interviewed by Mike Wallace on *Night Beat*, DuMont Television, November 7, 1956. Despite some writers' assumption that there was tension between Holiday and Helen Forrest during the period in which they both were singers with the Artie Shaw band, each later spoke well of the other.

101 **Schiffman, owner of the Apollo** Abbey Lincoln at the Jazz Seminar, Columbia University, Frank Schiffman interviewed on "Lady Day: Billie Holiday," May 1967, Pacifica Radio, KPFA.

101 **"I'm telling you, me and my old voice"** *The Complete Billie Holiday on Verve, 1945–1959*, Verve Records 517 658-2, 1993, disk 4, track 32.

104 **"If you find a tune"** Holiday and Dufty, *Lady Sings the Blues*, pp. 43–44.

104 **She made you accept her song** Kuehl notes, Rutgers University–Newark.

104 **Linda Kuehl, Holiday's would-be first biographer** Ibid.

105 **"A great actress but one who never had an act"** Martin Williams, *The Jazz Tradition*, second revised edition (New York: Oxford University Press, 1993), p. 86.

105 **"In sensing her mortality, we sensed our own"** Studs Terkel, "Afterword," in Nelson Algren, *The Man with the Golden Arm*, fiftieth-anniversary edition (New York: Seven Stories, 1999).

105 **"You had to have someone with you when you listened to Billie"** Darryl Pinckney, "Dancing Miss," *New York Review of Books*, March 4, 1976.

105 **said the words differently with each interpretation** Kuehl notes, Rutgers University–Newark.

106 **"She didn't even glance at it"** Timme Rosenkrantz and Inez Cavanaugh, liner notes to *Billie Holiday's Greatest Hits*, Columbia CL-2666, 1967.

106 **"nearer to North Africa than to West Africa"** "Billie Holiday: Singer Presents a Concert in Town Hall," *New York Herald Tribune*, February 17, 1946.

106 **"She was nervous and perspiring freely"** Vail, *Lady Day's Diary*, p. 105.

106 **The next day, however, Van Vechten wrote to himself** Quoted in Stuart Nicholson, *Billie Holiday* (London: Indigo, 2000), p. 166.

107 **The singers we see in performance are not the real persons** Simon Frith, *Performing Rites: On the Value of Popular Music* (Cambridge, MA: Harvard University Press, 1996), p. 215.

107 **We expect to see a performer maintain a consistent face** Paul Auslander, "Musical Personae," *Drama Review* 50, no. 1 (Spring 2006), pp. 101–19.

108 **speaking critically of singers who imitated other singers** Leonard Feather, "Lady Day Has Her Say," *Metronome*, February 1950, p. 16.

110 **"the first time I ever heard anybody sing"** Holiday and Dufty, *Lady Sings the Blues*, pp. 9–10.

112 **the use of vocalese** "Vocalese" is not to be confused with "vocalise," singing with one single vowel so as to eliminate words altogether.

113 **While music of verse may already be present in the lyrics** Kenneth Burke, "On Musicality in Verse: As Illustrated by Some Lines of Coleridge," *Poetry*, October 1940, pp. 31–40. My thanks to Susan Stewart for help in understanding Holiday's use of written lyrics.

CHAPTER SIX: The Singer II

115 **"A lot of singers try to sing like Billie"** Quoted in John Chilton, *Billie's Blues* (New York: Stein and Day, 1975), p. 229.

115 **"She could just tear you up"** Quoted in O'Meally, *Lady Day*, p. 52.

115 **Compare Holiday's "lagging" vocal** Holiday's "St. Louis Blues" was recorded on October 15, 1940; Bessie Smith's was recorded January 14, 1925.

115 **bridge, or middle section, of "Foolin' Myself"** Teddy Wilson and His Orchestra (with Billie Holiday), "Foolin' Myself," 1937.

116 **When she reaches the next two lines** Holiday is fond of this form of stress, the spondee, which in poetic terms is a foot of two syllables, both of which are stressed. (A foot in poetry is something like a measure in music, a grouping of rhythm and sounds.)

117 **"She sometimes sang entire vocals outside the beat"** Whitney Balliett, "Jazz: Teddy Wilson," *New Yorker*, July 19, 1982, p. 67.

117 **"The first night she handed me some tattered lead sheets"** Artie Shaw, *The Street That Never Slept* (New York: Coward, McCann and Geoghegan, 1971), pp. 303–4.

118 **"two beat systems functioning simultaneously"** Hao Huang and Rachel V. Huang, "Billie Holiday and Tempo Rubato: Understanding Rhythmic Expressivity," *Annual Review of Jazz Studies* 7 (1994–1995), pp. 188–89.

118 **"two parallel strands organizing the passage of time"** This may be what musician and film director Mike Figgis meant when he said that he learned to listen to Billie Holiday's vocal lines along with Lester Young's tenor saxophone commentary and phrasing when they were playing with a drummer "who was profound *because* you couldn't hear him." Ibid., p. 193.

118 **"What Is This Thing Called Love?"** Ibid., p. 184.

120 **instrumental jazz is a speech-inflected music** LeRoi Jones, *Blues People* (New York: Morrow, 1963); Sidney Finkelstein, "Inner and Outer Jazz," *Jazz Review* 2, no. 8 (September 1959), 19–22.

120 **interview she did with talk show host Tex McCrary** Holiday had taken McCrary's request for "her songs" literally and recited three she had written. When the host asked her if she didn't know any happy songs, she replied, with a laugh, "I know some happy songs, but I don't write them." *The Tex and Jinx Show*, WNBC Radio, November 8, 1956.

120 **performances "live phrase to phrase"** Chilton, *Billie's Blues*, p. 232.

120 **singing in Chicago and Frank Sinatra was there** Earl Wilson, *New York Post*, May 26, 1944, quoted in Vail, *Lady Day's Diary*, p. 70.

121 **developed a kind of speech-song** Hao Huang and Rachel Huang, "She Sang as She Spoke: Billie Holiday and Aspects of Speech Intonation and Diction," *Jazz Perspectives* 7, no. 3 (December 2013), pp. 287–302.

121 **Piaf, for example, sometimes stops singing** Rutkowski, "Cabaret Songs." Another Euro speech-song form occurs in early-twentieth-century works by Viennese composers Arnold Schoenberg and Alban Berg, who called on singers of their vocal works to deliver some lines in *Sprechstimme*, a form of spoken singing with relative pitch. But there seems to be no relation between this modern classical practice and either the Euro cabaret style or Holiday's style.

121 **tempting to look for the source of Holiday's style** Ashton Stevens, music critic for the *Chicago Defender*, raved about Ethel Waters's performance in *Plantation Days* in 1924 by comparing her singing favorably to Yvette Guilbert.

122 **Jefferson suggests that this emotional distance** Ken Burns's *Jazz* Transcripts, www-tc.pbs.org/jazz/about/pdfs/Jefferson.pdf.

123 **"Lester sings with his horn"** Holiday and Dufty, *Lady Sings the Blues*, p. 66.

123 **Gordon sometimes spoke a few lines of a song** Hear Dexter Gordon, *Live at Carnegie Hall*, Columbia/Legacy 65312 CD.

123 **Holiday and Young each chose to avoid** See the comparison of Holiday and Young's improvisations on "These Foolish Things" in André Hodier, *Toward Jazz* (New York: Grove, 1962), pp. 191–95.

124 **Holiday's and Young's shared musical affinity** Will Friedwald, *A Bibliographical Guide to the Great Jazz and Pop Singers* (New York: Pantheon, 2010), p. 224.

125 **recording and alternate take of "Me, Myself, and I"** This is not the song of the same name recorded by Beyoncé in 2003.

125 **a fully improvised, freshly created solo** Among other examples of the same musical relationship are "I'll Never Be the Same" (1937), "Time on My Hands" (1940), "A Sailboat in the Moonlight" (1937), and "He's Funny That Way" (1937).

126 **"the only ones who can take a solo"** Feather, "Lady Day Has Her Say." My discussion of obbligato and Billie Holiday is indebted to an invaluable tutorial with Loren Schoenberg.

126 **Hurston heard in preachers' prayers** "Spiritual and Neo-Spiritual," in Cheryl A. Wall, ed., *Zora Neale Hurston: Folklore, Memoirs, and Other Writings* (New York: Library of America, 1995), p. 862.

126 **Hurston goes on to say** Ibid. Buck Clayton, the elegant trumpet player who also accompanied Holiday on many of these early recordings, seemed to have a different view of the obbligatos they played: not as an essential part of the music, but as a decorative option, and used only to fill in the blanks: "When she would record I would watch her mouth and when I saw that she was going to take a breath or something I knew it was time for me to play between her expressions. It's what we call 'filling up the windows.'" Yet the recordings show that he, too, improvised distinct, related lines at the same time as she sang, and seldom if ever played only between her phrases.

128 **Compare the versions of "All of Me"** Cynthia Folio and Robert W. Weisberg, "Billie Holiday's Art of Paraphrase: A Study in Consistency," in *New Musicology (Interdisciplinary Studies in Musicology)* (Poznan, Poland: Poznan Press, 2006), pp. 247–75; Huang and Huang, "She Sang as She Spoke"; Robert Toft, "Lady Day the Torch Singer: The Vocal Persona of a 'Woman Unlucky in Love,'" in *12th Biennial IASPN International Conference, Montreal 2003 Proceedings*, International Association for the Study of

Popular Music, pp. 916–22, www.sibetrans.com/public/docs/Actas
_IASPM_Montreal.pdf.

CHAPTER SEVEN: The Songs I

132 **"instrumental[ized] the material at hand"** Schuller, *The Swing Era*, p. 116.
132 **so powerful and affecting in the best of Holiday's art** Ronald Schleifer, *Modernism and Popular Music* (Cambridge: Cambridge University Press, 2011), pp. 164–69.
133 **"In those days 133rd Street"** Holiday and Dufty, *Lady Sings the Blues*, p. 37.
134 **such small venues could have significant influence** Shane Vogel, *The Scene of Harlem Cabaret* (Chicago: University of Chicago Press, 2009).
134 **points of attraction for white musicians** Rudolph Fisher, "The Caucasian Storms Harlem," *American Mercury*, August 1927, pp. 393–97.
136 **don't take this recording seriously** Kate Daubney, "Songbird or Subversive? Instrumental Vocalization Technique in the Songs of Billie Holiday," *Journal of Gender Studies* 11, no. 1 (2002), pp. 22–23.
137 **"The Teddy Wilson small group sessions"** Teddy Wilson, *Teddy Wilson Talks Jazz* (London: Cassell, 1996), p. 24.
140 **"Good" jazz songs do not always make for great jazz** John Szwed, "Doctor Jazz," liner notes to *Jelly Roll Morton: The Complete Library of Congress Recordings by Alan Lomax*, Rounder Records 11661-1888-2 BK01, 2005, p. 19.
140 **Holiday sings it in a key high enough** Schuller, *The Swing Era*, p. 538.
142 **version of "Porgy" she sang was extracted from the opera's duet** Steven Lasker, liner notes to *Billie Holiday: The Complete Decca Recordings*, MCA D2-601, 1991.
143 **"I just made some records for Decca"** Interview on the *Curfew Club* radio program, recorded in late December 1948 and broadcast on January 8, 1949, on *Billie Holiday at Stratford '57*, Baldwin Street Music BJH 308, 1999, track 16.
143 **she did own records by Gershwin** Blackburn, *With Billie*, p. 97.
143 **At one point Aronowitz asked Billie** Al Aronowitz, "The Saddest Song Ever Sung," First of the Month, www.firstofthemonth.org/music/music_aronowitz_saddest.html.
145 **She avoids the birdcall-like dips** Humphrey Lyttelton, *The Best of Jazz* (New York: Taplinger, 1978), pp. 209–11.
145 **All the while she is phrasing across the beat** A second take of the song at a slower tempo exists but has less energy behind it. In a radio interview Phil Schaap asked Eddie Durham, the guitarist on the record, why the tempo was dropped on the second take. Durham replied that they'd taken a break to smoke a joint.
147 **Preston Love said that she always listened** Preston Love, *A Thousand Honey Creeks Later: My Life in Music from Basie to Motown and Beyond* (Middletown, CT: Wesleyan University Press, 1997), p. 219.

147 **"Fitzgerald, entering the microphonic arena"** "Chick, Basie Battle," *New York Amsterdam News,* January 28, 1938.

148 **"The reason for her dismissal"** "Hammond Did Not Have Holiday Fired!" *Down Beat,* September 1938, p. 6.

149 **Shaw wrote a short story** Artie Shaw, *The Best of Intentions and Other Stories* (McKinleyville, CA: Daniel and Daniel, 1989); Willie the Lion Smith, *Music on My Mind* (New York: Doubleday, 1964).

149 **"In a corner sat a distinguished-looking fellow"** Timme Rosenkrantz and Inez Cavanaugh, liner notes to *Billie Holiday's Greatest Hits.*

150 **"I gave her a record of Debussy's"** Blackburn, *With Billie,* p. 97.

152 **"She treated me well"** Helen Forrest, *I Had the Craziest Dream: Helen Forrest and the Big Band Era* (New York: Coward, McCann & Geoghegan, 1982), pp. 58–59.

154 **nightspot without racial barriers** "Mixed Band at Café Society: Joe Sullivan Organizes 1st Name Negro-White Orchestra Downtown," *New York Amsterdam News,* November 25, 1939, p. 1.

156 **"I always looked on Billie as a finished performer"** Kuehl manuscript, Rutgers University–Newark.

157 **Holiday's recording of "Strange Fruit" was released** The best source for information on this song is David Margolick's *Strange Fruit: Billie Holiday, Café Society, and an Early Cry for Civil Rights* (Philadelphia: Running Press, 2000), but additional material has been added here from the author's research. See also Nancy Kovaleff Baker, "Abel Meeropol (a.k.a Lewis Allan): Political Commentator and Social Conscience," *American Music,* Spring 2002, pp. 25–79.

157 **earlier pieces such as Bessie Smith's "Haunted House Blues"** Adam Gussow, *Seems Like Murder Here: Southern Violence and the Blues Tradition* (Chicago: University of Chicago Press, 2002).

157 **Lead Belly's "Hangman's Blues" and "The Gallis Pole"** *New Masses,* January 1931, p. 17; Lawrence Gellert, *Negro Songs of Protest* (New York: American Music League, 1936), pp. 10–11; *Workers' Song Book, No. 2* (New York: Workers' Music League, 1935), pp. 23–26.

158 **the night in 1958 that she sang it for Maya Angelou** Maya Angelou, *The Heart of a Woman* (New York: Random House, 1981), pp. 13–14.

159 **"spell out all the things that had killed Pop"** Holiday and Dufty, *Lady Sings the Blues,* p. 94.

159 **She undoubtedly also knew the widely told account** Chris Albertson, *Bessie,* revised and expanded edition (New Haven, CT: Yale University Press, 2003), pp. 255–71.

159 **A few years later James Baldwin would write** James Baldwin, "Many Thousands Gone," *Notes of a Native Son* (Boston: Beacon Press, 1955), p. 25.

160 **"separating the straight people from the squares"** Holiday and Dufty, *Lady Sings the Blues,* p. 95.

160 **interview that Holiday gave to *PM* newspaper** Harriott, "The Hard Life of Billie Holiday"; Holiday and Dufty, *Lady Sings the Blues*, p. 94.

161 ***PM's* editors printed a response** "Letters: 'Strange Fruit,'" *PM*, September 23, 1945, p. 19.

161 **Herzog Jr., a publicist and writer of song lyrics** When the book first appeared, Herzog said that he had written a piece that would give "an accurate accounting of what occurred referring to incidents Billie presents quite differently," which he'd titled "Blue Lady Sings Off-Key." It was apparently never published. Letter from Arthur Herzog Jr., to Leonard Feather, August 31, 1956, Institute of Jazz Studies, Rutgers University–Newark.

161 **"If Allan wants to come into court with his sheet music"** Letter from William Dufty to A. D. Weinberger, Esq., October 21, 1956, p. 2, H. Dennis Fairchild archive. As far as Milt Gabler was concerned, the band at Café Society had worked up the music.

161 **"nothing happened until Miss Holiday did the song"** Letter from William Dufty to Le Baron Barker, Doubleday and Co., October 26, 1956, p. 1, H. Dennis Fairchild archive.

162 **"When black face is lifted"** Gellert, *Negro Songs of Protest*, pp. 10–11.

162 **"For years both American fellow travelers and the FBI"** Dufty to Barker, October 26, 1956, pp. 1–3, H. Dennis Fairchild archive.

163 **"We give this statement to clarify the facts"** www.icollector.com /BILLIE-HOLIDAY-D-S_i559529.

163 **"I can understand the psychological reasons"** Quoted in Margolick, *Strange Fruit*, pp. 128–29.

164 **not based on making a social statement** Gilbert Millstein, "For Kicks: I," *New Yorker*, March 9, 1946, p. 34.

165 **there are downward arcs of notes** Robert Cogan, *New Images of Musical Sound* (Cambridge, MA: Harvard University Press, 1984), pp. 35–37.

165 **The melody she creates is quite different** William T. Dargan, *Lining Out the Word: Dr. Watts Hymn Singing in the Music of Black Americans* (Berkeley: University of California Press, 2006), pp. 218–20.

166 **White had never met Billie** Josh White, "A Fighter: That's the Billie I Remember," *Melody Maker*, August 8, 1959, p. 5.

166 **An article titled "Strange Song"** "Strange Record," *Time*, June 12, 1939.

166 **African American press was far more sympathetic** *Atlanta Daily World*, June 19, 1939, p. 2.

167 **Breit later wrote in a review** Harvey Breit, "Implanting Bitterness," *New York Times*, July 21, 1956.

167 **"It was one of the first modern blues"** Kuehl notes, Rutgers University– Newark.

168 **the music she told him she wanted to sing** Milt Gabler quoted in John McDonough, "On Disc: The Three Voices of Billie," *Wall Street Journal*, December 16, 1991, p. A12.

169 **The original version of "Gloomy Sunday"** "Gloomy Sunday" was composed in 1933 by Rezső Seress, whose title in Hungarian translates as "The World Is Ending." A later version with new Hungarian lyrics was written by László Jávor and retitled "Sad Sunday." "Gloomy Sunday" was first recorded in English with lyrics by Sam M. Lewis, and rewritten again with another set of English lyrics by Desmond Carter. Billie Holiday's version used Lewis's lyrics.

169 **It could also be played by an orchestra** Paul Bailey, "Tong Sung Long," *Times Literary Supplement*, October 29, 2004.

CHAPTER EIGHT: The Songs II

172 **"But then he contradicted himself"** Clarke, *Wishing on the Moon*, p. 191.

173 **"We changed the lyrics in a couple of spots"** Holiday and Dufty, *Lady Sings the Blues*, p. 101.

174 **"Trav'lin' Light" was an instrumental tune** Thomas A. DeLong, *Pops: Paul Whiteman, King of Jazz* (Piscataway, NJ: New Century, 1983), pp. 251–52.

177 **It is a song that has had a long life** For a deeper look at this song, see the excellent chapter on Holiday's and Crosby's versions of "I'll Be Seeing You" in Brackett, *Interpreting Popular Music*, pp. 54–74.

179 **feelings she may have had about her drug use** Albert Murray interviewed by Robert O'Meally, unpublished, n.d., Robert O'Meally archive.

179 **The song on the other side of the Decca single** "Roger Ramirez" in Stanley Dance, *The World of Swing* (New York: Charles Scribner's Sons, 1974), p. 327.

183 **She paused frequently** Maya Gibson, "Alternate Takes: Billie Holiday at the Intersection of Black Cultural Studies and Historical Musicology," PhD dissertation, 2008, University of Wisconsin–Madison; Mistinguett, *Mistinguett: Queen of the Paris Night* (London: Elek Books, 1954).

184 **she remained in a torch mode** Toft, "Lady Day the Torch Singer," pp. 917–21.

190 **"She'd walk over"** Quoted in Chris Ingham, *Billie Holiday* (London: Unanimous, 2000), pp. 30–31.

190 **"We never had time"** Ibid., p. 102. An amateur recording of a 1955 Rowles-Holiday rehearsal is included in *The Complete Billie Holiday on Verve, 1945–1959*.

190 **"display the complete interplay between us"** Ibid., p. 96.

192 **best audiences had been white** Blackburn, *With Billie*, p. 302.

193 **The strings were a comfort** Ibid. For the record, Marilyn Moore, a singer with the Woody Herman and Charlie Barnet bands in the late 1950s, said she was very close to Billie at the time this record was being made and claimed that Billie said she had nothing to do with the planning of the *Lady in Satin* album, did not know who Ray Ellis was before this, and hated the

songs she did with violins because there were too many of them and she couldn't hear herself. When the record began to get airplay and reviews, however, she changed her mind about it (Ted Ono, liner notes to *Billie Holiday at Stratford '57*). There is a possibility that this is true, since Ellis said when she first saw how many string players there were she left the studio in tears and had to be talked into coming back. Such contradictions in accounts such as this one are not uncommon when the subject has not given many interviews and most of what we know of her comes from others.

193 **The "ideal accompaniment for a jazz vocal"** Glen Coulter, "Billie Holiday," in Martin Williams, ed., *Jazz Panorama* (New York: Crowell-Collier, 1962), p. 147.

194 **Brooks's comments for the same CD reissue** Michael Brooks's notes were dropped from the digitally remastered CD reissue in 1997.

195 **The results may sound a bit weird** My thanks to Andrew Homzy for his discussion of this recording on the Jazz Research List, August 29, 2013.

196 **If that was so, Billie suggested** Earle Zaidins, quoted in Blackburn, *With Billie*, p. 307.

198 **"I'm Billie Holiday"** Max Jones, *Talking Jazz* (New York: Norton, 1988), p. 257.